CUSTOMER-FOCUSED MANAGEMENT BY PROJECTS

Customer-Focused Management by Projects

Ronald Vaupel

Gernot Schmolke

and

Andreas Krüger

Foreword by Hans-Ulrich Küpper

This edition published by
MACMILLAN PRESS LTD
Houndmills, Basingstoke, Hampshire RG21 6XS
and London
Companies and representatives
throughout the world

ISBN 0–333–92050–3

A catalogue record for this book is available
from the British Library.

This book is printed on paper suitable for recycling and
made from fully managed and sustained forest sources.

10   9   8   7   6   5   4   3   2   1
09 08 07 06 05 04 03 02 01 00

Printed and bound in Great Britain by
Antony Rowe Ltd, Chippenham, Wiltshire

Contents

List of Figures

List of Tables

List of Case Studies

Foreword

Rapid changes and increasing globalization are making unprecedented demands on managers. As a result, they need efficient tools to tap the knowledge and motivation of their staff as well as to reach their corporate goals. This becomes particularly necessary and difficult in the case of innovative tasks aiming to open up new markets, create new products and access new expertise. Project management represents a powerful tool for tackling such assignments. It is therefore used increasingly widely and is recognized as a valid object of scientific study.

This insight lies behind the publication of this book. It was written in close cooperation between leading German companies and a university institute. The necessary background material was obtained by combining the experience gained within the Siemens company with the latest theoretical results in the domain of project controlling.

The idea was to realize a *project* that was both scientifically sound and also oriented to direct applications. During their work, the authors became increasingly aware that project management goes well beyond the planning, monitoring and control of projects. The managing *of* projects can be seen as part of a more comprehensive scheme of managing *via* projects. In addition to budgeting, target systems and steering prices, the latter represents an unusually effective and comprehensive control tool. If it is applied within a suitably organized corporate culture, the company acquires a powerful set of tools for use in a dynamic and innovative environment. This handbook represents a guide, which can be applied directly in practical situations

Munich   PROF. DR HANS-ULRICH KÜPPER

Introduction

This book examines the topic of project management in some detail by presenting it as a management concept with a customer orientation. It has been subdivided into four main sections:

Part I clarifies the basic concepts and points out the advantages of management *with* projects. The principal elements of a management approach to projects are initially introduced in outline. They are then treated in detail at a later stage. Finally, it is explained how a project-oriented company selects projects for implementation in a focused way.

The successful execution of individual projects – i.e. the actual management *of* projects – is treated in Part II. This section examines the planning, control and successful termination of a project.

In Part III it will become clear that a consistent project orientation must be reflected not only in individual projects but also in all a company's management practices. An important aspect of this approach is that the corporate management must support the projects run in the company with the aid of suitable structures and tools.

The employees play a special role in project-oriented companies. Successful project management is the fruit of the day-to-day efforts of the team members and must be intimately integrated into the corporate culture. This important aspect will be covered in Part IV.

The range of topics covered obviously means that this book is directed at a very disparate target readership. It aims to give newcomers a complete overview of the nature of project management and the relationships it involves. Readers who are already familiar with this field will gain an additional business-oriented perspective over the full range of topics involved.

The main text of the book is presented in compact form. It is designed to provide an easy overview to users who are already familiar with project management. In addition, fundamental topics such as schedule network planning technology and target costing are presented in separate inserts as highlighted text. Other inserts give additional examples and details of specific tools. This allows less experienced readers to access everything they need to acquire an in-depth understanding of project management.

RONALD VAUPEL
GERNOT SCHMOLKE
ANDREAS KRÜGER

Part I   Management with Projects

Project management in the past

Early on in management practice it became clear that the usual somewhat rigid organizational structures were not well suited to deal with tasks that were both new and complex. The idea therefore arose to create temporary organizational units in order to realize such tasks as efficiently as possible in the form of **projects**. Over the years, the concept of **project management** was developed as a set of tools designed to plan and control projects.

Has project management proved useful?

Despite the positive experience that many companies have gained with project management in the past and continue to do in the present, this approach has never acquired the same high profile in the business world as related concepts such as *lean management* or *business re-engineering*. This neglect is clearly unjustified in view of the fact that project management has proved so useful in practice over many years. And yet, this low-key focus actually works in its favour. For in contrast to its siblings, which have attained celebrity status, project management has been able to prove its worth over the long term. Whereas other management concepts turned out to be little more than short-term fashions, project management has been successfully applied in companies for many years.

What can project management do?

This book examines the positive results obtained with project management in order to show that this approach can and should be more than a collection of tools designed to deal with new tasks of limited duration. If it is released from its technocratic moorings, project management becomes an appropriate management concept for companies with a distinct customer orientation. It then forms an ideal complement to techniques such as lean management or business re-engineering and extends beyond these in time.

1 Management with projects as an expression of customer orientation

What problems does project management solve?

Many companies suffer from the fact that they possess considerable resources but are unable to apply these optimally to satisfy their business targets. One example is the inefficient application of in-house expertise and the ideas developed by employees in the research and development sector to create innovative products that are successful in the market. Other problems often arise in the attempt to create services, which are customized to the individual needs of the client. As Figure 1.1 shows, this is exactly the point at which management with projects is applied.

Figure 1.1   Projects to focus a company's resources to the customer

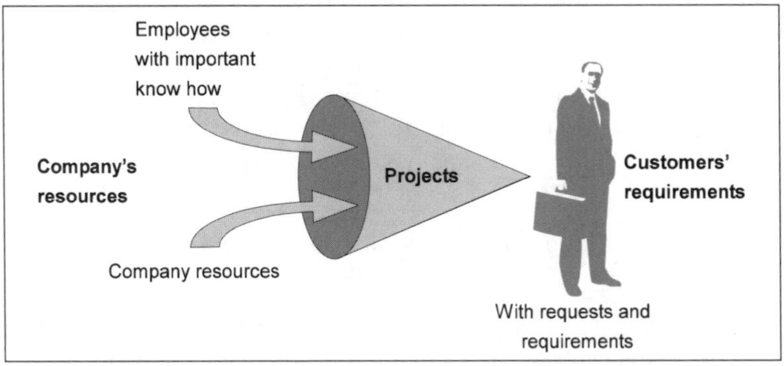

Employees with important know how

Company's resources

Company resources

Projects

Customers' requirements

With requests and requirements

> *Does project orientation imply customer orientation?*

Projects are a very flexible form of organization, which focuses all the necessary company resources to the customer and his requirements within a limited time frame.[1] They thus represent one of the most efficient forms of customer orientation. The customer may be **external**, such as a company planning to set up a communications system. But he may also appear in the guise of an in-house entity such as a department, which designs and installs a software system for another department, or perhaps a business unit, which commissions the development of a new product.

> *Why management **by** projects?*

The basic function of any company is to satisfy the requirements of its customers, and in particular of external ones. If it fails to do so, it will as a rule be unable to reach its corporate goals in terms of profits, growth or shareholder value. Project-oriented companies attempt to satisfy customer requirements and thus their corporate goals by means of the focused application of project management. The reasons why projects offer an advantage over rigid corporate structures from the **customer's** perspective are summarized in Figure 1.2. But a project-oriented company also has numerous advantages from the standpoint of the other parties involved. Flexibility in the manufacture of high-quality products to customer specifications secures long-term market success for the **company**. The value of the company then increases from the standpoint of the **lenders of equity and debt capital**. The lean structures and integrated task structuring typical of projects can motivate the **employees** more strongly and promote their development more effectively than is possible within conventional hierarchical structures. The flexibility of service provision represents a positive value not only for the customers; it also leads to interesting and challenging tasks for the company's **subcontractors**.

> *Why are stakeholders important?*

Project management can satisfy the requirements of a series of a company's **stakeholders**. It is important for a company to have a

Figure 1.2   Advantages of managing by projects for different stakeholders

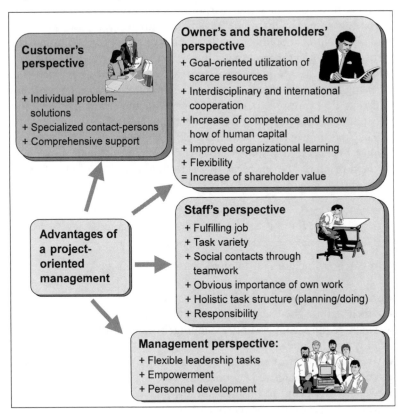

stakeholder-friendly philosophy, which goes beyond customer orienta-tion.[2] This is because stakeholders are strategic partners who have the power to seriously affect the well being of the company. For example, a company will get into difficulties if its customers turn away, if it loses its attractiveness for qualified employees or if investors shun it.

What does project orientation mean? What does it not mean?

Despite these notable advantages of management with projects, it is important to avoid **project inflation** within the company. Certainly, a **project-oriented company will** deliberately and repeatedly create new organizations for limited periods of time (projects) in order to implement its business policy and corporate strategy. But project-oriented corporate management or management with projects does *not* mean that all activities should be handled exclusively via projects. In fact, the term **project orientation** implies the necessity of continually checking whether the goals set might be better reached by initiating projects than by being implemented within an existing hierarchy. Project orientation will thus be expressed to varying degrees in the company's activities depending on the proportion of **project-capable tasks**.

The question as to which tasks can be implemented via projects cannot be answered globally. However, a number of **indicators** points to the possibility or even necessity of dealing with a task in the form of a project:

> *How are project-capable tasks recognized?*

This category includes all unique or non-recurring tasks:

- for which clear goals can be formulated
- which require the use of complex and/or new technologies
- which require cooperation extending over multiple organizational units and technical sectors
- which are urgent or subject to limited time frames
- which are characterized by uncertainty
- which are relevant to business policy, and
- which are necessary for reasons of business structuring.

As well as tasks:

- which represent a commercial risk to the company
- for whose implementation limited resources are available
- whose requirement for resources is above the average for the functions otherwise performed by the company, and
- which must be monitored in terms of results.

Or those tasks

- with a high proportion of external input, or
- for which the customer already has a project organization.

> *Will the number of project-capable tasks increase?*

The increasing pressure to solve individual customer problems and the growing complexity of products and services will tend to increase the number of tasks amenable to being handled by projects. In a whole series of sectors, projects already form the basis for successful business developments – for example, in the pharmaceutical industry, in the construction sector, in parts of the telecommunications industry as well as in some service sectors. Project management is also applied in the public service sector in order to ensure efficient workload handling.

> *Which projects does this book cover?*

We have seen that a number of highly diverse tasks can be realized in the form of projects. As a result, a book which deals with the basic idea of management *with and of* projects faces a major problem: namely to present material which is applicable to at least the majority of projects while avoiding an excessively abstract description which is well-nigh useless in practical situations.

To resolve this problem we will assume that the basic procedures involved in project management can be applied to almost all projects. After all, the ultimate aim is always to provide a service to the customer. That is why project management can help companies in very disparate sectors to achieve a high level of customer orientation. This book aims to introduce the reader to this management concept in more detail.

> *Which project types can be distinguished?*

Despite their common points, specific projects and project types naturally differ considerably (cf. Table 1.1). In individual cases, therefore, additional indications will be given wherever project types differ significantly. For the sake of simplicity, however, a distinction will henceforth be made only between **customer-order** and **product-innovation projects** without going into the details of all conceivable intermediate forms. This interpolation will be left to the reader.

Table 1.1   Differences between project types

	Pure customer-order project	Intermediate forms	Product-innovation project
Client	Concrete external customer	External customer or internal client	Internal client (with external target group)
Product	Manufactured from existing components	Must be adapted or newly developed	Completely new development
Target effect	Operative-tactical with strategic effects	Mixed	Strategic with operative-tactical effects
Special risks	Unexpected customer requirements, socio-cultural and political risks	Mixed	High technical risks, risks from market and competition
Example	Installing a communications system in an airport	Internal software development, reorganization projects, developing a product for an individual customer	Development of new communications terminals

NOTES

1   The German Standardization Institute (DIN) defines a project as having a non-recurring character, unique objectives that are subject to temporal, financial, personnel or other limitations and is delimited from other activities by a specific organization (cf. DIN e.V. [1987], p. 1).
2   Cf. de Wit [1988], p. 167. Bühner/Tuschke [1997] for a critical comparison of stakeholder and shareholder orientation.

2 The basic structure of project management

What are the elements of the project management concept?

Figure 2.1 gives an overview of the project-management concept, which will be explained in this book. It will be immediately apparent that this concept goes far beyond what is generally regarded as the domain of project management (PM). Sure enough, the **management of projects** forms the core of this concept. But it also specifically implies that appropriate form of corporate management designed to ensure successful project orientation over the long term must support individual projects. Such an appropriately structured **management system** then ensures that a company will attain its objectives efficiently with the aid of individual projects.

The basis for the success of a project-oriented company is its employees. That is why the fostering of a **project-oriented corporate culture** represents a critical success factor for management with projects.

Finally, consistent **customer orientation** is at the very heart of the concept of project management. It will be explained in detail in the following sections how this approach will affect the selection and implementation of projects in the company.

What's the basic structure of project implementation?

The basic structure involved in the preparation and implementation of a project is identical for all types of projects. It is illustrated in Figure 2.2. At the beginning of the cycle of managing *by* projects stands the **definition cycle**. Its first step is the **collection of project proposals**. Such proposals may be decision packages for developing new products or real orders from internal or external customers.

9

Figure 2.1   Overview of the project-management concept

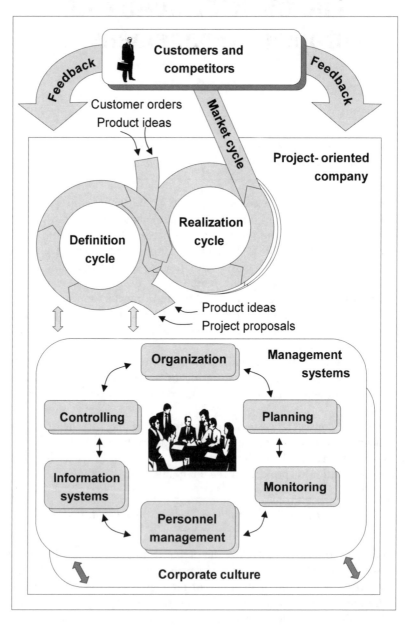

Figure 2.2   Basic structure of the preparation and implementation of a project

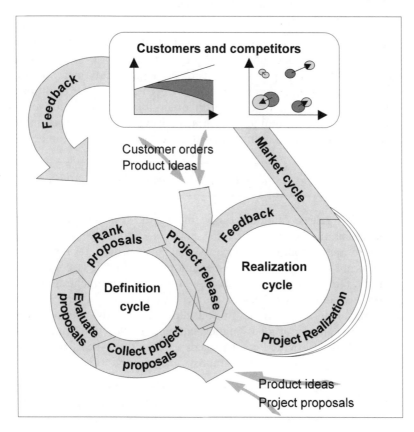

Once collected, the individual **proposals** are **evaluated**. In particular, they are checked for any positive or negative consequences their implementation may have in a project-oriented company.

The results of this evaluation are then used to arrange the proposals on the basis of priority. This **ranking procedure** is designed to create an initial basis for deciding which projects would be most promising for the company. A decision to select or reject suggested projects must be made if it seems likely that the company may have insufficient resources (installations, funds, etc.) or personnel (employees, know-how) to implement all projects that are given the go ahead in principle.

What does 'project release' mean?

The **project release** represents the real start of an individual project. This may be a product-innovation project that aims to implement a package of the most promising customer requirements in a specific product. But a project that had previously been evaluated as profitable may also be initiated to execute an order for the installation of a computer system for another corporate division or the construction of a detached house or nuclear power plant for an external customer.

---
*Where does the transition take place to management **of** projects?*

The project release simultaneously implies the transition to **project management** in the sense that this term is commonly used in the literature and corporate practice. Managing a project means above all ensuring its successful implementation – i.e. that it is completed from its start to its successful conclusion. But the implementation of a project also implies **feedback** to the definition process. This feedback from managing an individual project allows the positive and negative experience gained during its implementation to flow back into new projects. Project-oriented companies depend on this type of organizational learning to continuously improve their procedures.

---
*What part does the market process play in management **by** projects?*

A project is finally concluded when its results are handed over to the customer. These results may be a service performed or a product newly developed for an internal or external customer. Ultimately, the most important feedback for a project-oriented company flows from this **market process**. For this is where it becomes apparent whether the business results originally planned for the product are actually realized when it is manufactured. These results may take the form of a specific profit margin, an early break-even point, a planned market share or a sales target for a newly developed product. **Feedback** about the degree of attaining such targets and the reasons for a positive or negative deviation yields important information for the definition process, as much can also be learned from this for selecting and handling future projects.

What will the next chapters show?

The following sections will go into the details of the project management concept whose elements have merely been introduced briefly so far. The process of running projects in project-oriented companies outlined in Figure 2.2 will initially be examined in more detail. As already indicated, correct selection of the projects to be implemented is the very first step.

3 The definition cycle: selecting projects as a basis for project-oriented corporate management

The aim of systematic project selection is to distribute the available resources optimally among those projects, which are most important for the company. The first step in selecting projects is to collect project proposals (cf. Figure 3.1).

3.1 COLLECTING PROJECT PROPOSALS

> *What are proposals for customer-order projects?*

For **customer-order projects**, the collection of **project proposals** simply means the successful acquisition of orders as understood in the sales and marketing sector. Because it refers to orders for products already manufactured by the company, the collection of such project proposals is relatively straightforward from the standpoint of project management.

> *How are proposals collected for innovative products?*

Matters become somewhat more involved when it comes to collecting proposals for **innovative products**. In purely customer-order projects, a project proposal is present from the outset because a description of the product[1] to be manufactured already exists or is specified by the customer. Other types of projects must initially catch up with this head start, above all when it involves innovative products. Here, the nature

Figure 3.1   Integration of the definition cycle into the management concept of
a project-oriented company

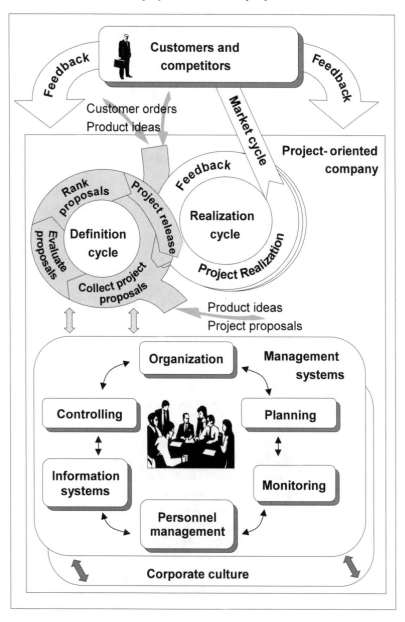

of the product and its properties, which are to become the object of a project, must still be decided. In order to obtain **project proposals**, **decision packages** must be assembled from a series of **product ideas**.[2] These decision packages describe a potential new product and its diverse features in a form appropriate to a project proposal. The multi-stage process required to develop them will be described below.

> *What are sources of product ideas?*

Product-innovation projects play an important part in a company's mid- to long-term competitiveness because they shape the product programme and thus have a critical effect on the future direction of the company's development. Product-innovation projects must therefore aim to include hitherto unsatisfied customer requirements in new products so that the attractiveness of a company's products is increased from the customer's perspective. Figure 3.2 shows that a series of internal and external sources may be tapped to generate ideas for new and promising products. However, the highest priority must be the requirements of current and prospective customers.

Figure 3.2   Sources of ideas for new and promising products

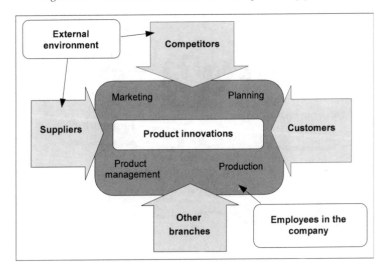

> *Do companies take note of customer requirements?*

A British survey of UK and Japanese companies[3] showed that 76 per cent of British and 70 per cent of Japanese businesses regard the satisfaction of customer requirements as *the* success factor for new products. However, only 24 per cent of British and 15 per cent of Japanese companies make systematic use of customer proposals as a source of product innovations. So whereas companies recognize the necessity of customer orientation as a critical success factor, they fail to act on it in practice! A similar pattern is seen among companies in other countries.[4] The collection of product ideas, especially of customer requirements used to initiate successful product-innovation projects, will consequently be examined in more detail after the following case study.[5]

Case study 3.1   Applying TopInfo in the definition process

TopInfo is a Groupware system running under Windows and designed to support project-oriented corporate management (see *TopInfo*, p. 268). Thanks to its comprehensive performance features and user friendliness, it places the reception and evaluation of customer requirements on a systematic basis and thus makes a significant contribution to a company's customer orientation.

TopInfo is a system into which a company's *requestors* located anywhere in the world can either enter customer requests made to them or submit their own proposals for improvement. They are particularly motivated by the fact that they can track the *fate* of their own proposals directly within the system. For the company, TopInfo offers a universally applicable system for supporting the selection of projects.

THE FUNCTIONAL RANGE OF TOPINFO

TopInfo is based on an ORACLE database system. In principle, any number of users can access the system via the company-wide INTRANET. To ensure that the request collection is effectively coordinated, their submission can be limited to persons (such as product line managers) who are designated as *requestors* in the system. They can then enter the information linked to the request by means of simple forms available in TopInfo. The extent of the minimum data to be entered (such as only a specific problem area or the economic effects of the proposal as well) can be centrally defined by means of mandatory fields.

The requests collected world-wide can then be assigned by administrative assistants (representing the single entry point) to individual business sectors or their relevant definition teams. Each request is assigned to a mentor in the definition team who acts as a contact person within TopInfo. He is the direct contact person for all matters regarding individual requests. This procedure assures transparency in processing customer proposals and requestors can keep track of the details of request processing at all times. After a request has been assigned to a definition team, only members of that team have write access to the requests (all other departments continue to have read access to relevant data).

TopInfo supports further processing of the requests within the definition team. The contact person can therefore transfer the rights to process individual requests both to fellow team members and to external experts so that specific technical or business comments may be added to them. The system describes the current status of a relevant request (from initial input up to rejection or inclusion in a decision package) by assigning work-flow points.

This status information is also used to control the further processing of the requests. Thus only requests with a certain minimum status (such as *specified, evaluated* and *prioritized*) may be permitted for inclusion in decision packages.

Any requests rejected by the filtering process in the definition cycle are marked accordingly. However, they are not necessarily deleted, but are available for possible re-use at a later stage.

The IRMS/CMS document management system running behind the user interface makes TopInfo particularly useful. All documents linked to a request, whether CAD design drawings or feature specifications (FDBs), can be integrated and managed directly in the system. The job hand-over, either between various experts or between team members scattered around the world, is facilitated by allowing the current processing status of a customer request to be viewed in the system within minimum delay.

Moreover, the data integration allows data storage free of redundancies and inconsistencies.

TopInfo is rounded off by extensive export and import functions as well as mail links. This makes it possible to exchange notes between other team members for dispatch or feedback.

3.1.1   A pro-active approach to obtaining product ideas

> *What is a pro-active approach?*

In order to anticipate changing needs in the target groups, it is of crucial importance not only to **passively** accept customer requirements but also to seek them out **actively**. Employees at the customer interface such as the sales or service sectors should be motivated by means of suitable incentives to approach customers pro-actively and keep a constant look-out for proposals for improving existing products as well as ideas for new products.

> *What are the advantages of special user groups?*

It has proved most useful to bring together particularly important and experienced customers, known as **lead users**, in specifically established groups and to devote intensive attention to them. The **JUST** user group within the Communications Group of Siemens AG is a typical example. For the customers, membership in these groups offers a way of actively influencing the company's product policy where this is of relevance to them. This increases customer satisfaction with the company and creates helpful personal links. It also opens up a source of extremely valuable product ideas to the company.

> *Where should pro-active acquisition of ideas be applied?*

The pro-active acquisition of product ideas also involves utilizing the additional sources of ideas shown in Figure 3.2. Valuable information about potential fields of activity, current technology streams and weak points of the products developed thus far is available not only from employees but also from external partners such as subcontractors. Suitable incentives and an efficiently operating company proposal scheme can help make this know-how accessible to the company.

3.1.2   Reception of product ideas at single entry points

Why are single entry points needed?

If projects are to emerge from the ideas for new product features available in the company or acquired from external sources, they must in the first place be passed on to the responsible agents. This in turn presupposes that such agents exist and that their existence is also well known within the company.

How do single entry points work?

In view of the importance of collecting product ideas, it makes good sense to create special contact points for this purpose. These **single-entry points** receive all product ideas coming in from around the world for a particular business sector and assign them to the teams responsible for processing them further. They therefore form the starting point for the selection of projects for innovative products and play a strategic role within a project-oriented company. Accordingly, it is important to provide them with appropriate computer support. Group-ware systems such as **TopInfo** offer an excellent way of systematizing and speeding up the entire process of the world-wide collection of product ideas (see applying TopInfo in the definition process, p. 17).

How can the efficiency of idea collection be increased?

In order to facilitate the further processing and analysis of product ideas, it makes good sense to specify a standardized format for them. Figure 3.3 shows an example of such a **request form**. A standardized

Figure 3.3 Example of a request form

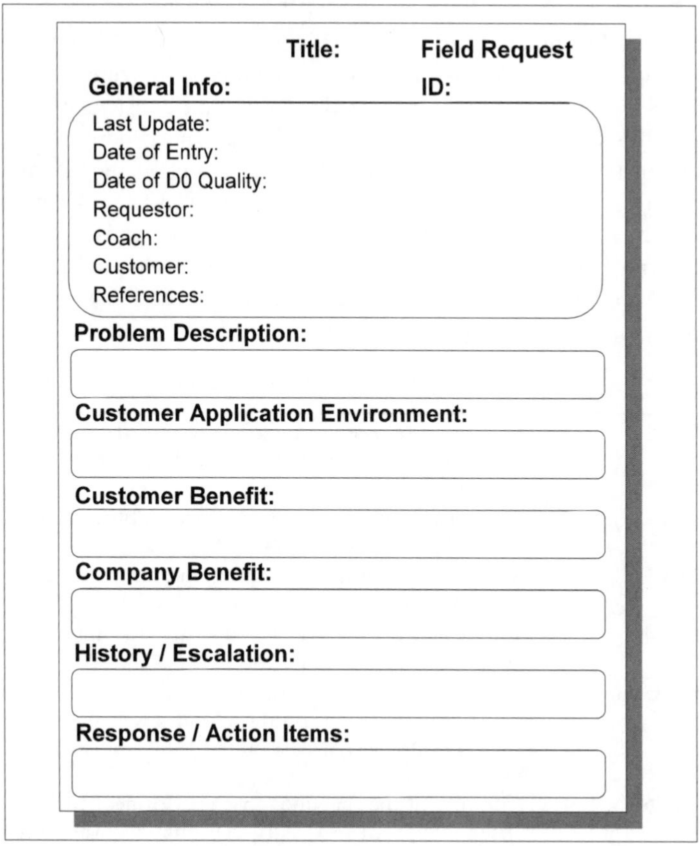

	Title:	Field Request
General Info:		ID:

Last Update:
Date of Entry:
Date of D0 Quality:
Requestor:
Coach:
Customer:
References:

Problem Description:

Customer Application Environment:

Customer Benefit:

Company Benefit:

History / Escalation:

Response / Action Items:

form obliges the applicant to proceed in a systematic way by specifying which basic information must be entered in order to make these ideas useful. In practice, a standard form also channels the information search by guiding customer-service or sales employees to the relevant information and thus simplifies the selection of useful product ideas. Computers offer a way of permitting only fully completed request forms to be passed on for further processing from the outset. Thus a form might require details of the customer in question, of the existing system environment as well as the anticipated effect (inclusive of its expected duration) on this customer of acting on the proposal.

Case study 3.2   Feature Documentation Building Blocks (FDBs)

Feature Documentation Building Blocks (henceforth abbreviated to FDBs) form the basis of project documentation referred to a specific product. They describe the individual constituents and features of a planned product derived from the product break-down structure (see Structure plans, p. 91) as well as the activities required for its manufacture. Because the product description becomes increasingly detailed as the project proceeds, and the information available about it also becomes increasingly specific, it is recommended to split the FDBs up into several classes. This procedure is illustrated in Table 3.1.

Table 3.1   Contents of specifications

FDB1:	Description of a performance feature of the planned product from the viewpoint of the potential or acutely affected client.
FDB2:	First description of the performance feature from an internal technical viewpoint.
FDB3:	Definition of user interface of the performance feature to be manufactured.
FDB4:	More detailed concept as to how the performance feature is to be implemented.
FDB5:	Clear definition of the distribution of the product feature among various product complexes (subsystems) as well as complete specification of the associated interfaces.
FDB6:	Definition of the functions to be performed within the various complexes as well as their interfaces (important communications object for those involved in the project).
FDB7– . . . (e.g. 14):	Increasingly specific documentation of the routines required for the final system test of the individual product components as well as their interaction.

The various FDBs can be easily linked to the schedule and resource plan. Responsibilities must be assigned to the individual FDBs and their completion must be specified at the various milestones. An example would be to define FDB1-4 as mandatory for a decision on implementing a product feature (project release). This then ensures that reliable information will be available as a basis for decision-making.

3.1.3 Filtering and selecting product ideas

> *How can project selection be supported by a suitable organization?*

Encouraged by suitable incentives, numerous product ideas will tend to stream into the single entry points. A multi-stage filter process must then be applied on a step-by-step basis to describe them in specific terms, to evaluate and select them and finally to collect the most promising ideas as project proposals (decision packages). This process runs continuously in project-oriented companies. An obvious approach is to set up special teams of experts to support the selection of product ideas and later of project proposals. Such **definition teams** should be interdisciplinary and comprise members with all relevant expertise including in development, sales, product management, manufacturing, service and commercial procedures.

A step-by-step filter process for selecting product ideas

> *Why should selection be made in writing?*

Such a step-by-step approach is necessary for selecting incoming product ideas because the effort required to process them increases exponentially as they acquire more specific contours. The more detailed the information that must be obtained for a product idea, the greater the investment lost to the company if the final decision goes against implementing the project.

> *How is preliminary selection made?*

In order to limit the investment of effort, an **incoming inspection** must be introduced as the first step in the filtering process. This is where the incoming requests are pre-selected. After examining the contents of the product ideas, experts must check whether the costs resulting from their acceptance (project costs, subsequent manufacturing costs, sales and service costs), as well as their revenues and strategic effects justify a more precise analysis. Only economically interesting and technically feasible customer requirements are then passed on for further processing in a second selection stage.

Table 3.2 Contents of a draft specification from the customer's viewpoint (FDB1)

General information	– Source – Global description – Responsible team members – Range of affected products etc.
If an *external* product idea: customer requirements	– Description of product features required by customer – Possible description of the *problem* (not the possible solution) that led to the suggestion – Description of the customer's current situation (capacity utilization etc.) – Any special requirements (secondary conditions such as: no new hardware should be required etc.) – Customer's competitive situation (are other competitors interested in this product idea?) – Interface requirements – Special features at local/international level – Forecast (how important would implementation of the idea be to the customer) – Customer benefit (savings, time benefits, etc.)
Interdependencies with other technical sectors	– Training/personnel – Logistics – Production – Service etc.
Interdependencies with existing products	– To which current products is the idea relevant? – Would cannibalization effects result? – Can synergies be utilized? – Relationships to third-party products
Competitive factors	– Current and future competition in this sector
Make or buy	– Subcontracting also possible? – Synergies with existing products (suppliers, economies of scale)
Business opportunities	– Market potential/attractiveness – Entry barriers, etc. – Risks
High-level plan for market launch	– Product positioning – Distribution channels – Pricing strategy
Cost saving	– Estimates of expected cost saving

> *How is the customer effect of an idea analyzed?*

The next filtering stage focuses on the procedures for translating the evaluated product ideas from customer requirements to corporate specifications. The relevant technical experts thus elaborate the ideas available for selection in detail from the customer's perspective. For this purpose, it is recommended to prepare an initial rough specification (see Feature Documentation Building Blocks, p. 22). A completed rough specification from the customer's perspective (FDB1) should comprise the data on the subject areas listed in Table 3.2.

> *How can the efficiency of idea selection be enhanced?*

An analysis of the product ideas on the basis of specified criteria allows the significance and long-term consequences of accepting them to be examined from the customer's perspective. But it also helps to show up the weak points of these ideas (such as excessively short-term results) at an early stage. A regular reworking of the FDB1 topics allows the experience gained in the past implementation of product ideas to flow into the current process. The utilization of this experience enhances the learning capability of the company and thus the efficiency of project selection.

> *When does the technical specification take place?*

The presentation from the customer's perspective is followed by a description of the product idea from an **internal technical perspective** in the form of an FDB2. The consequences of implementing the requirements are then worked out in cooperation with experts from each of the relevant technical sectors:

- Initial project cost estimates (see Project cost estimate, p. 28),
- Initial economic feasibility study (see Profitability analysis, p. 40)
- License and patents situation,
- Necessary training programmes etc.

Together, FDB1 and FDB2 provide sufficient criteria to evaluate and prioritize the ideas available for selecting potential new product features in a next step.

A ranking system for evaluating ideas for product features

> *How are ideas made comparable?*

A **ranking system** derived from the **scoring method**[6] offers a good way of selecting those ideas for new product features that are to be included in decision packages. Because numerous possible ideas must be compared on the basis of diverse criteria, a systematic presentation of these criteria and alternatives is needed to make well founded decisions. In a first step, therefore, the criteria, which will be used to evaluate and compare the various product ideas are listed. In a second step, they are assigned an individual scale (numeric, ordinal or cardinal). The targets can then be evaluated in terms of the degree of attaining the individual customer requirements, which are to be compared. In a third step, the individual criteria are weighted in accordance with their importance, for example by being assigned a factor between 0 (irrelevant) and 1 (very significant).[7]

> *Which ideas go into the package?*

Finally, classifying the available ideas in this ranking model, which may become a permanent institution within the company or the definition team, supports the selection of product ideas to be included in a package. The weighting of the product ideas yields a prioritized list, which can be used as a basis for making the final decision. An example of a ranking system is shown in Tables 3.3 and 3.4.

> *What are the advantages of scoring?*

A significant **advantage** of using the benefit value method for selecting projects is the use of *a single* model for all the comparative criteria (such as quantifiable cost parameters and the strategy-compliance, which is difficult to measure). Because it is independent of the ease with which these criteria can be quantified, it allows *a single* overall benefit value to be obtained for the various alternatives. In addition, a method of this kind, which has become an established institution within the company, ensures that project proposals are always checked on the basis of all relevant criteria irrespective of the source from which they were submitted.

Table 3.3 Ranking system to choose from customer requirements (I)

(1) Choose criteria
(2) Assign a scale to each (for example: US$, high–low)

(4) Evaluate requirements

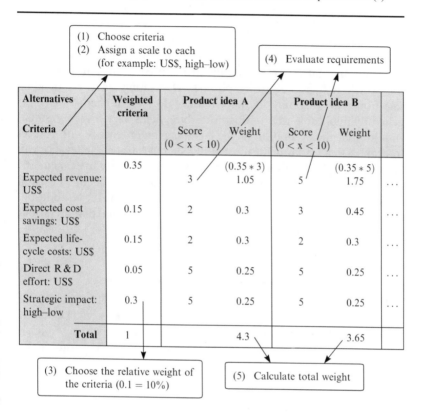

Alternatives / **Criteria**	**Weighted criteria**	**Product idea A** Score (0 < x < 10)	**Product idea A** Weight	**Product idea B** Score (0 < x < 10)	**Product idea B** Weight	
Expected revenue: US$	0.35	3	(0.35 * 3) 1.05	5	(0.35 * 5) 1.75	. . .
Expected cost savings: US$	0.15	2	0.3	3	0.45	. . .
Expected life-cycle costs: US$	0.15	2	0.3	2	0.3	. . .
Direct R & D effort: US$	0.05	5	0.25	5	0.25	. . .
Strategic impact: high–low	0.3	5	0.25	5	0.25	. . .
Total	1		4.3		3.65	

(3) Choose the relative weight of the criteria (0.1 = 10%)

(5) Calculate total weight

Table 3.4 Ranking system to choose from customer requirements (II)

Product idea	**Weight**	**Ranking/Priority**
Product idea A	4.3	1
Customer requirement C	4.1	2
. . .	. . .	. . .
Product idea B	3.6	9
. . .	. . .	. . .

> *What must be considered in a scoring run?*

The **danger** of this approach lies in its apparent objectivity. The instrumental character of benefit value analysis and its results in the form of quantitative scores lend the procedure the illusion of objectivity, which it does not really possess. Depending on the individual selection and weighting of the criteria – for which there can be no generally applicable rules – this procedure yields very diverse results.[8] In addition, the evaluation of the customer requirements with respect to criteria that are difficult to quantify such as strategic relevance can hardly be checked objectively. Nor is it sufficient merely to evaluate the individual features in isolation in order to produce the decision package, as was done in the ranking system shown here. In addition, the decision must also include the effects of a **combination of various product features** (such as on market success or costs).

> *What can scoring achieve?*

The scoring method should therefore be seen as a highly informative and easily visualized tool for supporting selection decisions. However, it can never fully exempt the decision authorities from the responsibility for the final decision as to which product ideas should be included in the decision packages.

Case study 3.3   *Project cost estimate*

Every project represents a new process for the company. This creates a problem, namely that in the early phases of a project no precise information is yet available on the activities to be performed, their scheduling or their exact resource requirement. As a result, it is not easy to plan the project costs. However, information about the expected project costs is also required in the early phase of a project: in order to accept or reject an order, to release the project, for make-or-buy decisions or for distributing the budget among subprojects (Figure 3.4). Various ways of *estimating* project costs have thus been proposed and applied. Because extensive literature is already available on this topic, it will suffice here to merely give a brief overview of a number of particularly interesting approaches.[9]

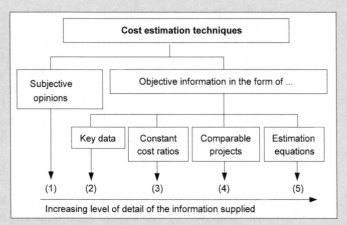

Figure 3.4   Cost estimation techniques

(1) **Subjective procedures** estimate costs on the basis of expert opinions, e.g. by drawing on the expertise of particularly knowledgeable employees. They can also be used where very little starting data is available or is present only in an unstructured form. They are particularly fast and flexible. Because of their subjectivity, however, the results derived from them cannot be analyzed or checked objectively. Among the best-known subjective procedures are team estimates and the Delphi method.

(2) **Key data procedures** attempt to summarize the experience gained in finished projects in the form of key data in order to estimate the costs of new projects. This is done by first estimating a *reference parameter* (such as kg or lines of code) for the project. This reference parameter is then multiplied by a cost factor that may, for instance, reflect the previous costs of each unit of this reference parameter. A key data procedure frequently used in development projects is the *expenditure estimate:* the manpower expenditure for the project is estimated in PY (person years) and the overall expenditure is then extrapolated on the basis of an hourly rate.

    The simple applicability and speed of this procedure must be offset by the strong dependence of its reliability on the measured reference parameters and their connection with the actual project costs.

(3) **Ratio procedures** are based on the constant relationship existing between specific cost relationships in similar projects. Thus the *percentage rate technique* assumes a similar distribution of costs among the various phases of a project. If the average cost of the definition cycle in previous projects was found to be, say, 20 per cent of the total project costs, then the total costs of a current project can be extrapolated on the basis of the actual data from its definition phase. Similar procedures can be used to determine the structure of the various types of cost involved in a project (material cost share, etc.).

These procedures can give very accurate results in projects of similar structure. However, they require initial data measurements, which may be very extensive (e.g. expenditures in the definition phase), thus limiting their applicability in the early phases of a project.

(4) **Adaptation procedures** are very popular in practice. These procedures also make use of the experience gained from earlier projects. The first step is to find a project or subproject which is similar to the current one. The differences between this and the current project are then identified in order to determine the costs of the new project. This is facilitated by the fact that data resources from past projects are usually administered in computer systems. *INVAS* is an example of an adaptation procedure developed at Siemens AG as an integrated process for estimating project costs. This computer-based system is used to forecast the manpower costs of software development projects by identifying suitable comparative projects. Parameters such as the time required for the development, the cost centres involved and their productivity are then used to estimate the expected costs of the project.

The speed, adaptability and quality of these procedures must be offset by the high information input required to obtain a cost forecast. However, this drawback can be minimized by the use of powerful computers.

(5) Parametrical cost estimates, also known as **cost estimation relationships (CERs),** use regression analyses to determine the relevant version of the parameters in CER equations which are either available commercially or are developed within the company.

One of the best known CERs for determining the costs of software developments is the *constructive cost model* (*COCOMO*). Its basic variable is the number of lines of code that must be generated. The basic version uses the simple regression equation $A_{base} = C1 * U^{C2}$. It allows the development expenditure Abase to be determined on the basis of the source code instructions (in units of 1000) as well as the regression constants $C1$ and $C2$ obtained from previous projects. Various extensions are available for obtaining more precise forecasts.

Another widely used CER is *function point analysis* from IBM. A function value is determined for a new project and is subsequently used to estimate the expected manpower expenditure. The function value is in turn calculated from function points, which are assigned on the basis of the complexity and dimensions of the project. These are then multiplied by an effect function that reflects the cost-increasing or decreasing effect of the environment.

The quality of the estimate and the speed of application of existing CERs are offset by their drawback of low adaptability – i.e. completely new estimates must be made in the event of changes in the project.

In practice, a number of these procedures are combined (e.g. team estimate plus plausibility checks via CERs) in order to obtain a reliable estimate for the expected project costs.

3.2 EVALUATING PROJECT PROPOSALS

Project proposals are collected continuously. This process is an automatic part of the acquisition of customer orders but also exploits every other source of project proposals. Specific project proposals are derived from strategic planning, for example. In other cases, the process described above is used to create decision packages from a series of product ideas. These packages then also have the character of project proposals.

> *What is the evaluation for?*

In order to select those projects, which will actually be released from a series of diverse project proposals, these must initially be made comparable by means of an **evaluation**. As Figure 3.5 shows, this evaluation must be based on both **strategic** and **operative** criteria. Specifically, the following aspects should be covered:

- The suggested projects should be examined for their **compliance** with corporate **strategy.**
- An evaluation of the project proposals from the **customer's perspective** should show:

  (a) which customers would be affected
  (b) which market segments would be served by the project
  (c) what other effects (image, customer satisfaction, etc.) would result for the customers.

- From the **employees' perspective**, a check should be made as to whether the existing know-how would be optimally applied in the suggested projects and how attractive these are for the employees. This is important, because otherwise resources would be left unused and employee expertise would be developed more slowly than is desirable. Moreover, the assignment of employees to demanding projects encourages their motivation and work satisfaction and thus their productivity.
- A specific evaluation from the **process viewpoint** would also analyze the internal core processes, which the project will have to traverse. This involves an estimate of the probable duration of the project as well as of the expected project costs.
- Finally, the profitability of the projects must be assessed from a **financial viewpoint**. This might include the following aspects:

  (a) The profitability of the project (see Profitability analysis, p. 40)
  (b) Its potential contribution to the shareholder value – e.g. the attainable return on investment
  (c) The necessity and possible ways of financing the project.

Case study 3.4   The s-curves concept[10]

Technologies, and thus the products based on them, are subject to a life cycle. This means that they do not have an infinite life but leave the market after having traversed a number of typical life phases. This insight is used by the concept of *s*-curves to clarify the need to develop replacement technologies at an early stage. Figure 3.5 shows this concept graphically. It is assumed that the output of R&D activities (in particular the performance of the resulting technology) initially increases faster than the funds invested in this sector. From a certain turning point, however, it begins to increase at a slower rate than this investment (known as the declining marginal rate of return of R&D expenditure). In other words, the expenditure required to reach an additional unit of performance of a technology increases with the age of the technology. This means that it tends to be more difficult to attain an additional boost in performance for a mature technology than for more recent technologies.

Figure 3.5   Technology *s*-curve

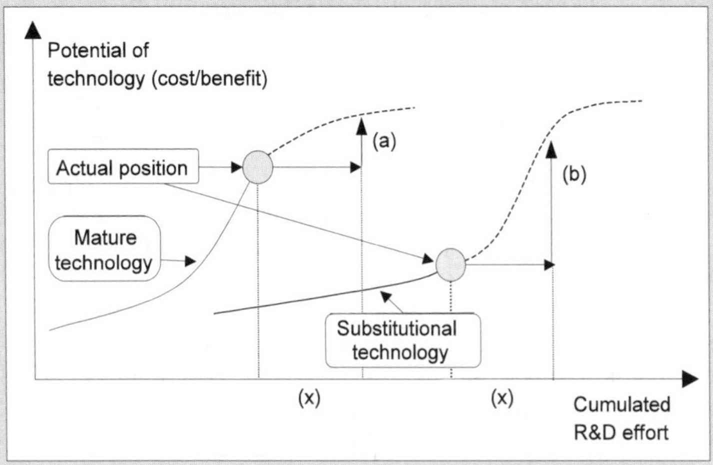

The goal of strategic planning is derived from this *s*-curve concept – namely, to determine the optimum time at which the transition should be made from an old technology to a substitution technology. The point must therefore be identified from which additional R&D expenditure (marked in the diagram with (x)) promises more output (marked with (b) and (a)) when it is invested in a new technology than in an old one.

The great difficulty here is the impossibility of forecasting the future development of a technology with any reliability. After all, it depends just as much on the behaviour of the competitors as on developments in other sectors. And the results of basic research also affect the future market success of a technology.

Floppy disks for computers offer an example of the poor predictability of the life cycle of a technology. Their marketability will in the future depend very significantly on how CD-ROM technology develops. If it has become possible to make these devices recordable at little cost, floppy disks may quickly disappear from the market together with all their associated products.

3.2.1 Strategic aspects of evaluating project proposals

The role of strategic planning in selecting projects

> *Does project selection have a strategic significance?*

The strategic dimension of project selection is particularly clear in the sector of product innovation. Ever shorter product life cycles mean that companies must plan well in advance to identify the products they wish to use to secure market shares in the immediate future. For example, as early as 1996, products that had been developed less than two years earlier accounted for 90 per cent of all sales in the sector of telecommunications terminals at Siemens AG. This trend will intensify in the new millennium.

> *What does strategic planning do?*

Strategic planning examines the future development of the corporate environment by means of market and competitiveness analyses both within and outside a particular sector. It also attempts to anticipate changes in this environment by means of early warning systems. The information obtained in this way is then used to select the business fields on which the company should focus its activities in the mid to long term. Strategic orientations, known as **roadmaps**, are elaborated. They outline the technologies and promising markets on which corporate groups should concentrate in the immediate future. (see s-curves concept, p. 32).

(see s-curves concept, p. 32)

Which projects are strategically important?

However, this strategic dimension is not limited to projects for innovative products alone. All projects focus corporate resources on the satisfaction of customer requirements. In doing so they tie up employees and resources over several months or years. So the decision in favour or against a project always implies the question as to whether it makes sense for the company to apply its resources to this specific objective. Thus if a company were to decide to opt out of nuclear energy, it may make sense to deploy part of its workforce principally in projects for customers in other technology sectors, such as hydro-electric power. After all, the work pursued in a project always affects the direction in which the know-how of the employees involved is developed.

- The selection of a project proposal affects the mid-term development of employee qualifications. Selecting a project thus always means identifying the main markets onto which the company will focus its activities.
- The basic emphasis of strategic planning must be reflected in the portfolio of implemented projects in order to attain the strategic targets.

What are the functions of strategic planning?

In order to realize this aim, two functions are performed within the scope of strategic planning for the collection and evaluation of project proposals. In the first place, criteria are developed for checking existing project proposals to ensure that they comply with corporate strategies – i.e. the proposals are **verified**. Secondly, specific product ideas and/or proposals are generated within strategic planning. For example, the development of an innovative product or the implementation of a desirable reorganization may be proposed. Despite their prominent character, product ideas and proposals derived from strategic planning must traverse the same evaluation process. This will now be described.

Figure 3.6   Evaluating project proposals

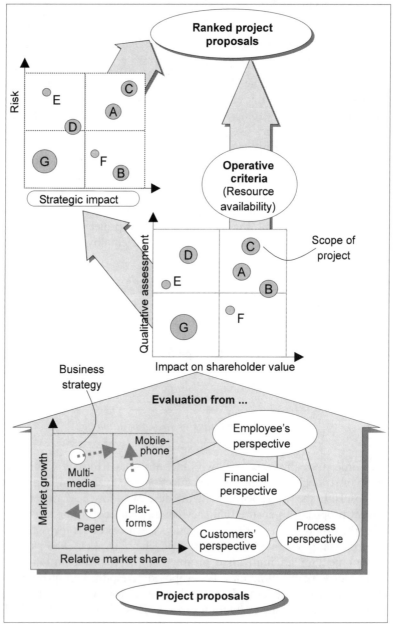

Strategic planning tools for evaluating project proposals

Portfolio method

> What are portfolios?

The most widely used way of visualizing the planned strategic development of a company is the **portfolio method**[11] (cf. Figure 3.6 and Figure 3.7). A portfolio is a two-dimensional grid used for classifying the previous and planned activities of a company. Its great advantage lies in its suitability as a presentation tool. However, its simplicity is at the same time a major drawback wherever it is used as the sole basis for a decision in favour of or against specific activities.

> What part do portfolios play in selecting projects?

In selecting projects, portfolios nevertheless act as an important aid for checking the correct orientation of all current and planned projects with respect to corporate strategy. Project proposals can thus be classified on the basis of their contribution to individual fields of

Figure 3.7   Business-field portfolio

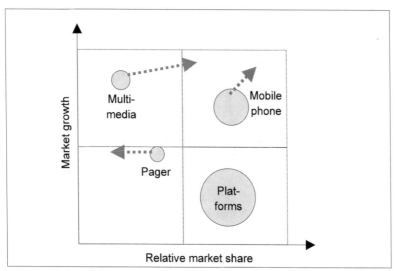

activity within a business-field portfolio or other portfolio methods. The distribution of critical corporate resources (employee capacity and know-how as well as capital) among the projects should then correspond to the strategic importance attached to these fields of activity.

> *What are strategies for the example?*

In the example shown in Figure 3.7 it would make little sense to tie up a large part of product development capacity in the fields of pagers and industrial installations. Instead, the strategic orientation should stipulate that know-how be concentrated on expanding the multimedia and mobile phone sectors. The platforms sector makes a significant contribution to the business results by acting as a *cash-cow*.[12] Customer-order projects acquired in that sector could thus finance the strategically important mobile phone and multimedia sectors and balance the risks taken by the company.

Strategic gap analysis

> *How can the need for new projects be visualized?*

A project is a problem-solving process. The problem to be solved is that a desired future state (such as a target profit) will clearly not come about automatically. The forecast development of the company does not agree with the desired goal. In fact, a project is needed (e.g. to develop a new product or to manufacture an installation for a customer) in order to close the gap between the goal and current projections. This idea is clarified by *strategic gap analysis* (cf. Figure 3.8).[13] In this procedure, the target specification derived from strategic corporate planning, e.g. with regard to the profit to be realized in the future, is compared with the projected results of developments in existing products and current projects. In view of the product life cycles, however, a decreasing development must be expected with time.

> *How do the strategic and operative gaps differ?*

Gap analysis makes a distinction between two categories of gaps. The term **operative gap** designates the shortfall between current projec-

Figure 3.8   Strategic gap analysis and project planning

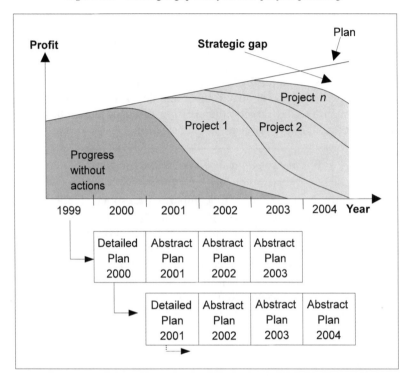

tions and targets which can be covered with projects that have already been initiated. In Figure 3.8,[14] for instance, a current product-innovation project (Project 1) could make an additional impact on the results from the year 2000. In contrast, the **strategic gap** is a target/actual deviation for whose coverage no steps have yet been taken. This gap must be closed by means of longer-term strategic planning via projects and other activities.

> *What are deferred costs and revenues?*

It should not be forgotten that a *current* project (No. 1) incurs costs *now* and will not yield revenues until *after* it has been completed (for example, in the form of new products or sales revenues from external customers). This delay is also important for commercial project planning, such as for the financing and profitability analysis of a project. This will be examined at a later stage.

> *Can only profit gaps be visualized?*

Gap analysis can naturally be performed not only on a target such as increased profits as was shown in this example. Other targets may also be set – such as sales targets, the creation of corporate value or the securing of a high level of customer satisfaction.

> *Where can gap analysis be usefully applied?*

Gap analysis can be used to compare the estimated effect of a suggested project with the company's strategic targets in order to clarify the **long-term benefit** of a project. It is a tool for managing *with* projects because it does not focus on processes within individual projects but on their aggregated effect on corporate targets. This means that the release of new projects should not be oriented solely to currently available technical, personnel and financial resources. Gap analysis also links the decision for or against a project to its longer-term effect.

Case study 3.5   Profitability analyses

Projects represent investments in which initial expenditures are made in the expectation of future returns. The procedures used in investment planning can therefore also be used to analyze the profitability of projects.[15]

In a profitability analysis (Table 3.5), a distinction can be made between static and dynamic procedures. These differ in the manner in which they deal with the time lag in the payments, costs and revenues associated with a project and which may be distributed over several years. The following projects and their payment flows can be used to illustrate these procedures.[16]

STATIC METHODS OF PROFITABILITY ANALYSIS

Static methods of analyzing the profitability of projects ignore the time aspects involved in the pattern of payments, costs and revenues.

Table 3.5   Example for a profitability analysis

FY	1998	1999	2000	2001	2002	2003	2004	
Project 1	−200	−200	−150	70	100	280	230	[K$]
Project 2	−250	−250	−180	270	420	80	30	[K$]

	Project runtime Expenditures		Market cycle Income from sales	
Cost comparison	Profit comparison	Profitability calculation	Amortization calculation	Net present value method
Costs [K$]	Profit [K$]	Return on sales	Amortization period	NPV with imputed interest = 5%; [K$]
−550	**130**	**19%**	> 3 years	7.23
−680	120	15%	**< 2 years**	12.48

In **cost comparison calculations,** the total costs incurred in various projects are compared and the most cost-effective alternative is selected. **Profit comparison calculations** represent the logical extension of this procedure and also include the total revenues associated with the project.

Amortization calculations determine the period of time over which the expenditures associated with a project are recovered by corresponding revenues. A project with the shortest amortization period is regarded as the best bet. The problem is that this approach completely ignores what happens to the products after the end of this amortization period.

Cost-effectiveness calculations determine the sales revenues (results/sales) or the return on investment (ROI) of various projects. The ROI of a project is calculated as the mean profit yielded by the project divided by the mean capital tied up in the project.

Because of their simplicity, these static methods are the most widely used ways of analyzing profitability. They also include *economic product planning* (*EPP*) which attempts to present the results attainable by a project as well as its final product in a transparent form (Table 3.6).

Table 3.6 Example for economic product planning (EPP)

Fiscal Year	1998	1999	2000	2001	2002	2003	2004
Sales volume (items)	0	0	0	232	352	80	40
Unit price	–	–	–	1.5	1.5	1.5	1.5
Turnover	–	–	–	348	528	120	60
Manufacturing costs	0	0	0	23.2	35.2	8	4
R&D costs	230	230	160	20	20	20	20
Sales costs	0	0	0	23.2	35.2	8	4
Other costs	0	0	0	11.6	17.6	4	2
Operating profit	−230	−230	−160	270	420	80	30
Cumulated profit	−230	−460	−620	−350	70	150	180

Values in K$ **Return on sales:** 17.0%

DYNAMIC METHODS OF PROFITABILITY ANALYSIS

The dynamic ways of analyzing the profitability of projects also consider the times at which the payments are made and revenues are received. These procedures are based on the assumption that sales revenues occurring at a closer point of time should be assigned a higher valuation than those received at a later stage. One reason for this is the possibility of re-investing capital flowing back to the company at an earlier stage in new projects or making it available to another profitable investment.

In the **net present value (NPV) method**, therefore, future expenditures and revenues are discounted on the basis of the current time of planning. The NPV then represents a parameter that is adjusted for the temporal incidence of the payments and thus allows a fair *comparison* between various projects. This also becomes clear in the above example. In view of the early incidence of the payments in Project 2, this would obviously be preferred to Project 1. In the evaluation of *individual* projects, a positive NPV means that the relevant project is profitable in principle.

Whereas the net present value method uses an imputed interest rate to discount a series of payments in a project, the **internal rate of return method** calculates the interest rate, which yields a NPV of zero. This marginal yield reflects the marginal interest rate at which the discounted payments for a project exactly equal the discounted revenues. If the internal rate of return exceeds the minimum yield desired by the company, the project should be evaluated as positive.

In addition to this procedure, a whole series of other methods and variants are available for examining projects from the standpoint of profitability. However, as these are less widely used, the interested reader is referred to the relevant literature.[17]

3.2.2 Operative criteria for evaluating project proposals

Which criteria should be applied?

The tools used in strategic planning reveal the basic suitability of a project proposal to contribute to attaining the company's strategic goals. The actual decision on whether a suggested project should be implemented requires additional and more detailed information. In particular, the **profitability of the project** must be subject to critical analysis. This is done by comparing the costs involved in the project (see Project cost estimate, p. 28) with its expected returns. Various procedures are used to perform these profitability analyses in practice (see Profitability analysis, p. 40).

What must be considered in profitability analyses?

In order to obtain reliable and commercially well founded information on the profitability of a project, the following aspects must additionally be considered:

• A project initiated today may have positive effects for follow-on projects. Thus the development of a new product component does not benefit only the product for which it was designed. Follow-on projects can also make use of this new technology, thus yielding considerable cost savings. The same holds in the sector of customer-order projects, where current projects may bring in considerable service orders at a later stage. That's why it would be wrong to reject a current project if its costs cannot be covered by the revenues coming from the sale of the resulting product, without including its possible effects on follow-on projects.

- In the same way, a planned project may well have economic consequences for parallel projects within the company: either through the consumption of scarce resources, or perhaps due to future cannibalization effects of the products on the market.
- The project life cycle must be considered when checking its feasibility with respect to the budget. This is because a specific if generally non-linear cost pattern is linked to the life cycle of a project, which must be covered by the budgets of the following fiscal years.

> *Why are risk aspects important?*

The profitability of a project always represents an **anticipated parameter**. Diverse risk sources can affect the profitability in both positive and negative ways. As a consequence, it would be wrong to equate relatively safe projects with high-risk ones by merely comparing their (expected) sales revenues, for example. In fact, **risks** must be explicitly included in the evaluation of project proposals (cf. portfolio in Figure 3.6). The foundation stone for risk-aware project management is laid by establishing project risk catalogues (see Risk-aware project management, p. 47).

3.3   RANKING PROJECT PROPOSALS

> *When is prioritization required?*

When the projects have been selected, an authorized agency in the company (department management, sector management, project balance teams, etc.) must decide which projects should be released for implementation. In order to facilitate the task of this agency, the various project proposals must be suitably classified – i.e. they must be **prioritized**. This is needed in order:

- to provide a decision-making basis for selecting projects in the event that resources are insufficient to implement all suggested projects, and
- to assign a priority to the projects actually released at a later stage, which lays down which projects should have preference in obtaining critical corporate resources.

> *What does a scoring model do?*

In project-oriented companies in which the various decision-making bodies may be confronted with numerous suggested projects, it makes sense to support this prioritization in a methodical way. A good way of doing this is to use a **scoring model** (Figure 3.9). This way of prioritizing is similar to that used for the product ideas discussed in subsection 3.1.3. Despite the problems pointed out in that section, it is useful to weight the suggested projects with respect to each other in order to obtain an additional decision-making criterion for prioritizing and selecting projects. A scoring model provides a basis for weighting individual project proposals by combining operative and strategic information and clarifies the effect of each proposal on the corporate goals.

> *Which elements should a scoring model cover?*

The specific structure of the scoring model will depend on the company, the product and the technical sector involved. In general, however, the following perspectives should be covered:

- Strategic perspective
- Customer perspective
- Employee perspective
- Process perspective
- Finance perspective.

> *What might a scoring model look like?*

Figure 3.9 shows a possible structure of such a scoring model. The project proposals are evaluated on the basis of their contribution to the various objectives pursued by each sector (score from 0 to 5). Care is taken to include the mutual linkage of the individual objectives (arrows). The overall evaluations of the individual project proposals (score * contributions summed over all targets) will differ depending on the current mutual weighting of the targets (x per cent).

Figure 3.9   Possible structure of a scoring model

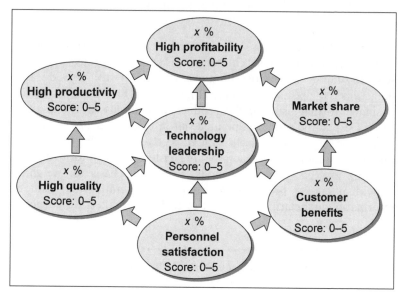

What are the limits of a scoring model?

It must again be stressed that a scoring method can merely offer support in making decisions. This model cannot automatically lead to prioritizing the projects and proposals, let alone yield a decision for or against specific proposals. Any attempt to make it do so would almost certainly lead to incorrect results.

How should emergency projects be treated?

Some projects appear to be unprofitable on the basis of the defined criteria but must nevertheless be implemented. Examples of such **mandatory projects** are conversion of the company to the euro, preparing for the Y2K problem or urgent emergency projects. However, because mandatory projects also consume resources, they cannot be excluded from the overall process of project selection. Because they *must* be implemented, they acquire a special status in subsequent procedures.

Case study 3.6 Risk-aware project management

Because a project represents a new task for a company, at least in subjective terms, it always involves risks:

- **Deadline risks**: such as those due to unexpected complications in individual work packages.
- **Cost risks**: such as those due to price increases in externally bought-in services.
- **Risks from market and environment**: new competitors, drop in demand, global legal stipulations, etc.
- **Technical risks**: problems in the realization of individual product components.
- **Risks from the project-management process**: unsuitable forms of organization, planning uncertainties, etc.

If these risks actually occur during a project, they can jeopardize its profitability and in extreme cases even necessitate its abortion. This is why risk awareness must be developed in project management – i.e. potential sources of danger must be explicitly included. A risk orientation can be ensured in the following way:

(1) Identification of project risks

A danger identified means a danger averted: this motto can also apply to project management. That's why potential sources of hazard should already be identified in the early phases of a project. The most efficient way of doing this is to use **risk checklists** that include data from earlier projects. Such lists should be assigned to individual sectors or to the entire company and must give the project director or controller a fast overview of potential risks. All risks recognized as being relevant to the project in hand are then documented in the form of a **project risk catalogue**.

This catalogue has a hierarchical structure similar to that of the project structure and schedule plans. It contains high-level information on the risks occurring at overall project level as well as more precise details of the risks present in the individual work packages. In order to cover the various levels of detail, comments on the different risk categories should previously have been obtained via questionnaires during the preliminary phase of the closed estimation session together with descriptions of the work packages.

The project risk catalogue (Figure 3.10) forms the basic documentation for risk-aware project control and should thus be continuously updated. This can be done in special risk audits or within regular status meetings, project rounds or group discussions.

Figure 3.10   Project-risk-catalogue

Project Beta - Risk Catalogue					
Aggregation: Overall project			Last changes:	Date:	
Category:	Description:	(A/B/C)	Impact:	Probability%:	Action Items:
Technical risks	Hardware and Software integration not possible	A	–200.000 US$	25	Audit at 20.10.
Market and environment	Company Z enters market in 2001	B	– 50.000 US$	10	Additional capacity
Cost risks	Supplier A rises prices	B	– 20.000 US$	30	Fallback supplier C
Time risks	Supplier B fails	B		20	Fallback supplier D

(2)   Evaluating the project risks

An **ABC analysis** is a good way of classifying the identified risks. Those risks whose occurrence could seriously jeopardize the profitability of a project are designated as *A risks*. Most risks may be classified as *B and C risks*. These include potential disturbances that can obstruct the course of the project to a greater (B) or lesser (C) extent.

To classify the risks into one of these three categories, an estimate must be made of the **probability of its occurrence** as well as its **effect** in such an event. Only experts can make such estimates. Depending on the phase and level of the current project, special expert teams (such as the definition team at overall project level in its early phase or auditor teams during its implementation) or relevant work groups (for risks at work-package level) provide an obvious answer.[18]

(3)   Handling risks by risk-aware project control

A risks in particular need to be watched in the course of the project, as they represent either very likely or very dangerous sources of hazard. The project management should therefore ensure regular reporting on the development of these risks.

A major task of risk-aware project management is to establish such awareness in the individual project teams. These should therefore receive direct feedback about all identified risks, their possible consequences as well as ways of bypassing them. Special incentives can be linked to the avoidance of particularly serious risks, such as preventing technical problems in an important subcomponent, in order to focus the attention and commitment of employees.

Further ways of handling project risks are:

- by incorporating buffer times into particularly critical project components
- by including a risk surcharge in the profitability analysis and the preliminary calculation
- by assigning specially qualified employees to critical activities
- by establishing additional reviews for critical product components and specifications, as well as
- by running special risk audits during project implementation.

3.4 PREPARING AND INITIATING PROJECT RELEASE

It has already been described in the preceding sections how incoming project proposals or those packaged within a subprocess are initially evaluated with the support of a definition team. The proposals are subsequently prioritized depending on their importance for the company. The processes of collecting and evaluating project proposals should run continuously so that they become established as routine functions in the company.

> *How is a project release initiated?*

This preliminary work now provides the basis for the relevant decision-making body (sector management, project balance team, etc.) to designate projects for release. The release ultimately takes the form of a project agreement in which the designated manager of the incipient project is officially assigned to this task. However, as will be shown in Part II, this does not necessarily mean that the project teams should not already start working on an individual project even before its release. On the contrary, the information obtained by the project team in the course of project planning is often required for a project release.

3.4.1   Selection of projects for release

> *What must the decision-making body do?*

The decision-making body has to apply the available corporate re-sources in a way to optimally reach the overall objectives of the company. To do this, it must assign the available budget as well as capacities, material resources and employees principally to those projects, which are particularly urgent, strategically important or particularly promising. As Figure 3.11 shows, in addition to the available budget, the main critical factor here is the available know-how of the employees.

Figure 3.11   Decision on project-release

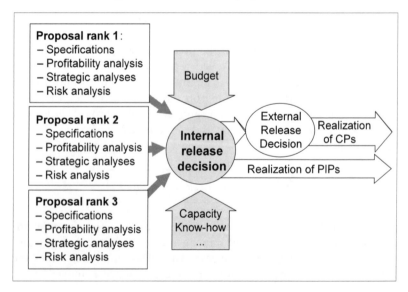

> *What information is needed?*

Three types of information are therefore needed as a basis for making the decision to select the projects to be released. It has already been shown how they are obtained in the preliminary phase of the release:

- Information about the submitted **project proposals**, in particular:

    (a) The ranking of the proposals against the background of the operative and strategic corporate goals (cf. the previous chapter).
    (b) A compact summary of the most important operative and strategic evaluations of the project proposals. To ensure better comparability between projects, a standardized form should be used for this purpose. An example of such a form is shown in Figure 3.12 (overleaf).
    (c) Risk catalogues for all project proposals (see Risk-aware project management, p. 47).

- The available **budget** for the period concerned.
- Information on available **capacities**, especially:
    (a) Information on available employee capacity as well as to their know-how (see Resource allocation planning system, p. 97).
    (b) Information on other expected bottlenecks in machines or resources.

> *How detailed should the information be?*

Depending on the business sector and type of project in question, information of differing detail and reliability may be required. Determining the level of detail of the requested information stands in close relation to the selection of the time of release. This question will now be examined.

3.4.2 Selecting the time of release

> *Why is the time important?*

The release of a project represents a major decision for the company, because it means that resources will be assigned to specific tasks for a

Figure 3.12   Information to support the release of project Beta V1.0

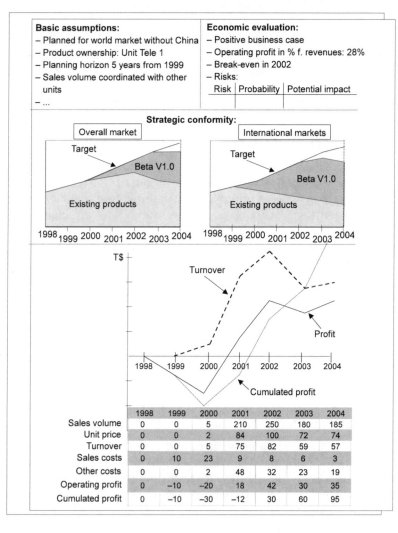

Basic assumptions:
– Planned for world market without China
– Product ownership: Unit Tele 1
– Planning horizon 5 years from 1999
– Sales volume coordinated with other
  units
– ...

Economic evaluation:
– Positive business case
– Operating profit in % f. revenues: 28%
– Break-even in 2002
– Risks:

Risk	Probability	Potential impact

Strategic conformity:

Overall market

International markets

	1998	1999	2000	2001	2002	2003	2004
Sales volume	0	0	5	210	250	180	185
Unit price	0	0	2	84	100	72	74
Turnover	0	0	5	75	82	59	57
Sales costs	0	10	23	9	8	6	3
Other costs	0	0	2	48	32	23	19
Operating profit	0	−10	−20	18	42	30	35
Cumulated profit	0	−10	−30	−12	30	60	95

long period of time. The choice of date for the project release is ultimately a decision about what demands should be made on the quality of the information specified as a precondition for the project.

> *What must be considered in selecting the release date?*

The data used in subsection 3.2.2 for anticipated project costs or sales revenues may be merely predictive in character. The more detailed the information on the planned project, the more accurately can the project expenditures be estimated and the required material and financial resources be released. If a decision on project release is already taken shortly after the project proposals come in or are made, then the profitability analysis will be limited to the data available up to that point. In this case of an early project release, such data may be no more than estimates by experts. However, if the project release is delayed until the completion of the bottom-up outlay estimate described in the following chapters (or if these subprocesses are run in parallel), then more precise data will be available for the profitability analyses from the closed estimation session.

In making the decision on the release date, therefore, all the aspects listed in Table 3.7 must be weighed up.

3.4.3 External project releases as a special feature of customer-order projects

> *Why is an external project release initiated?*

In contrast to product-innovation projects, the decision about the release of a customer-order project lies in two different sets of hands. An internal agency (departmental managers, project balance teams, etc.) must decide which projects should be carried out within a specific time frame. This **internal project release** corresponds to the descriptions so far given. In customer-order projects, however, an **external project release** must be added. Here, the customer who commissioned the project decides on its implementation.

Table 3.7   Early versus late project release

	Early project release on basis of approximate information	Later project release on basis of more detailed information
Examples of required inputs for product innovation projects	– First feature specifications – Strategy compliance checked – Top-down expenditure estimate by experts	– Feature specifications – Logistics concept – Service concept – Training concept – Product design etc. – Expert session (bottom-up cost-estimate) – Risk analysis etc.
Advantages	– Time benefits – Fewer policy problems if a proposed project is rejected	– More accurate and detailed data ⇒ more solidly based project decision ⇒ more accurate budgeting, financial planning etc. possible ⇒ lower risk of later target overruns
Disadvantages	– Danger of expensive project failures or fundamental deviations from the plan – Danger of budget overrun – Complex plan adjustments	– Danger of cognitive-dissonance avoidance: the more time already invested in examining suggestions, the greater the unwillingness to subsequently reject them – High planning expenditures – Motivation problems (if detailed and work-intensive suggestions remain unrealized too frequently)

> *What demands does the customer make?*

The demands made by the customer on the release of a project may be very diverse. In contrast to an internal department, the customer is less interested in the profitability of the project for the company but rather in its benefits for himself. He is concerned that the company should deliver a package with the desired quality at the desired date and at the desired costs. If he approaches several companies, it will be vital to realize these goals more efficiently than the competitors, who may be unknown.

Overall, this situation means that the managers of a customer-order project will face the following problems:

- The need to prepare in a flexible way the information which the customer requires for the external release of the project – e.g. schedule and deadline plans, cost plans, quality plans, etc.

> *Why is flexibility important?*

This flexibility refers not only to the contents of the project but especially also to the duration, type and accuracy of their implementation. Thus a customer may insist that his own project management processes be observed or that his own planning tools be used. A customer-oriented company must be able to respond to such demands.

- Great time pressure for the internal release.

> *Responding to time pressures*

External customers tend to set the company a tight time limit by which they expect an offer (a project proposal). All the information required by the customer must be available by that time.

Despite the focus on information for the customer, a decision must initially be made about the benefits that the project will bring to the company. This must consider all relevant matters as well as those covered in this section. However, a tight schedule for external release puts the process of defining customer-order projects under great pressure to ensure their efficient implementation. This makes it all the more important to systematize and implement this process in a defined way in a project-oriented company as well as to support it by means of suitable tools. These will include the release checklists described in Section 3.5.

- Parallel definition and implementation.

> *How useful is it to run processes in parallel?*

In practice, the definition and implementation processes of a project are run in parallel to some extent. This aspect will be examined more closely in Chapter 4 of Part II. Such parallel execution is unavoidable in view of the time pressure on the release of a customer-order project and to allow the internal release to take place at the optimum time. In concrete terms this means that a large part of the planning of an individual project is already completed before the internal and external release. This naturally involves the risk of investing efforts in a project that may ultimately not be implemented. However, this measure is absolutely unavoidable if the company is to be genuinely customer-oriented.

3.4.4 The contents of a motivational project agreement

> *What goes into a project agreement?*

At the internal release, corporate resources are officially assigned to the individual projects. The project agreement defines the rights and obligations of the corporate management and the designated project management. The project head(s) are granted corresponding powers of decision-making and delegation so that they can manage the '*sub-company' project* assigned to them independently as entrepreneurs within the company (cf. subsection 4.1.1 in Part II). At project release, the project managers are also set the initial objectives which they must attain via the project:

Initial objectives as the basis of a project

> *What part do the initial targets play?*

Defined **project targets** must comprise the starting point of every project. Their formulation can be seen as the basic foundation for the project. Just like a house, a successful project cannot be built on foundations which are soft, porous or unclear.

> *What must be the starting point for formulating the targets?*

The targets making up the foundations of a project must always be based on maximizing **customer satisfaction**. This is obvious in the case of customer-order projects, as the customer specifies the initial goals to a considerable extent. It is not quite as easy to focus on customer satisfaction in the product-innovation sector. However, the definition process includes a routine showing how this objective can be systematically achieved. In both cases, the objective of creating customer-oriented performance will be given concrete form in the project agreement by asking the following questions:

> *What types of project targets are defined?*

- **Product and quality targets**: Which product should be developed or manufactured and which performance features should it have? In the product-innovation sector, the quality target also covers the total manufacturing costs of the future product (see Target costing, p. 62).
- **Time targets**: When must the project be completed? The completion deadline is frequently a critical target parameter of a project. It is either derived from the optimal market window for a newly developed product or is specified by an external or internal customer.
- **Cost targets**: What is the maximum permissible cost of the project? This target is set by the project budget. Depending on the type of project, it covers the maximum project costs inclusive of any costs of production or market launch.

> *How do targets mutually affect each other?*

In formulating the initial targets, it must always be considered that project targets will mutually affect each other.[19] This also applies during the top-down development of the initial target ideas. Figure 3.13 shows possible **relationships between targets**. Thus the realization of a larger number of performance features may be possible only with additional costs, which may be excessively high, and longer project duration. The relationship between deadline and cost targets must also be considered. Excessively narrow deadline targets may lead to higher project costs – for instance, in the form of overtime or by having to

Figure 3.13   Possible relationships between project targets

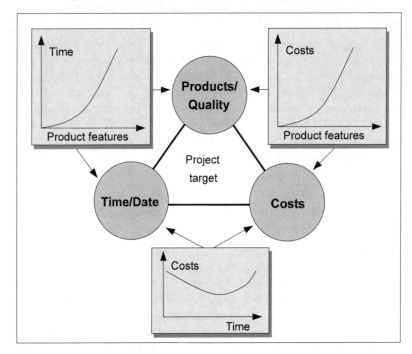

bring resources in externally. But excessively long project times also give rise to additional costs, either because of the longer tie-ups of personnel or by the loss of market potential or sales due to late market entry, penalty clauses, etc.

> *What is a target system?*

Consideration of such possible target relationships in the early phase of project planning allows a **target system** to be created for the project. The project contents, their dimensions and the time frames of the targets are recorded in this system.

> *Why must project targets be frozen?*

Because the initial targets form the foundation of a project, they must be frozen at project release. It is not easy to change this foundation after the project has started. The members of the project team must receive clear instructions as to what is to be attained by what means. If these instructions are unclear or are frequently changed, the motivation of the employees is jeopardized from the beginning and with it the success of the project.

What is the target system for?

The target system fixed in this way will be used later in the course of the project to break down the global targets into specific targets for the actual implementation of the project, i.e. it is the basis on which the targets for the individual project team members are elaborated.

Like the initial targets, the detailed targets must also satisfy the following conditions in order to act as motivators:[20]

What must be considered in formulating the targets?

- **Operationally**: The targets must be clear and understandable to the persons addressed and if possible be quantifiable. This involves three dimensions: the target content ('reduce costs'), the target extent ('by 15%') and the time frame ('by the end of 1999').[21]
- **Controllability**: The point of formulating the target is to give employees clear points of orientation for their actions. To allow the success of these actions to be monitored, the project targets must be formulated so that their attainment can be reliably checked. Thus milestones should be defined in terms of '100% results' whose attainment can be unequivocally evaluated with a 'Yes' or 'No'.
- **Possibility to be influenced**: In order to ensure employee motivation, only those targets may be specified which are within the power of the team members to change. To make people responsible for things which lie outside their power can have a negative effect on their commitment in other fields of activity too.

Motivational effect of other parts of the project agreement

What other contents are included?

In addition to the project targets, the project agreement must also lay down the rights, duties and competence of the project leaders. The aspects of employee motivation specified in Part III, Section 10.1, cannot be ignored when attempting to enhance the motivation of these leaders. Figure 3.14 summarizes the essential contents of a motivational project agreement. It also indicates factors that must be considered in formulating the individual points.

> *Which contents can be motivating?*

The establishment of performance-related rules of remuneration or bonuses is not always an effective motivational tool. And if employees are intrinsically motivated, such extrinsic incentives may even reduce their motivation. Moreover, the responsibilities granted to the project leaders or team members must be matched to their functions and competence. It has a negative effect on motivation if employees are made responsible for things they cannot control (see Motivation theories, p. 256). If a project leader has no authority over his subordinates, for instance, any attempt to motivate him in terms of remuneration based on the attainment of project targets will be to no avail.

In addition to the duties of the project leaders and team members, the responsibilities and duties of the top management must also be clarified at the start of the project. The resulting framework conditions then increase the reliability of the project implementation.

> *How can customer feedback be ensured?*

In order to ensure that the project management is genuinely customer-oriented, this must be written into the project agreement. Thus it may be stipulated that the leader of a customer-order project must define suitable yardsticks in order to measure the level of customer satisfaction. These may be defined within the project (e.g. obtain feedback from the customer about the product specification), or may go beyond the project (e.g. raising the quality of the product after the customer has used it for two years). Measures of this kind allow the **feedback** outlined in Figure 2.1 to be systematically utilized in the implementation and marketing processes. This in turn is an important element for motivating the employees for future projects.

Figure 3.14   Contents of a motivational project agreement

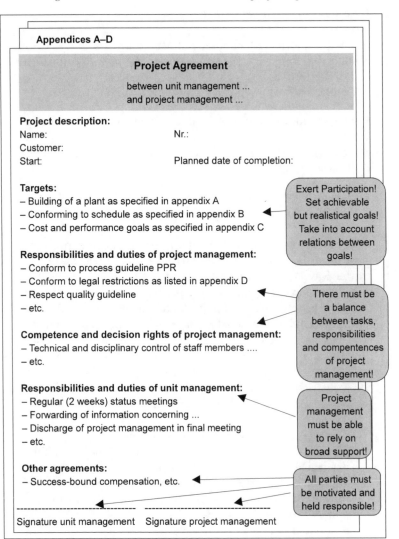

Case study 3.7   Target costing

A customer-oriented company must ensure as early as the product development stage that its products are both competitive and cost-effective.

The decisive factors for achieving this end are:

- the **quantities** of the new product which can be sold over its entire life cycle
- the **price** tag that can be attached to the product, as well as
- the **cost** of the product.

The **quantity** and the **product price** are affected by the quality of the product. As competitive pressures rise, a company is increasingly less able to influence these two factors.

However, products that are both successful and profitable must have the quality desired by the customer and be available at the lowest possible **cost**. Because up to 70 per cent of manufacturing costs and up to 90 per cent of the entire life cycle costs of a product are fixed in its development,[22] the profitability must be carefully considered at an early stage in product-innovation projects. Indeed, it lies at the very centre of the target costing procedure, which consequently has its broadest application in the early phases of product innovation, such as in the product design and construction stages. Target costing covers the following substeps:[23]

(1) *Deriving the upper cost limit for a product*
    The maximum price of the planned product is initially determined. This is to some extent set by the competition, and reflects the price that the customers are prepared to pay for the planned product.[24] If the planned profit per product unit is deducted from this figure, the costs of the planned product allowable by the market are obtained. These **allowable costs** are the costs that the resulting product must not exceed if the target profit is to be attained (Figure 3.15). They should comprise both the individual costs and the product-oriented overheads. But they will also include some utilization costs incurred by the customers in using the product (such as operating and disposal costs).

Figure 3.15 Determination of target costs

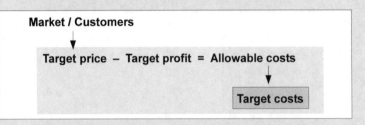

In the most usual *market-to-company* variant of target costing, the allowable costs are set directly in the form of **target costs** – i.e. as the upper cost limits of the planned product.

Sometimes the allowable costs are additionally compared with the **drifting costs** associated with the company (e.g. based on existing design drawings and given production conditions). The target costs are then finalized in negotiations whose object is the closing of the gap between allowable costs and drifting costs. Within product-innovation projects, such negotiations may well form part of the expert session mentioned in Part II (Section 4.1.3), after the drifting costs have been measured in providing a description of the work package. However, as this approach diverges from the desired customer orientation, the *market-to-company* procedure described above is to be preferred.

(2) *Deriving cost specifications for product functions and components*

A product must offer various **functions** (e.g. for a car: driving, being attractive and safe). It also consists of several parts (product **components** such as tires, steering wheel and seats). To ensure that the target costs are observed, the costs determined for the total product must be broken down among the individual product functions and later among the product components (Table 3.8).

The definition of a product-innovation project includes a specification of the **functions**, which the planned product must satisfy. The individual functions of the product are then **weighted** relative to one another – i.e. the relative importance of each function *for the customer* is determined.

Table 3.8 Target costs for different product functions

Function	Weight (%)	Target costs ($)
Driving comfort	30	3 600
Sporting optics	10	1 200
Security	30	3 600
(...)	(...)	(...)
Total	100	12 000

In our example, the target costing is performed for the interior fittings of a car. In the first stage of the product structure plan, the target costs of the interior fittings are estimated to be $12 000. Because driving comfort makes up 30 per cent of the total customer benefit attainable via the interior fittings, the target costs of the product functions will be $3600. This figure then represents the target costs for improving the motorist's comfort and convenience by means of the car's interior fittings (Table 3.9).

In the further course of the implementation process, the total product is subdivided into individual **product components**. The product and work breakdown structures detailed in Part II, Section 4.1.2 provide the tools for this purpose.

Table 3.9 Contribution of components to the fulfilment of product functions

	Driving comfort (%)	Optics (%)	Security (%)	(...)
Seats	60	20	30	
Gear box	10	5	10	
Steering wheel	20	15	15	
Dashboard	10	35	25	
(...)				
Total	100	100	100	

Table 3.10 Determining component weights

	Component weight (%)	Component target costs ($)
Seats	29	3.480
Gear box	7	0.780
Steering wheel	12	1.440
Dashboard	14	1.680
(...)		
Total	100	12.000

The target costs are broken down appropriately among the individual product components by evaluating the degrees to which the various components are responsible for various functions. In the example shown in Table 3.9, the seats make up 60 per cent of the motorists' comfort, 20 per cent of the optical impact and 30 per cent of the safety of the interior fittings. These figures provide the basis for the **component weights** (e.g. seat weighting = 60 per cent * 30 per cent + 20 per cent * 10 per cent + 30 per cent * 30 per cent = 29 per cent). In this way, the maximum costs of each component required for keeping within the target costs for the total product are obtained in steps.

In the example in Table 3.10 the costs of each seat set must not exceed $3.480 if the weighting of the components is to correspond to the importance assigned to them by the customers. The design, manufacture etc. of the seats must be oriented to this target parameter at an early stage. In a product-innovation project, the steps of breaking down the target costs among the individual components are performed within the process of deriving the low-level plans from the high-level plans as described in Part II (Section 4.1.4).

(3) *Monitoring and securing observance of target costs*
The target components specify the upper cost limits as guidelines for the members of the project team, such as the designers. They must observe these limits in planning and implementing the components. In order to be aware of any

divergence from the target costs at an early stage, it is a good idea to continuously keep tabs on them within the scope of the project monitoring. The members of the project team also estimate the subsequent cost effects of their work, such as the future manufacturing costs of a component. Interdisciplinary cooperation is thus encouraged between employees in the various sectors (development, sales, production, etc.) within the process of target costing. This information is then used in the project-monitoring phase for the

- observation of the target costs specified for the individual components, as well as for the
- correct customer-oriented weighting of the individual components in the total product.

Current forecasts of the cost shares of the various components are plotted on a **value control chart** (Figure 3.16). This shows whether the components are weighted in line with their contribution to the customer benefit of the product at a particular time. A funnel-shaped tolerance range is defined so that target divergence is not proscribed as rigorously for trivial components as for more important ones. If a component lies above a corridor this means that its

Figure 3.16   Value control chart

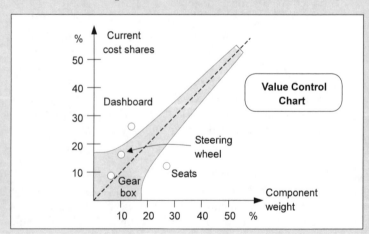

cost share is at that moment higher than the value corresponding to its contribution to customer benefit. Cost-reduction measures must be applied at this point. If a component lies below the control range, a check must be made to see whether further improvements are possible, as this may allow the customer benefit to be increased.

In this example, it should be examined whether greater focus on the development of customer-oriented seats may produce added value. In the same time a simpler and less expensive design of dashboard or steering wheel can be considered, possibly by using less costly materials.

By orienting the product design to customer benefit, target costing offers an important tool for the kind of customer-oriented management that is specifically called for in product-innovation projects. It is useful to avoid developing products with many technical components that the customer may not want at all. Within projects, it also acts as a tool for guiding the behaviour of the team members with respect to targets.[25] But target costing is also useful for continuously monitoring the customer orientation of existing products.[26]

3.5 SUMMARIZED DEFINITION RESULTS IN THE RELEASE DOCUMENTATION

> *What is the release documentation for?*

In the definition cycle, a project is selected and ultimately released for implementation. In order to ensure easy transition to the implementation stage, the results of the definition process must be summarized in a clear and concise form. This is an indispensable step for improving the flow of information between the various subprocesses, especially if at least some of the members of the project implementation team are different from those working on the project definition.

The release documentation may have various designations. Known conventionally as the **specifications sheet**, some companies prefer to call it the **master binder** or **M1 documentation**.

Release documentation for a product-innovation project may include the following contents:

What can the release documentation cover?

- A description of the performance features of the product to be manufactured and their interactions (such as FDB1-4)
- A definition of the user interface
- A design and implementation concept
- A rough draft for tests and trials
- Information on country-specific market introduction and certification expenditures
- The business data planned for the project/product
- An economic product plan (EPP)
- A high-level schedule network plan (**PERT CHART**) for all units involved, including the principal milestones and their results
- A manufacturing concept
- A service concept with service-relevant business data
- A logistics concept for market launch, tools and documentation
- The distribution channels involved
- A basic marketing concept
- Interdependencies with other products
- A rough price concept (see Target costing, p. 62)
- Other contents (e.g. information on requirements for approval, licence situation, recycling considerations etc.).

How are the specific contents defined?

It is clear that the release documentation forms an important part of a project agreement. This is because it summarizes the most important targets to be attained, plans to be realized and guidelines to be observed. Contents can be added or removed as desired, depending on the project type. A standard must be created which is applicable over all sectors and departments and contains at least the contents of the release documentation in order to facilitate the work of the **implementation teams** – i.e. those employees who are assigned to individual projects. This ensures that all-important aspects are considered as early as the definition process when finalizing the project proposals.

> *How can the efficiency be increased?*

Using a release checklist can increase the efficiency of preparing the release documentation and thus concluding the definition process. This covers all contents that are regarded as potentially important for a project on the basis of experience gained from earlier projects.

> *How should checklists be used?*

To be of any real use, a checklist must be seen simply as a helpful device. By no means all the documents and concepts listed in it should be created/acted on in each project and included in the release documentation. A release check list represents a maximum plan which helps users to benefit from the experience gained in earlier projects and to design a particular project more efficiently. When defining a project, a quick assessment can be made on the basis of a checklist as to which of the points listed are required in the current project and which are not. This speeds up project execution and gives the project management the assurance that no important contents have been left out of the project release.

> *What happens after the release?*

The transition to the process of **project management** takes place at the latest with the release of the project and hand-over of the release documentation to the implementation team. Part II will cover this aspect in detail.

It has already become clear from Figure 2.2 that project release does not represent the final conclusion of the definition process. A number of basic ideas are implicit within the circular representation of this process:

- Product ideas and proposals that were rejected should not be deleted immediately from the corporate memory
- The definition process itself must be allowed to evolve continuously.

3.6 SYSTEMATIC RECYCLING OF PROJECT PROPOSALS AND IDEAS

> *Why are rejected proposals still needed?*

Suggested projects, which could not be implemented for technical reasons, as a result of poor market prospects or on the basis of other criteria should not be finally rejected out of hand. The dynamics of the markets and of technical advances may well lead to a situation in which formerly non-feasible or inappropriate alternatives may yet turn out to offer interesting and stimulating indications for potential developments. The same applies to product ideas, which were examined more closely but were excluded from decision-making packages. And customer orders that were rejected internally or externally may well provide valuable clues for subsequent improvements. They may, for instance, reveal a need to catch up in technology or weaknesses *vis-à-vis* competitors and thus represent important input for future product-innovation projects.

> *How are rejected proposals processed further?*

Rejected project proposals or the product ideas they contain should initially be classified, for instance into purely *nice-to-have features* and *problem-solving features*. Within these individual categories, the product ideas can then be prioritized so that their feasibility may be re-examined in subsequent projects. Here too, a computer-aided approach would appear desirable (see Applying of TopInfo in the definition cycle, p. 17).

3.7 CHECKING THE SELECTION FILTER

> *How can the selection process be improved?*

The last phase of the overall project-selection system examined here ensures the establishment of a **continuous learning process**. This implies a regular check of the filters addressed or the criteria used in them to select projects.

Although this question may appear obvious, it is nevertheless observed in practice that monitoring the quality of the filter criteria is frequently neglected. Project leaders are regularly judged on the basis of their success, but the selection filters used to choose specific projects are assessed much more rarely.

An appropriate feedback process must therefore be applied to check whether the selection criteria used are really suitable for releasing successful projects. This step also initiates a learning process in the selection of projects: it continually improves this process phase whose great importance has already become clear. The first step in this direction has already been mentioned, namely to include measurement points in the project agreement. Further points will be examined in Part III (Chapter 9, Project-oriented monitoring).

NOTES

1 The terms used here should be briefly clarified: a **process** is a chain of interconnected activities which convert a definable input into a definable output. A **product** is a combination of production factors, as a rule the output of a process. Various processes and subprocesses are traversed in the course of a **project**. A project thus represents the path to a product.

2 In the following treatment, a distinction will be made between product ideas and project proposals: **product ideas** are proposals for new product features. Unlike **project proposals**, however, individual product ideas are not yet sufficiently far advanced so that the product features they describe can be directly implemented in a project. In contrast, a project proposal comprises the description of a result (such as a product or a service together with their subcomponents) which can be implemented directly in the form of a project. Examples are orders to set up a plant, to instal software or to perform a consulting service, as well as **decision packages** for developing a new product. Project proposals therefore usually comprise several fully elaborated product ideas and become projects directly after their release.

3 Cf. Edgett, Shipley, Forbes (1992).

4 Pavia (1991), p. 19 draws on several empirical studies that confirm the great importance of customer orientation in selecting projects in the product-innovation sector. At the same time, she points out that companies almost never make systematic use of such customer orientation.

5 The following structure was created on the basis of a system presented by Reichert, Kirsch and Esser (1991), p. 583 for identifying new areas of activity for companies.

6 Cf. the scoring method in Küpper (1997), p. 74 f. as well as the references given there.

7 In the ideal case, the weights should be assigned so that their sum over all criteria amounts to 1 – i.e. the individual criteria should be evaluated on the basis of their pro-rated importance.

8 Thus in the example in Table 3.4 a lower weighting of the strategic relevance would result in a significantly higher ranking for customer requirement B.

9   More comprehensive sources on the topic of project cost estimates include
     Burghardt (1995), pp. 130–89, as well as Schulz (1995) to which reference
     will be made in the following presentation and from which (p. 86) the
     diagram above was also taken.
10   This concept and its roots are presented by Stock (1990) among others
     (p. 114 ff). The statements made him refer back to Michel (1987), pp. 70
     ff. from where the diagram was also taken.
11   Cf. in general Dunst (1983). An overview is given in Küpper (1997), pp. 82
     ff. as well as in Gälweiler (1990), pp. 76 ff.
12   In strategic management, the term *cash cow* refers to a business field or
     product which has as a rule already existed in the company for a long time
     and is well positioned in a mature and thus slow-growing market. Owing
     to its long experience in these sectors, the company can skim off profits
     without having to invest too much in expanding its activities.
13   Gap analysis is a classical instrument of strategic company management.
     Cf. Ansoff (1976), p. 131 as well as Kreikebaum (1993), p. 43.
14   The diagram is based on Stockbauer (1991), p. 136 ff.
15   A complete overview of the procedures used in investment planning may
     be found in Blohm and Lüder (1991).
16   It is assumed in the following presentation that payments over the same
     period lead to costs of the same magnitude. This is quite usual in projects.
     Where this is not the case, a distinction must be made between procedures
     based on costs (EPP, cost and profit comparison calculations) and those
     based on revenues and expenditures (investment planning procedures such
     as the net present method).
17   Examples are Perridon and Steiner (1993) p. 34 ff.; Seicht (1994),
     pp. 346 ff.; Burghardt (1995), pp. 53 ff.
18   The literature offers a whole series of sophisticated tools that can support
     an evaluation of risks. The interested reader is referred particularly to
     Franke (1987, 1993); Gong and Hugstead (1993); Yeo (1991); Halman
     and Keizer (1993) and Diekmann (1992).
19   Details may be found in Küpper (1997) p. 67 ff.
20   Cf. the statements made in the motivation theories covered in Part III,
     p. 256.
21   Cf. Küpper (1997) p. 67.
22   Schweizer and Küpper (1998) p. 663.
23   A comprehensive comparison of target-costing variants is given by
     Seidenschwarz (1993) p. 115 ff.
24   Finding out how much the customer is prepared to pay is one of the most
     difficult steps in target costing. Conjoint analysis represents a particularly
     useful tool for this purpose. It can be used to determine the customer
     benefit of a product as well as the price that the customer is willing to pay.
     An example of the conjoint analysis procedure is given by Backhaus *et al.*
     (1996) p. 521 ff.
25   Cf. details in Riegler (1996).
26   Cf. Schweitzer and Küpper (1998), p. 662 and the literature given there as
     well as Horváth, Niemand and Wolbold (1993), pp. 1–27.

Part II Management of Projects

*What does management **of** projects mean?*

Part I showed how a project-oriented company selects projects in order to focus its resources to its customers' needs. The project release was described as the point at which the official handover to the management of an individual project takes place. This section will examine the successful management of projects (cf. Figure II.1).

What does the management of projects comprise?

In order to realize this objective, two processes are necessary: the **planning** (Chapter 4) and **continuous control** (Chapter 5) of projects. The following sections present the substeps indispensable to successful project management in process terms. Although they cannot be transposed to every project in unmodified form, they do provide useful indications for structuring an individual project.

Figure II.1   Integration of the realization cycle into the
project management concept

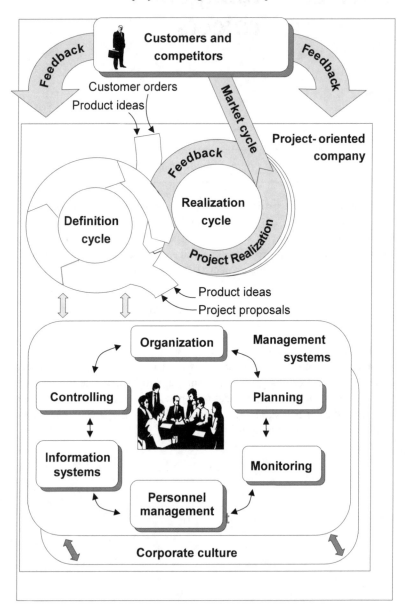

4 Planning a project

> *What is project planning for?*

A project focus offers an effective way of creating a customer-oriented company. Every project aims to make corporate resources available for satisfying a customer's specific requirements. Project planning is an indispensable technique to attain this goal. It is designed to obtain information about the future execution of the project in a systematic way and to anticipate the action that must be taken to achieve that goal. It thus involves the creation of measures designed to attain the project targets as effectively and efficiently as possible (Figure 4.1).

> *Can definition and implementation overlap?*

Project planning is a complex task, which accompanies the project all the way from its beginning to its end (cf. Figure 4.1).The creation of projects was described in Part I. Figure 4.2 shows that parts of the definition process already belong to the domain of (individual) project planning. For example, an analysis of the cost-effectiveness of projects may require basic knowledge about the activities associated with these

Figure 4.1 Project processes relevant to planning

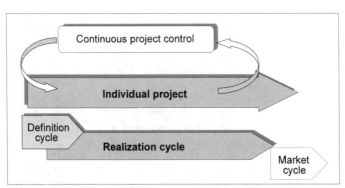

Figure 4.2   Reach of project planning

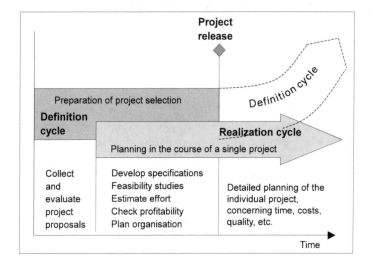

projects. To obtain such knowledge, the initial results of project planning will already be required.

The more rigorous the requirements made on the data needed for the project release, the closer the links between the definition and implementation processes. As a result, the contents of these two processes will overlap.

- There is no distinct interface between the management *with* projects and the management *of* a particular project. The latter is an integral part of the concept of management by projects. A company can be a market leader with the aid of projects only if it masters the art of project leadership.
- The intersection of the contents of the definition and implementation processes should also be reflected in the project organization. Thus members of the project team may act as experts who select the project and formulate its targets. If the project is implemented, they will play a key role in it.

Why are definition and implementation run in parallel?

One way of utilizing the relationships between the definition and implementation stages is to run both processes in parallel in terms of their schedules and contents. This approach may even be unavoidable, especially in customer-order projects, if the customer requires relatively precise data for the external release of the project. The relevant plans will then have to be elaborated during the implementation stage.

4.1 PLANNING TO INITIALIZE A PROJECT

What are the functions of project initialization?

Initialization forms the starting point of every project (cf. Figure 4.3). Even if this subprocess is not explicitly delimited in a project, its contents are essential for successful project management. It is at this stage that the project targets are formulated and their feasibility is ensured by planning appropriate activities. The success of a project is already largely programmed at initialization. Alterations can still be made at this stage during the elaboration of the project plans in ways that are no longer possible in the later course of the project. As altering existing plans is always problematic this should remain the exception during the execution of a project.

Figure 4.3   Initialization as a subprocess of the realization cycle

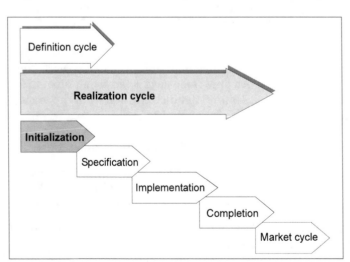

Figure 4.4   Subprocesses of project initialization

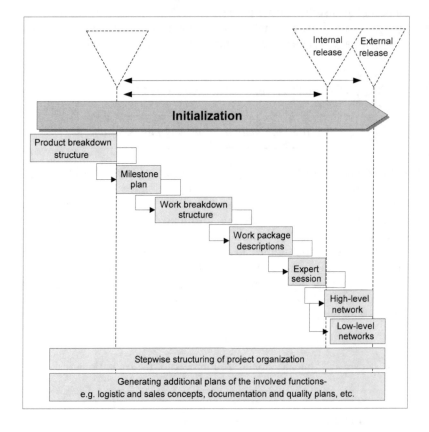

Figure 4.4 shows that the initialization of a project comprises several subprocesses. An important stage is the definition of the project organization and its more detailed formulation in a step-wise procedure.

4.1.1   Selecting a suitable form of project organization

From what point are organizational plans needed?

It was observed in Part I that information as to whether the project targets can really be attained with the company's available resources is needed for the project release. As a rule, agreement on an official project release and the associated allocation of the project budget can be reached only when it has become clear that appropriate capacities are available to realize the planned activities. For this reason, an initial organizational plan should be issued as early as the project definition cycle. It should comprise at least the following elements:

> *What are the contents of an organization plan?*

- Assignment of the main tasks to **function holders**
- Information about the planned **organization** of the project, as well as
- Information about the planned **processes** of the project.

Assignment of tasks to function holders in the planned project

> *How can the feasibility of the planned tasks be assured?*

The scope of a planned project represents an essential initial target and is thus already determined in the definition process. In customer projects it emerges in the course of negotiations with the customer, whereas in the product-innovation sector it is selected on the basis of the strategic and operative criteria already explained. The main components, which must be made available for manufacturing the product, can then be identified. In order to ensure the feasibility of the project in good time, function holders must already be assigned to each main function at this stage.

- Specific function holders should be assigned to each main function by name as far as possible.

> *Is personal contact required?*

It is not sufficient merely to identify potential function holders who appear to be suitable for the planned project activities. The project leader must ensure that these function holders are available and are willing to cooperate on the project. Therefore initial contacts with potential team members, corporate units or external suppliers are essential.

What are the functions of the project managers?

The appointment of suitable team members always involves considerable effort for the project managers. Potential team members must be personally interviewed and their interest in working on the project must be aroused. Finally, the selection of employees requires negotiations with the line departments, which frequently have the actual authority to delegate an employee to a project.

Case study 4.1   Basic forms of project organization

Figure 4.5   Staff organization of a project

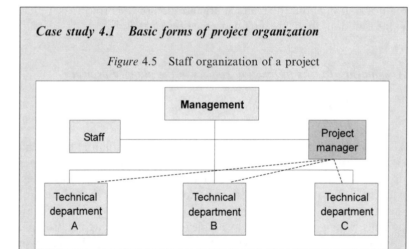

In a **staff organization** (Figure 4.5), all the activities required for a project are performed within existing technical departments. They are coordinated by a project leader whose management position gives him no direct authority *vis-à-vis* the technical departments. Although he monitors the technical, scheduling and cost aspects of the project development, he is not responsible for attaining the project targets. This responsibility lies with the individual technical departments involved.[1] In order to perform his job, the project coordinator is granted relevant information and consulting authority so that he can continuously monitor the course of the project in the line departments.[2] As this form of organization is rarely selected in practice owing to the weak position of the project leader, it will not be treated in any further detail in the main part of this book.

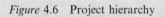

Figure 4.6 Project hierarchy

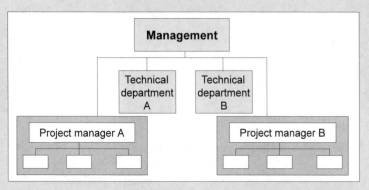

In a **project hierarchy** (Figure 4.6), all the resources required to satisfy the project activities, i.e. machines, employees etc. are transferred to a specially created temporary organizational unit. The project leader has, like a line supervisor, unequivocal authority *vis-à-vis* the project team members assigned to him.[3]

Finally, in a **matrix hierarchy** (Figure 4.7), a horizontal structure is superposed onto the function-based organization. The project leader then coordinates his project via all the technical sectors involved. The function-based authority of the technical department heads thus exists side by side with the project-based authority of the project leader. The employees of the relevant technical departments therefore receive directives from their line superior and project-based specifications from the project leader.[4] Many different forms of project matrix organization are

Figure 4.7 Matrix hierarchy

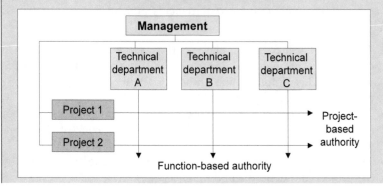

found in corporate practice, ultimately covering all nuances between the extremes of project hierarchy and staff organization.[5]

Beyond the ideal types of project organization just described, project-based activities may also be handled within the **original corporate hierarchy** without making any changes to the organization.

Selecting a suitable organizational structure for the planned project

> *When is an organizational structure required?*

In looking for suitable people to fulfil the main functions in the planned project, the project managers should already prepare their ideas about the ways in which the team members are to be integrated into the project. These considerations form part of the selection of a suitable project organization that will now be discussed.

The case study Basic forms of project organization (p. 80) shows four different ways of organizing a project. Each of these basic forms has specific advantages and disadvantages that should be considered when opting for ways to run a project.

> *When to keep the existing hierarchy?*

It makes good sense to handle **projects within the existing corporate hierarchy**, such as within a department if they are small and can be implemented using the technical expertise and functions of a single organizational unit. If these requirements are satisfied, a number of advantages follow:

- The project leader is also the superior of the team members in a disciplinary or technical sense for the unit's other operational business. This simplifies the authority relationships and reporting procedures within the project.
- The team members already know each other before working together in the project. This coherence enhances the efficiency of the teamwork.
- The project affords an easy overview and hence effective control by the project and departmental managers.

> *What alternatives are available for complex projects?*

Complex projects exceed the limits of individual technical depart-ments, and thus require the establishment of a specific project organi-zation. Possible forms of organization are reduced to two alternatives: a project hierarchy or a matrix organization. The fourth basic form, the staff organization, will not be examined in more detail as the weak position of the project leader makes it unsuitable for handling complex projects.

> *Projects or matrix hierarchy?*

A comparison of a **project hierarchy** with a **matrix organization** brings out their respective advantages and drawbacks. A project hierarchy tends to motivate the employees by assigning all resources and team members to a single project leader. Clear lines of authority and transparent teams some of which are located in the same place allow a more efficient process execution than is possible in matrix organizations.

> *What are the advantages and drawbacks?*

As against this, Figure 4.8 shows the advantages of the matrix organization: above all, it allows more efficient utilization of corporate resources. The various projects can access know-how in a flexible way

Figure 4.8　The efficient organization of a project[6,7]

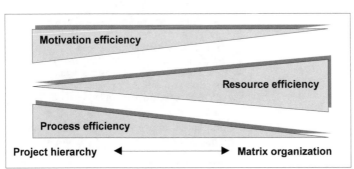

without tying all capacities up in a single project, as would be the case in a project hierarchy. This fundamental difference results in specific advantages and drawbacks of the two forms of project organization for the various parties involved. They are summarized briefly in Figure 4.9 and Figure 4.10.

• The managers of a project should try to combine the advantages of both types of organization by carefully selecting the team members and the type of organization.

Figure 4.9 (Dis-)advantages of a matrix organization

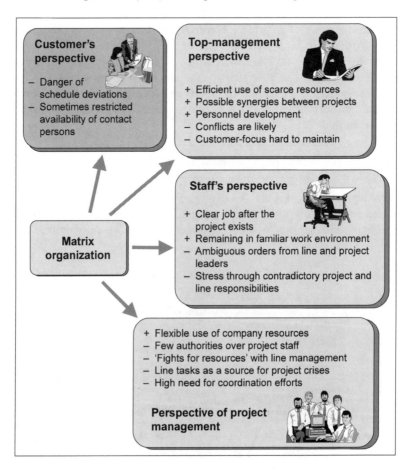

Customer's perspective

− Danger of schedule deviations
− Sometimes restricted availability of contact persons

Top-management perspective

+ Efficient use of scarce resources
+ Possible synergies between projects
+ Personnel development
− Conflicts are likely
− Customer-focus hard to maintain

Matrix organization

Staff's perspective

+ Clear job after the project exists
+ Remaining in familiar work environment
− Ambiguous orders from line and project leaders
− Stress through contradictory project and line responsibilities

+ Flexible use of company resources
− Few authorities over project staff
− 'Fights for resources' with line management
− Line tasks as a source for project crises
− High need for coordination efforts

Perspective of project management

Figure 4.10 (Dis-)advantages of a project hierarchy

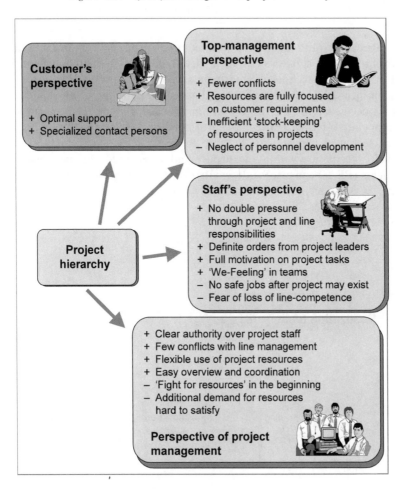

What are core teams?

A number of employees from all the technical departments involved in the project (development, sales, commercial sector, controlling etc.) should be concentrated in a **core team** as understood in a pure project organization. In contrast, other **project participants** remain anchored in their line departments but are explicitly assigned to the project and its management.

> *How are the coordination problems of a matrix mitigated?*

Special institutions are set up in complex projects to coordinate the overall project activities despite a partial or complete matrix structure. For example, technical departments can be induced to delegate a **subproject leader (SPL)** who coordinates the handling of all subactivities necessary for the project within this department. These form an important interface between the project managers and the employees in the technical department. Because they are delegated from the line, their acceptance within the department is ensured. **Product feature agents (PFAs)** can also be designated for the technical coordination of the various technical departments. Their task is to coordinate the

Figure 4.11   Example of a complex matrix hierarchy

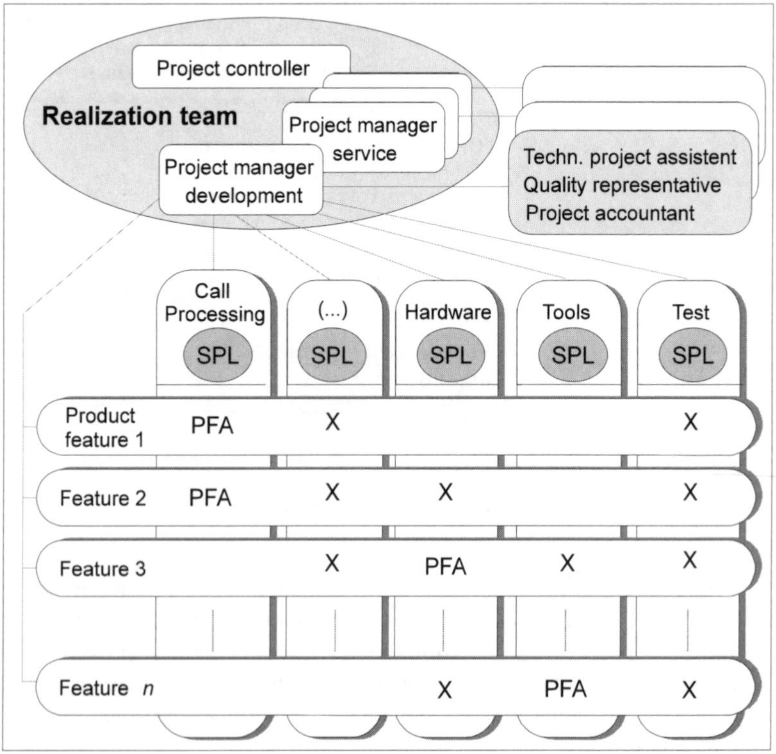

implementation of a product component across all the technical departments involved (cf. Figure 4.11).

Depending on the importance of the project for the company, it will tend to opt either for a project hierarchy or a matrix organization.

Case study 4.2 Forms of process organization

The classical form of running projects is the **waterfall model** or life-cycle model (Figure 4.12).[8] A project is subdivided into several subprocesses, which are executed in sequence. In general, the product to be developed is initially completely specified and the requirements emerging from this specification are defined. The necessary subactivities are then analyzed and implemented in steps. After the product is manufactured, tested and if necessary modified, it is handed over to the market or to the customer.

Figure 4.12   Waterfall organization

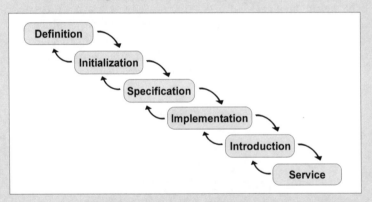

A second way of running a project is **prototyping** (Figure 4.13). Here, too, the requirements on the product and its performance features are initially recorded. After a rapid design, an initial product model, the **prototype**, is created. This may be a product, which already satisfies many of the required functions. Thanks to recent advances in IT, early prototypes now tend to be designed as PC-based models that simulate the product functions for the customer. After feedback has been obtained from the customer, the prototype is re-worked in steps until it completely satisfies the customer's requirements.

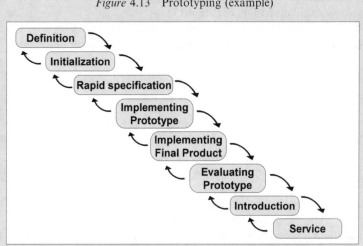

Figure 4.13   Prototyping (example)

The **spiral model** (Figure 4.14) represents a form of process organization developed in the software sector to combine the advantages of prototyping with the waterfall model.[9] In a slightly modified form, it may also be applied to other projects in both the product-innovation and customer-order sectors.

Figure 4.14   Spiral model

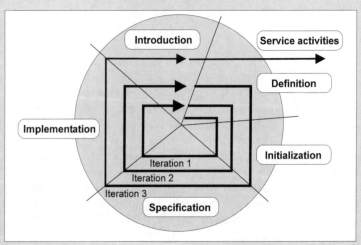

Like the waterfall model, the spiral model is based on a multi-stage process. An example might be the subdivision made in this book into definition and implementation processes. These main processes are themselves composed of subprocesses, as explained in Parts I and II.

In contrast to the waterfall model, the spiral model subdivides the overall project into a number of stages (also known as **runs**, **iterations** or **subprojects**). The individual subprocesses – i.e. the definition, evaluation and selection of the requirements and the planning and implementation of each step – are traversed in each of these stages. Each iteration ends with the completion of an operational product (prototype) and its presentation to the customer. The feedback subsequently obtained provides the input for the next project stages.

Selecting a suitable process organization

> *What does the process organization involve?*

For project release, information must be available about the way the project is executed in addition to its organization. Whereas the hierarchic organization determines the teams and their members who will be used to implement a project task, the process organization defines the subprocesses by which this takes place. The object of process organization is thus to structure the subprocesses of a project in an integrated and target-oriented way. The case study *Forms of process organization* (p. 87) shows the most widespread basic forms.

> *What does it mean for the customer?*

The selection of the process organization is important for the customer of the project because it determines a number of factors, including:

- the point in time at which the customer is able to explicitly affect the future development of the project (go/no-go decisions)
- the time at which the customer can expect the first physical results of the project.

> *On what basis is the form of process organization chosen?*

As in the selection of a project organization, the decision for a project execution involves weighing up various advantages and disadvantages, as is shown in Table 4.1.

Table 4.1   Comparison of different forms of process organization

	Advantages	**Disadvantages**	**Application fields**
Waterfall	– Simple systematic configuration – Highly structured – Easily understood	– Real projects cannot be executed in a strictly sequential way – Risky in very new and uncertain projects because not everything can initially be planned – Customer only sees the product at the end	– Further and adaptive developments – Projects with a low to medium degree of novelty – Projects without excessive uncertainties
Prototyping	– Increased customer satisfaction due to close cooperation – Early feedback from customer	– Fast prototype development at the cost of higher-order project targets – Prototype may cover up deficiencies	– Where insufficient product description possible at the outset – e.g. new products – If required by the customer
Spiral model	– Customer can release each stage separately – Profitability and risk analyses possible for each stage – Step-by step feedback from customer	– Requires efficient processes, otherwise uneconomical – New, thus may be difficult to convince the customer	– Very complex projects – Uncertain projects – E.g. for new developments under great time pressure (first version must come out early)

Who makes the decision?

A decision can only be taken individually for each project. In customer-order projects the customer can also affect the selection of the process organization. For example, she may insist that the project be executed on the basis of a process scheme that is already established in his organization. In such cases, the company running the project must have the flexibility to respond easily to such requirements.

Case study 4.3   Structure plans

Structure plans help to present a complex set of circumstances in a transparent way. In project management, particular use is made of product and work breakdown structures:

THE PRODUCT BREAKDOWN STRUCTURE (PBS)

Product breakdown structures give a systematic and complete overview of the various components of a product. The depth to which the product is subdivided will vary depending on its purpose (for outline or detailed planning).

THE WORK BREAKDOWN STRUCTURE (WBS)[10]

A WBS is used as a project-planning tool in order to make complex projects with many different but strongly interdependent subfunctions more transparent and easy to follow. It is helpful to derive the detailed functions that this requires via a deductive procedure (from the general to the specific) on the basis of the higher-level project subfunctions.

The aim of the WBS is:

- to obtain a **complete** overview of all project functions and tasks
- to display the main **interrelationships** and **interfaces**
- to supply a **systematic basis** for the subsequent planning in terms of expenditures, execution and resources, as well as
- to provide a basis for risk analyses and further detailed plans.

A distinction is made between the following *types of work breakdown structure*: **Object-oriented WBSs** have a form resembling that of the product structure plans. They break a project down on the basis of its various planned results (Figure 4.15). This approach is appropriate when the project function largely agrees with the object to be implemented.

Figure 4.15   Object-oriented WBS

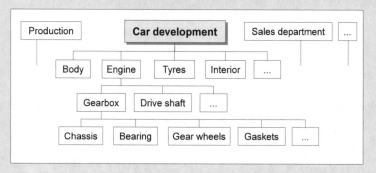

Function-oriented WBSs break a project down into individual functions (Figure 4.16). This approach has obvious advantages when aspects of the project go significantly beyond its material object.

Figure 4.16   Function-oriented WBS

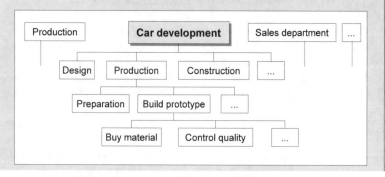

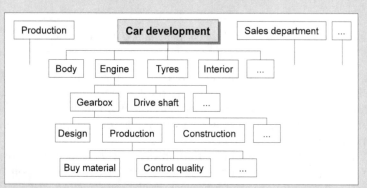

Figure 4.17   Mixed form of a WBS

In practice, a **mixed form of WBS** often delivers the best results (Figure 4.17), as it allows all the activities involved to be covered in a really comprehensive way.

The lowest-level activity bundles in the WBS, which are no longer subdivided, any further are designated as **work packages**. They should comprise only associated activities that can be executed by a smaller organizational unit (such as a work group). Their scope and level of detail can be determined by observing the following points: a work package should represent a concrete function, which can be transferred completely to a responsible unit and can be specified with the relevant precision. However, the subdivision should not be pursued too far so that the cost-estimate and monitoring activities based on this work package do not become too complex.

Where goods or services are to be bought in externally, specific work packages must always be defined in order to ensure more effective planning and monitoring.

Standard structure plans or **templates** (e.g. for performing tests) can rationalize this planning step by summing up the know-how gained in preceding projects with similar tasks. They also prevent any omission of individual subfunctions or work packages, which may jeopardize the further progress of the project.

4.1.2 Project structuring

> *How are **all** components of the planned product covered?*

It was shown in the definition cycle how projects are released. The release documentation contains the most important starting targets from a top-down perspective, especially the first rough schedule plans for the main milestones and the structure of the product to be manufactured.

If no generally applicable definition cycle has been institutionalized in a company, which is naturally undesirable from the viewpoint of customer orientation, then a **product breakdown structure (PBS)** must nevertheless be created at the beginning of the project planning phase (see Structure plans, p. 91. It shows the complete basic structure of the product to be developed as well as the necessary subcomponents, which it comprises. The product breakdown structure forms the starting point of every successful project planning process, as it precisely defines the product to be implemented, i.e. the planned output of the project.

> *How are first schedules derived?*

The knowledge of the scope of the planned end product must be followed by the specification of a planned schedule from the customer or market side in the form of a **milestone plan**. The most important milestones are set as orientation points for further planning on the basis of the targeted time of completion and rough estimates of the project expenditures.

> *How are **all** necessary project activities planned?*

In the next planning step, the product breakdown structure is transferred to the **work breakdown structure (WBS)** (see Structure plans, p. 91). The WBS is one of the most important tools in project management. It offers a complete hierarchical listing of all the tasks required for successfully executing the project. The **work packages** form the lowest level of a WBS and cover the bundle of tasks that can be transferred to a department for processing under its own responsibility.

> *Is a WBS important?*

The work breakdown structure forms the basis for the later scheduling and execution planning. Correct structuring of the project tasks is of great importance for the execution of the project.

> *How is a WBS characterized?*

- The work breakdown structure must include **all** the function sectors involved in the project together with all the tasks they must fulfil.
- The WBS is created **in steps**. As the degree of detail of the planning increases, the individual tasks can be subdivided into individual steps.
- As a rule, four to six **levels** suffice for a work breakdown structure applied to complex projects.
- The definition of the **work packages** is the most detailed level and hence the last step in structuring a project.
- Work packages should be defined so that their contents can be implemented as completely as possible by a single organizational unit. This implies that the creation of the work breakdown structure must be oriented in line with the planned **project organization**.
- The structuring of the WBS should reflect the **management style** aimed at in the project. Thus a WBS which is already function-oriented at the upper levels requires a centralized form of decision-making in the project. This follows from the strong dependencies between those functions that make decentralized coordination difficult. However, if the project is to involve a delegation of responsibilities, an object-oriented structure is recommended.[11]

> *How are tasks systematically distributed?*

During the creation of the WBS, the tasks should be assigned in organizational terms to the agents who will be responsible for them at a later stage. Coordinating the WBS with an organization breakdown structure does this and assigning the work packages to various function holders (Figure 4.18). It is important to appoint the responsible agents by name and to discuss the details of the various task groups and work packages with these people and units. This avoids any vagueness, misunderstandings and conflicts at a later stage.

Figure 4.18   Work breakdown structure with assignment of organizational terms

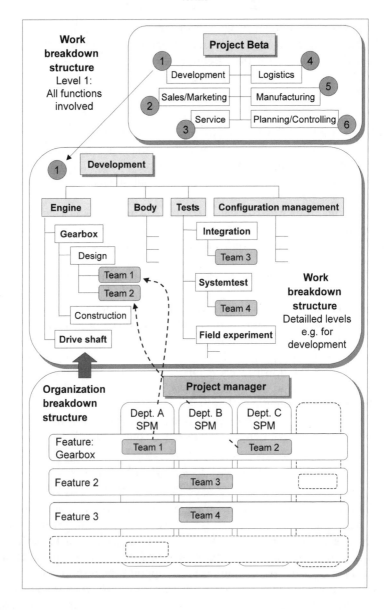

Case study 4.4   Resource allocation planning system (RAPS)

The managers of project-oriented companies must be informed of the manpower capacity utilization in the various projects and for non-project activities at all times. RAPS is an example of a tool designed for **resource allocation planning** that can supply this information (Figure 4.19).

Figure 4.19   RAPS spreadsheet

EXCEL-Worksheet for one person in a group

Manpower - Planning		Mr Jones			Status: Oct 97									second fiscal year		
		Values given in pers.-months (PM)														
Project	Total PY 97/98	Oct 97	Nov 97	Dec 97	Jan 98	Feb 98	Mar 98	Apr 98	May 98	Jun 98	Jul 98	Aug 98	Sep 98	Total PY 98/99	Oct 98	
R 6.3/600ECX; Large node	0.10	0.2	0.2	0.2	0.2	0.2	0.2									
R 6.3/600ECX; Basis LM	0.05	0.1	0.1	0.1	0.1	0.1	0.1									
Entkoppelte Länderfreigaben																
Hicom 300 - V 3.3+																
Service-PC V 3 (für H300 V3.4)																
Service-PC China																
Hicom 300 - V 3.4																
Service PC Betr.																
ATM P2																
ATM P3																
DMS V 2.1	0.33	0.5	0.5	0.5	0.5	0.5	0.5	0.5	0.5							
DMS V 2.2	0.23	0.2	0.2	0.2	0.2	0.2	0.2	0.5	0.3	0.2	0.2	0.2	0.2	0.05	0.2	
DMS V 3	0.18								0.2	0.5	0.5	0.5	0.5	0.05	0.2	
Generiertool H 300 Betr.																
DMS-Kundenprojekte	Max. = 1.0 PY					Max. = 1.0 PM									
others / education																
Total	**0.90**	**1.0**	**1.0**	**1.0**	**1.0**	**1.0**	**1.0**	**1.0**	**1.0**	**0.7**	**0.7**	**0.7**	**0.7**	**0/10**	**0,4**	

Pers. months / 12

STRUCTURE

RAPS is an MS-EXCEL spreadsheet linked to a database. It allows the resource capacities of a project-oriented company to be centrally coordinated. Various display options offer compact overviews of current and future capacity utilization of corporate resources for project-based and non-project activities.

The data acquisition is structured on the basis of the organization of the relevant corporate sector. It allows transparent presentation of the various levels of aggregation, from individual employees via project teams up to main departments. RAPS thus complies with the information requirement of the different management levels, from groups via projects up to the sector head.

Figure 4.20   RAPS capacity overview

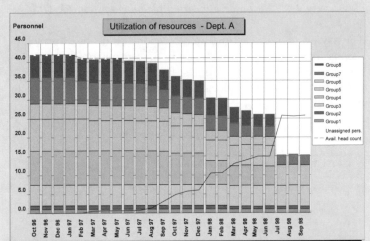

DATA ADMINISTRATION AND EVALUATION

The RAPS data is decentrally administered and centrally consolidated. Thus every group leader can access and alter the data
relating to deploying the resources assigned to him. The data is
administered in distributed mode and can be consolidated and
evaluated by the multi-project controller at regular intervals
(Figure 4.20).

RAPS allows a planning horizon of 12 months (for example)
across the board irrespective of the planning horizon of the
schedule plans of individual (sub) projects. This offers the benefit
of a longer-term overview of resource capacities. Information is
thus available as to which employees of which organizational
units will be available for deployment in the project as early as its
start phase – i.e. after initial expenditure estimates have been
made.

Moreover, the expenditure forecasts resulting from the aggregation of the various individual estimates can be coordinated
with the available manpower capacities recorded in RAPS. As
shown in Figure 4.21, it may become apparent here at an early
stage that the milestone deadlines planned from the top down
cannot be observed. Thus milestone T28-1 was planned

top-down for mid-December 1998. The results of the expert session show an expenditure of 40.0 PY by T28-1. According to the resource overview recorded in RAPS, however, these 40.0 PY can be reached by mid-January 1999 at the earliest, as no more employees are available (ascending bold line). In the same way, T28-2 cannot be reached until a month later. The project is thus not feasible from the viewpoint of department A with the planned scope within the specified time. Appropriate counter-measures must therefore be taken.

In the same way, the information available in RAPS can be used to decide whether and which new projects can be started with the resources available in the next plan periods.

Figure 4.21   RAPS feasibility study

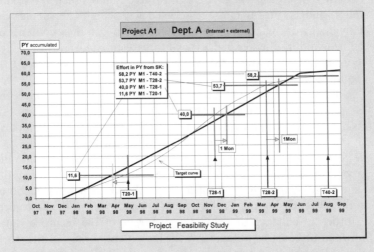

THE BENEFITS OF RAPS

Overall, RAPS allows cross-project as well as project-based planning and control of corporate manpower resources. However, this framework planning can also be used for making plausibility estimates and to check detailed project-planning processes (possibly performed with conventional project-planning tools), in particular the scheduling. RAPS thus represents a suitable tool for resource allocation planning in the mid-to-long term.

4.1.3 Work-package description and expert session

What must a work package description comprise?

In order to obtain a more accurate forecast of the costs associated with a project in an **expert session**, the contents of the individual work packages (WPs) must initially be described and the expenditures/efforts they involve must be assessed.

A number of rules should be followed when designing and **describing the contents** of the work packages:

- The **size** of a work package can be measured in units such as working hours, budget, etc. It must be selected with care. The smaller the individual work packages, the more accurately can their contents be defined and the associated expenditures estimated. However, the coordination effort required within the project then increases to a commensurate degree.
- The more detailed the definition of an individual work package, the less scope for executing it remains for the employees assigned to this task. However, as pointed out in Part III, this **scope of action** plays an important part in the intrinsic motivation of the employees.
- Because the work packages form the basis for estimating the expenditures/efforts, it is important in addition to executing the required tasks to include all **supporting activities** such as induction of staff and preparing the work results for hand-over to the customer.
- In order to enhance the explanatory power of the recorded data, information must be obtained about the potential **risks** of the work packages as early as this point. For example, the main assumptions under which the expenditures were estimated must be made explicit.
- In many cases, it may be equally important to explicitly mention elements, which are *not* included in a work package in order to avoid lack of clarity and any unnecessary duplication of work.

Who describes the work packages?

This task lies in the hands of the team members designated for this function in the work breakdown structure. Their job is to prepare **work**

Figure 4.22   Example of a work-package description

Department: Tele 1	Dpt. Manager: Goodman

Work package description

Project:

WBS-Number: A221

PARADE
Feature Package 1

Short description:
Feature: 500ZY
Complex: Keyboard
(...)

Responsible Group: Team 03	Name: Mrs Trautmann

Estimated Effort (Person Months): 10	Duration: 6 Month

Effort based on following Assumptions:
– Punctual availability of lab
– (...)

Identified Risks:	Impact:	Probability:
– New tools necessary?	+/– 1 PM	50%

WP-Content:
– Creation of detail-specifications FDB5-7   2.0 PM
– Customize interface   3.0 PM
– Modify keys to new standards   3.0 PM
– Test   2.0 PM

Effort in phase:
M0 – M1   4.0 PM
M1 – M2   3.0 PM
M2 – M3   3.0 PM
Total PM   10.0

package descriptions for use in the expert session. Figure 4.22 shows a suitable form for such a description. These descriptions forecast how much expenditure the relevant work packages will probably require in terms of time and resources. The relevant departments may then apply various estimation procedures, as already described in the case study *Project cost estimate* (p. 28).

> *How can project accounting be facilitated?*

In order to facilitate the interface to the project planning and control activities on the commercial and project-execution sides, the specifications should be based on the following criteria:

- Both **feature-related effort** and **non-feature-related effort** (such as for financial control and other overheads) must be recorded and as far as possible listed separately.
- The necessary effort must already be recorded at this point in accordance with the company-specific **cost type catalogue** in order to allow the expenditures/efforts to be converted to cost and subsequent parameters at a later stage.
- Another useful step is to divide the various activities and efforts on the basis of the **project phases** or subprocesses in order to facilitate their assignment to business years.

> *How can planning errors be recognized?*

The aggregation of all the work-package descriptions yields a detailed forecast, referred to both processes and departments, of the project effort anticipated from a bottom-up perspective. Figure 4.23 shows an extract from a relevant spreadsheet. The task of project controlling is to subject the data obtained in this way to critical scrutiny. In practice, the data on the resource expenditures planned for the scheduled implementation of the work packages is checked for feasibility – e.g. whether the manpower requirement stipulated as necessary to reach the targets is in fact available. Only a central department, such as the project-controlling agency, has an overview of the distribution of resources over time among the various projects running in parallel within the company. It can thus determine whether the relationship between target schedules and the resource requirement estimated by the teams is realistic (see Resource allocation planning system, p. 97).

> *What are the aims of the expert session?*

The **expert session** can now take place on the basis of these preliminary activities. The principal aim of this session is to determine

Figure 4.23   Part of an expert session spreadsheet

Project Effort PROJECT 1 Manpower Effort M1-M3 (PM), separated by departments Grand Total (1st FY to 3rd FY)							
Task / Job **Total effort: Development M1-M3**	**Dept. 1**	**Dept. 2**	...	**Dept. 6**	**Su. MUC**	**Su. USA**	**Total**
(APS from M1-M3)							
APS-Production							
0-APS / 2nd APS -Line Start up							
Simulator							
Total effort: APS M1-M3							
Test T28-M3 Testfield Support							
Documentation							
Total effort: Syst.Pl./Proj.Support							
Actuals before M1							
Grand Total (Pers.-Months)							

the total anticipated costs of the project as precisely as possible. Its other aims are:[12]

- To ensure that the future project team acquires a comprehensive understanding of the project target – i.e. one that goes beyond its own sphere of responsibility.
- To eliminate any misunderstandings about the scope of performance, interface requirements etc. as well as any information gaps.
- Finally, to create all the preconditions to ensure smooth cooperation between the various people and agencies involved in the project.

> *What happens in an expert session?*

In order to reach these goals, it is the task of the project controller in his capacity as moderator to summon the project leaders, team leaders and line managers as well as representatives from the commercial side to the expert session. The estimates for the various work packages are then presented and discussed in this session. In particular, a check is made of the completeness, correctness and coherence of the individual estimates. A project accountant converts the results of the expert session, which as a rule are specified in person months (PM) or person years (PY) for each project phase, to project costs distributed over the relevant fiscal years. These results therefore represent the critical interface to the project-planning and control activities on the commercial side (cf. the cost-effectiveness analyses in the project planning phase in Part I and during the project as described in Section 5.2.5).

> *What is the output of an expert session?*

The expert session finalizes agreement on the project targets. Depending on the time selected for the project release, these then go directly toward the project decision, or are used to check the data that were used as the basis of this decision. If a significant discrepancy is revealed between the top-down and the bottom-up planning, the plan must be revised, and the project customer must approve this revision.

Case study 4.5   Tools for schedule and execution planning

Project planning focuses on the sequence of individual steps to be performed in a project, their scheduling as well as the creation of the basic preconditions to assure effective project control. The tools that support this project phase are consequently among the best-known and most highly developed methods applied in project management. Network diagrams and bar charts are particularly widespread examples.[13]

NETWORK DIAGRAMS

Network diagrams depict a project in graphical form. A project is represented by *nodes* and *directed edges/arrows* which symbolize the processes, the dependencies existing between them as well as events (defined states in the project) (Figure 4.24). In principle, a distinction can be made between various types of network diagram. They imply various *planning philosophies*, but these will not be examined in any further detail at this point.[14]

Figure 4.24   Node/activity description

Nr.		Duration
Description		
Resource		
Earliest possible starting time (EPS)	Earliest possible completion time (EPC)	Buffer

Process node network diagrams are widely used in European countries (e.g. in Germany). The *Metra Potential Method (MPM)* is very popular thanks to its relative simplicity. It maps the required processes in the nodes and their dependencies in the arrows. The data recorded per node is illustrated in Figure 4.25.

Figure 4.25   Example of a MPM-network

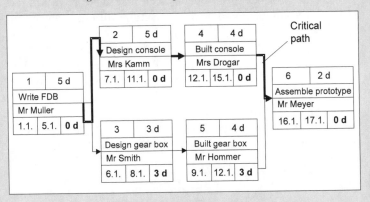

In a *forward calculation (1)*, the earliest possible starting times of all processes, as well as the resulting earliest possible completion times, are determined on the basis of the first services to be performed and on their duration. The following *reverse calculation (2)* takes the scheduled end of the project as its basis and determines the latest times at which individual processes must be completed in order not to overrun the final deadline. This method also yields the latest possible starting times of the processes. The *buffer time (3)* of a process is obtained from the difference between latest and earliest possible times that a process

Figure 4.26   Calculating a network

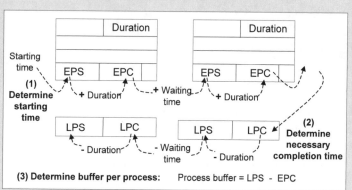

(3) Determine buffer per process: Process buffer = LPS - EPC

may end (Figure 4.26). It specifies whether the process can be delayed without extending the duration of the overall project. All processes with a buffer time of 0 are located along the *critical path* of the project.[15] Any delays occurring there have a direct effect on the completion date of the overall project and must thus be avoided.

Process network diagrams such as the best known and most widely used *Critical Path Method* (CPM) map the processes with arrows (Figure 4.27). All the processes are flanked by a start and an end result represented by nodes. The time-consuming aspect of this method is that it requires the use of *dummy processes* to display all the dependencies in the project.[16] The critical path is then calculated analogously to the MPM method.

Figure 4.27   Example of a CPM network

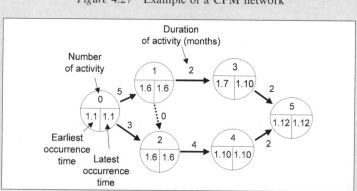

The *Programme Evaluation and Review Technique (PERT)* differs from the methods examined so far by not assuming that the process has a definite duration. Instead, a probable duration is estimated, its possible variance is determined, and an anticipated value for the project duration is then obtained from this. Another version of PERT is known as the *three times estimation:* three durations, a pessimistic, an optimistic and a probable one, are estimated for each process, and the expected project duration is then calculated from these.

In addition to these classical network methods, a number of extensions focus on specific subaspects. However, as these are still little used in practice, only the *Graphical Evaluation and Review Technique* (GERT) will be mentioned at this point. It allows the use of stochastic process sequences and relationships.

BAR CHARTS/GANTT DIAGRAMS

Bar charts are among the oldest tools used in project management and certainly represent the most widespread form of project-based schedule and execution planning (Figure 4.28). Their main advantage is their simplicity. They are extremely easy to grasp and learn to use and are thus particularly well suited to communicating the schedule and execution plans created on their basis. Another advantage is that individual tasks can be displayed graphically within a time grid. Network diagrams do not offer this option.

Figure 4.28   Part of a bar chart

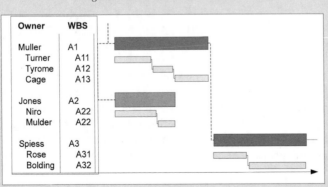

However, the simplicity of bar charts can also become a drawback, especially if they are created manually – i.e. without access to a computerized network diagram running in the background. As the projects become more complex, the transparency of this method is greatly reduced, thus increasing the danger of neglecting dependencies or omitting individual activities. This in turn can lead to unrealistic schedule and execution plans. Other negative features are the difficulty of integrating resource planning and of identifying time reserves in the execution process.

Attempts have been made to counter these drawbacks by representing projects with a mixture of bar charts and network diagrams. One such approach presents activities *and* their dependencies in a bar chart and shows elements such as buffer times in graphical form.

In computer-aided project management (CAPM) tools in particular, therefore, a network diagram is always run in the background and various forms of bar chart are also available as a communications interface.

Two ground rules should be noted for applying the tools of schedule and execution planning:

- **Completeness**: The project execution should be planned on the basis of previously created work breakdown structures. This is the only way of ensuring complete coverage of all activities.
- **Monitoring capability**: The degree of detail must be matched to each user, so that he can understand the information content and can monitor its implementation. Hierarchically structured network diagrams (high-level and more detailed low-level network plans) can offer useful support for this purpose.

TEMPLATES FOR FACILITATING SCHEDULE AND EXECUTION PLANNING

Projects always represent new processes in a company. However, they do occasionally yield subaspects, which need to be executed repeatedly in other projects. It is therefore a good idea to store **templates** for this kind of frequently used process routine (e.g. the execution of a system test) in a central database. The planners of a specific project can then access them in order to facilitate their work.

4.1.4 From high-level to low-level plans

In the following stage, the agreed objectives must be converted into detailed plans in a stepwise process. These detailed plans then provide the basis for implementing the project.

Creating high-level plans

> *How is a binding milestone plan created?*

The preceding steps were used to derive the project targets. These describe the performance scope of the product to be implemented and define the framework conditions agreed for its implementation in terms of schedules and finances. The original deadlines anticipated from a top-down perspective (planned by the definition team from market viewpoints) and the effort determined in the expert session from a bottom-up perspective represent a **countercurrent process** which leads to the definition of a **basic milestone plan.** It is binding for all parties and fixes the most important project deadlines that must be observed in order to complete the project successfully within the set schedule.

> *How is the network plan obtained?*

The existing work breakdown structures can now be used to create a **high-level network plan** (see Tools for schedule and execution planning, p. 104) for the project. This plan shows the aggregated steps, which must be taken in order to complete the project within the final deadlines in their correct sequence with respect to both resources and schedules. Figure 4.29 shows a high-level network plan in the transparent form of a bar chart.

> *How is under/over-planning prevented?*

A major challenge in creating project plans is to select the optimum **level of aggregation**. Complex projects are characterized by a large number of individual tasks with a high degree of mutual dependence and interaction. The project planner must thus master the art of

Figure 4.29   Transfer of a work breakdown structure into a high-level bar chart

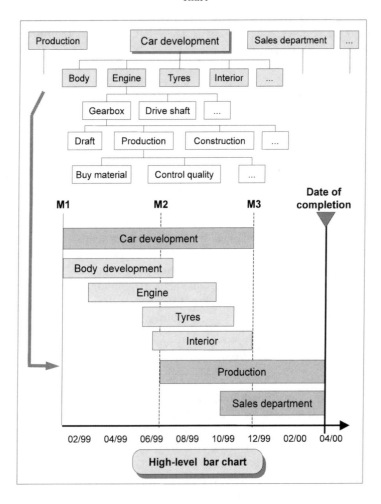

creating plans, which are accurate and complete as well as transparent and easy to follow. An excessively detailed plan (over-planning) can have as negative an impact on its implementation as one that is too abstract and thus provides insufficient information (under-planning). A **network plan subdivision** is a useful way of avoiding this danger. It simultaneously satisfies the need for information by the various groups of people involved in the project (cf. Figure 4.30).

Figure 4.30   Integration of low-level plans into project planning

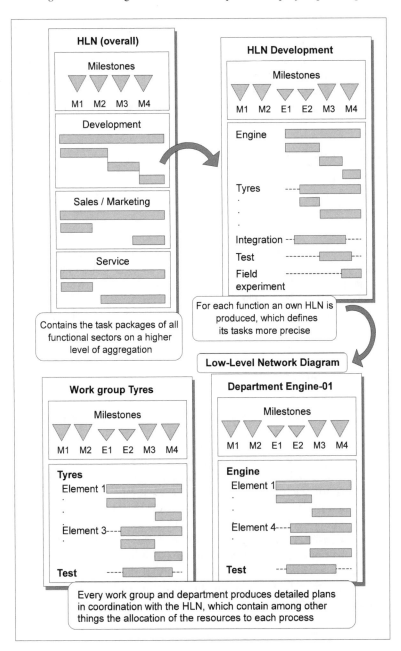

Instead of producing a *single* detailed plan encompassing all aspects of the project, the planners start with an abstract overall plan for the project, which is then subdivided in several stages into detailed plans focusing on specific subsectors. The high degree of aggregation of the initial high-level network plan satisfies the information need of its addressees, namely the project leaders or controllers assigned to the task of supervising the whole project. They also have the necessary overview and expertise to set up the high-level network plan.[17]

Creating low-level plans

> *What is the starting point for detailed planning?*

The high-level network plan forms a framework for the detailed planning which must be observed if the overall project is to be completed in accordance with its targets. As Figure 4.30 shows, this plan is now used by the individual project teams to detail the subactivities it contains. The subproject leaders and group leaders thus create the **low-level network plans** autonomously together with their teams. These plans define the activities to be performed by individual team members at their own responsibility, inclusive of their sequence and the allocated resources, in order to attain the targets of the high-level network plan.

> *Why is the detailed planning performed in stages?*

As Figure 4.30 shows, the detailed plans are elaborated in stages: starting from a high-level network plan of the overall project via high-level plans for each functional sector (development, sales, logistics, service, manufacturing etc.) down to the low-level plans for each department and work group. One reason for this procedure is to ensure that the high-level planning activities really are feasible at low level. There is no point in scheduling deadlines at a higher level of abstraction (e.g. the manufacture of a subassembly) if they cannot be adhered to at lower levels of detail (e.g. the manufacture of the individual parts for the subassembly, their integration, tests, etc.). And the same applies in the opposite direction: the detailed plans must be oriented to the high-level plans, too.

> *Who coordinates the high-level and low-level plans?*

For these reasons, the low-level network plans are created by individual departments and work groups on the basis of the drafts of the high-level plans. The subproject leaders coordinate this step. They elaborate the high-level plans for each functional unit and also participate in the lower-level planning activities. They thus coordinate these levels to ensure their mutual coherence.[18] Subproject leaders (or team leaders in other forms of project organization) thus act as an important interface between the overall project managers and the individual work groups.

> *What are the inputs for the detailed planning?*

Figure 4.31 and Figure 4.32 show possible ways of carrying out the actual low-level planning. Significant inputs come from the technical specifications in the release documentation as well as from the deadline targets from the high-level planning activities. In addition, more specific information about the total anticipated expenditures for each work package to be performed is already available from the expert session.

> *How is the detailed planning performed?*

The first step in the detailed planning is **task planning** ①: here, all the activities necessary for attaining the required output are listed. Next, the various dependencies between the individual functions are made explicit. This substep is important for the following **execution planning** ② step in which the activities are arranged in a logical sequence with respect to the required resources. This provides the basis for the **scheduling and capacity-planning** step. The latter is underpinned by two differing *planning philosophies,* which raise a number of problems depending on the size and type of the project:

> *How is resource-driven planning carried out?*

In the **resource-driven planning process** (cf. Figure 4.31), the manpower requirement is initially determined for each activity ③. This step is followed by allocating the resources to each process ④ – usually with the aid of specially designed software tools such as Primavera, Time-Line or MS-Project. Depending on the software product, the allocation is performed simply with the mouse (drag and drop) or by entering the resources manually into relevant table fields for the processes. In this procedure it can be determined, with which proportion of its net working hours each resource is allocated to a process (between 0 and 100 per cent). The program then calculates the duration of the process from the assigned manpower and resource capacity ⑤. A number of important factors must be observed here. If they are ignored, errors can already occur in the early phases of the project:

> *What errors may occur in the most common software tools?*

- The duration of a process is not obtained simply by dividing the required expenditure by the available capacities. For example, a process with an effort of 50 person-days cannot simply be shortened by assigning 50 employees to an overall period of one day. Co-ordination and matching problems also enter the equation. In addition to this, not all tasks can be easily subdivided.
- Incorrect deadline calculations can result if 100 per cent of the official work time of employees is assigned to a project. Experience shows that secondary administrative duties such as telephoning, organization etc. eat into substantial times earmarked for project activities.
- The system should include a separate schedule calendar for each employee in order to include vacations and out times at an early stage in the planning procedure. Most commercial software products support this function.

> *What are the advantages of resource-driven planning?*

Resource-driven planning activities in the form of integrated scheduling and capacity allocation allow project routines to be optimized with the aid of the comprehensive functions offered by commercial project management software. One example is the use of sophisticated algorithms for capacity smoothing as described below. However, the use of these planning methods is linked to a number of application conditions:

Figure 4.31   Resource-driven low-level planning

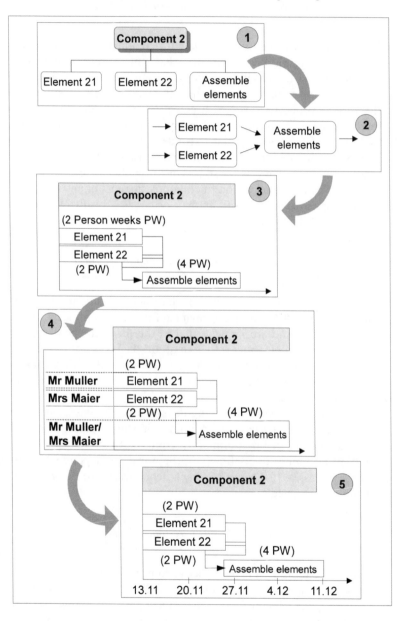

> *What are the limits of resource-driven planning?*

- It must be possible to quantify the effort required for the processes involved with relative precision. Also, this should not change significantly in the ensuing period as it represents the basis for all the subsequent scheduling and capacity-planning activities. Because the various processes involved become increasingly complex, which tends to happen during the development of new products, the usefulness of the resulting plans also declines.
- It must be possible to allocate resources to individual processes as exactly and exclusively as possible. Unexpected changes in available capacities can lead to major fluctuations in scheduling. In matrix organizations, such fluctuations may occur as a result of resource conflicts with line functions.

> *How does duration-driven detailed planning proceed?*

For the reasons already mentioned, **duration-driven** planning approaches (cf. Figure 4.32) are recommended for complex projects, which are liable to risks and are implemented in the form of a matrix. The focus of the detailed planning is then to attain the results of the project as early as possible. Particular emphasis is placed on the full participation of those managers who are indispensable for bringing the planning to a successful completion.

The process run times (in working days) defined to ensure that the results of the project are completed in line with the targets are entered into relevant computer programmes. In addition, the initial conditions of each programme are defined in the form of dependencies to preceding processes. If there are no such dependencies to be observed, a start date is assigned.

> *What part do software tools play?*

The software tools used here are designed principally to calculate the earliest possible final deadline and to identify the processes which affect the deadlines – i.e. which lie along the critical path ⑥. Capacities can also be allocated to individual processes in duration-driven planning, but without automatically affecting the duration of the process. In

Figure 4.32   Duration-driven low-level planning

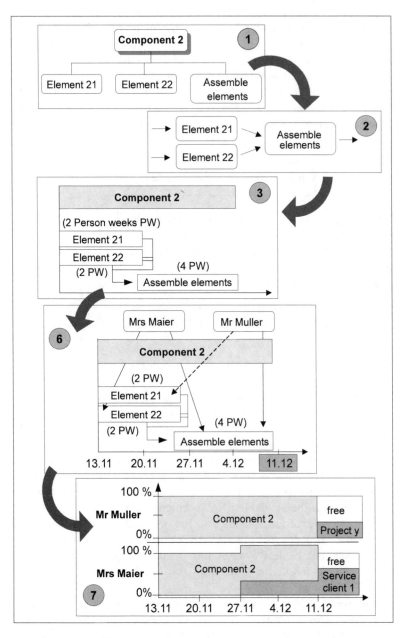

contrast, the allocation of personnel resources tends to have a more informative function ⑥. A representation of the resource capacity utilization, as in a **histogram**, is not useful in practice if tasks are processed in parallel. It makes more sense to plan resources via special resource planning tools (⑦ see Resource allocation planning system, p. 97), which tend to be established within an entire sector or company. It is quite sufficient to allocate the manpower resources for a specific project in the form of specific percentages. Any free capacities can then be used for other tasks. This applies particularly in a matrix organization.

What distinguishes the two approaches?

In duration-driven planning, the final deadline forms the starting point and the capacities needed to meet it are subsequently determined. In contrast, resource-driven planning starts from the estimated effort and available resources. Only then is the final deadline determined, which can be reached with their aid.

What are the advantages of duration-driven planning?

The duration-driven approach has the following main advantages:

- The scheduling process can focus exclusively on the attainable final deadlines without having to worry about allocating resources to every process in detail. A check is merely made every time the network plan is updated to ensure that everything is on schedule for the final deadline. This information is derived from the allocated personnel. It makes no difference what percentage of each resource is allocated to the process. The important thing is the assurance that the result will be available by a specific deadline.
- Because resources are allocated to the project as a whole and not to individual processes in order to determine the duration (see above), employees can be flexibly reorganized whenever plans are changed, a step which is frequently necessary to ensure that the final deadline is met.
- Not every minor change in allocating resources to individual processes, for example owing to the unexpected need for a team member to be delegated to short-term line tasks, will cause deadline

shifts in a (sub)project. Otherwise nearly unmanageable coordination problems would occur in complex projects.

- Because resources are allocated in a fixed way to the subproject but not to individual processes within it, a group leader can assign his capacities flexibly to the various processes. This is of particular importance in a matrix organization in order to balance out fluctuations in available capacity.
- The use of cross-project resource allocation planning tools in a matrix organization ensures that employees are not erroneously assigned to several projects or line functions so that their maximum capacity is exceeded. An example of over-capacity caused by line functions is shown in step ⑦.

> *How and by whom are capacity bottlenecks relieved?*

In both planning approaches, it is up to the subproject/group leader to coordinate capacity demand with capacity supply. This arrangement can lead to significant conflict potential in matrix organizations.

The example of Figure 4.32 illustrates the importance of capacity problems. In the case of the duration-driven planning in step ⑦, the capacity of Ms Maier would be exceeded by 10 per cent if the scheduled final deadline were actually to be met. Such capacity bottlenecks must be relieved by suitable countermeasures. These might include:

- Postponement or expansion of non-critical project activities
- Outplacement of project activities to external companies or third parties within the company
- Reassignment of staff between projects
- Postponement or expansion of critical activities, but only as an ultimate measure, as this would lead to project delays
- Overtime should not be included in the plans, as this would tend to jeopardize the project deadlines from the very outset.

> *What must be regarded in capacity planning?*

The following must be considered in this context:

- In the case of resource-driven planning, the automatic capacity-smoothing function offered in most software tools should be used with the utmost care. The automatic calculation of new process duration times as well as the distribution of capacities over time based principally on mathematical methods can lead to results that are far removed from practice, if not downright incorrect. Floating resource transitions between two processes present a particular problem, as they are very difficult to map in the system. They require subsequent manual correction, thus again clarifying the advantages of a duration-driven approach to planning. The example in Figure 4.32 shows how commercial software tools would calculate a later final deadline in order to relieve Ms Maier in ⑦ from the burden of her excess capacity utilization.[19]

- To employ new staff or introduce them to the project can have the negative effect of burdening existing employees with the task of mentoring the newcomers. This will tend to aggravate the capacity situation in the short term.

> *Do low-level plans affect on high-level plans?*

Low-level scheduling can lead to problems, which cannot be circumvented by any countermeasures. The deadlines laid down in the high-level plans then turn out under closer inspection to be untenable. Such cases absolutely require **feedback** from the low-level to the high-level planning activities in order to adjust relevant deadlines or sequences there.

> *How is the controllability of the plans assured?*

As soon as the scheduling and capacity planning have been completed, the profile of the project or subproject becomes apparent. In order to control and monitor the whole process effectively, **milestones** are set at particularly critical points along the project (cf. Figure 4.33). These points are located at intervals during a project at which the attainment of specific subtargets can be verified. The section on project control will cover this approach in detail. It will be shown that result checks at milestones offer a very good way of tracking the progress of the project:

- When schedule plans are set up, care should therefore be taken to place milestones at reasonable (not too lengthy) intervals during the project.

Figure 4.33   Milestones in the detailed schedule

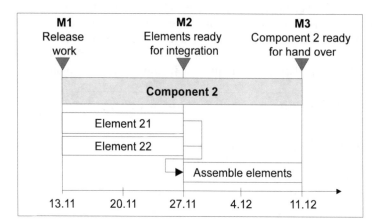

What is a baseline?

In order to allow the later progress of the project to be compared with the initial plan, the schedule and capacity plans are frozen to the **project baseline** after being set up and coordinated. Even if the plan is subsequently adjusted, a comparison with the original baseline can yield information about the progress of the project as well as reasons for any problems that may have arisen.

Planning quality in greater detail

How is the performance scope defined?

The definition cycle covers not only cost and time targets, but also above all sets targets with respect to the desired product quality. In the first place, these quality targets refer to the performance features of the relevant product. An initial product configuration is defined on the basis of the requirements of a specific customer or an addressed target group. This is done with the aid of the feature documentation building blocks described in the definition phase.

The initial configuration is frozen in the form of a **configuration basis**. However, it is typical of projects that it is rarely possible to describe the planned end product in full detail at their start. No more than rough specifications, which reflect the customer's requirements, are usually available at that point. These are then transferred stepwise into more concrete form at a later stage. The configuration basis offers a comparative yardstick for orienting the subsequent project control so that the original customer requirements are not lost from sight.[20]

> *Why is the configuration basis frozen?*

The configuration basis is elaborated in steps during the course of the project – i.e. it is gradually supplemented by detailed specifications. All the specifications received and approved at the various milestones must then be **irrevocably frozen**. In general, no changes should be made. Such a procedure has the following benefits:

- It allows a check to be made at the planned verification times as to whether the progress of the project corresponds to the current specifications.
- It thus ensures that the products/services really are implemented in exactly the form that the customer had commissioned in the first place.
- It allows those people who work on subcomponents to obtain reliable information from the configuration basis, such as that relating to interface requirements.
- It also saves time and costs and thus helps to ensure the success of the project. As a result, uncoordinated changes in the specifications of individual subcomplexes are prevented from generating problems at the later stage of integration into an overall product.

> *What other quality targets are relevant?*

The quality targets of a project refer not only to the configuration of the relevant product. In particular, they also include the **reliability** of the overall product. Thus a maximum **failure rate** is determined from the customer's perspective. It reflects the downtime as a percentage of the total operating life of the product.

This target parameter allows the mean time to repair (MTTR) and thus the specification parameter of **product availability** or mean time between failures (MTBF) to be calculated with the aid of a reverse calculation.

> *How are quality targets made verifiable?*

In order to achieve the desired product quality at the final project deadline, the attainment of the quality targets must also be continuously tracked during the project. Deviations from project targets must be recognized as early as possible so that suitable countermeasures can be taken. This problem will be examined in more detail in Section 4.3 on project control. When the quality plans are set up, therefore, the targets they contain must as far as possible be oriented in an operational way in line with the time frame for the project.

Problems frequently arise in attempting to make quality targets **operational**, because quality is not an easy parameter to measure during the execution of a project. In this case, a roundabout approach is useful. Instead of setting quantitative targets for each project task, qualitative targets may also be specified and verified by checklists. If quality targets are difficult to express in concrete terms, then at least binding targets should be set for the performance of the activities relevant to quality (tests, reviews, etc.).

> *How are quality targets scheduled?*

The **quality targets are arranged in a time frame** by defining quality-related targets for the main milestones of the project, which must be reached if these milestones are to be attained. The release checklist was an example of this kind. It allows those elements of individual projects to be defined, which must be attained if the project is to be released.

Another example: detailed specifications are elaborated in product innovation projects for performing field trials by defining a minimum period of customer experience (number of test customers * test time) which is mandatory for series delivery to take place. Similar parameters are defined for the individual milestones and are included in the relevant checklists, which were used to verify that a milestone was reached.

In order to verify the attainment of the quality targets between the main milestones too, the scheduling must be performed in greater detail. This can be illustrated by looking at software development. The *mean errors per thousand lines of code (kloc)* which will occur in the course of the development process are already known from past

Figure 4.34 Open errors in the course of a software-development project

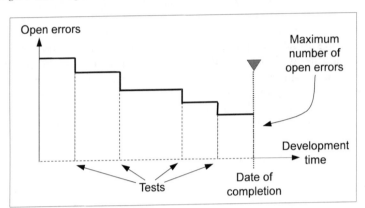

experience. Empirical data also shows how many of these errors can on average be detected and eliminated in a test phase. A histogram can be created with the aid of this information based on the complexity of the product to be manufactured, the maximum number of open errors specified in the final target and the test phases defined in the QA plan. The result is a quality curve of the subproject (cf. Figure 4.34) which can subsequently be used as the basis for quality-oriented project control.

> *How are the quality targets documented?*

The example of software development should not be taken to mean that quality targets can be set only in well structured sectors. Quality plans must also be set up for less easily formulated tasks and their observance then checked at a later stage.

In view of their importance, the quality targets for the overall project and the supporting in-house processes are recorded in separate documents known as **product quality agreements (PQAs)**. Global PQAs should already be available at the time of project release. Conflicts with the cost and time targets can then be detected and eliminated. It is therefore recommended to proceed as for the first product feature specifications, namely to appoint a neutral expert body (the definition team) with responsibilities across functional sectors to coordinate the issuing of the relevant plans.

How are quality targets converted into plans?

In order to express the quality targets laid down in the PQAs in concrete terms, more detailed plans must now be derived for attaining these targets during the execution of a project. A **quality assurance plan** (QA plan) visualizes this approach and forms the starting point for **project-accompanying quality control**. In the QA plan, the elements of the work breakdown structure are assigned to quality assurance measures (cf. Figure 4.35). Review partners may then be appointed for the specifications to be issued according to the work breakdown structure and integration and module tests may be planned for various software development phases.

Figure 4.35   Contents of a QA plan

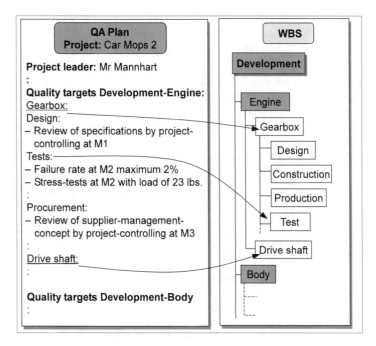

Which sectors does the QA plan cover?

The QA plan is very comprehensive. It contains detailed targets and specifications for all the departments involved in the project. In product innovation projects, quality targets may be included in the logistics, sales and manufacture stages: an example is the **dead-on-arrival rate,** which specifies the maximum percentage of products, which may fail after delivery and during the first start-up phase. In order to issue and monitor the QA plan, the quality manager for the project must have a comprehensive overview of all the sectors involved.

Documentation planning

> *Why is documentation planning required?*

Large numbers of documents of various kinds are generated in the course of project management. They range from basic strategy formulations via requests of different stages of detail, product specifications and profitability analyses up to the most diverse project plans. It is easy to see that complex projects generate a large number of documents, all of them more or less important for the project and hard to keep track of. If this flood of documents is not carefully organized from the very start of the project, its subsequent execution may encounter major difficulties. Inadequate updating of **project documents** (such as specifications, product descriptions) can lead to poorly organized records and may seriously impair the user's ability to operate the products. Thus missing documentation in software products frequently hinders troubleshooting operations. Well thought-out management of **project documentation** (agreements, project plans, development documents, protocols, etc.) helps to avoid this kind of unnecessary problems. All project employees are kept abreast of the latest status of the project planning in order to ensure that the project is implemented in line with the set targets.

> *How is consistent documentation ensured?*

The need to issue release documentation at the end of the definition cycle already represents an important aspect of documentation management. In the early phases of the project planning, however, a **documentation plan** must also be elaborated for the remaining part of the project. Figure 4.36 indicates its two main constituents. A **document requirements list** assigns the documents to be issued to each element in

Figure 4.36 Basic structure of a documentation plan

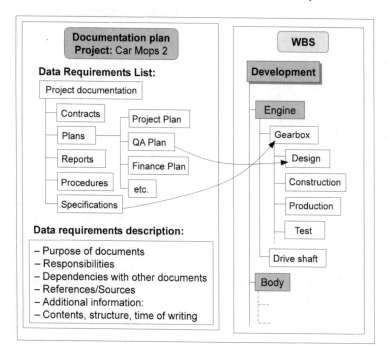

the work breakdown structure. Each document must contain the following information in order to ensure that this procedure runs smoothly:[21]

- A unique document number and designation
- The department responsible for its issue
- The planned deadline for its issue
- The recipients of the document (distribution list)
- Any release requirements (such as reviews of specifications, cf. a QA plan).

> *How is the comparability of projects guaranteed?*

It is also recommended that the document requirements be defined. For project-oriented companies, these are often fixed in a **document requirements description** which covers an entire project. By describing the minimum contents, issue cycle and explaining the meaning and purpose of the documents, it ensures that they are consistent through-out the project.

However, it also defines the classification status of documents that have already been issued. Examples are:

- 'Present and in use'
- 'In preparation'
- 'Currently being checked'
- 'Currently being altered.'[22]

The document requirements description is thus also of importance for management *with* projects, as it facilitates the comparison and the evaluation of different projects.

Consistent documentation of an individual project forms the basis for project control. Thus the current product and process plans also include the basic configuration described in the preceding section against which the actual progress of the project can be compared.

4.1.5 Summarized results of the initialization process in the planning documentation

> *Why is planning documentation needed?*

Like the release documentation issued at the end of the definition cycle, a compact summary of its results is prepared at the end of the initialization process. This **planning documentation** (also known as the project plan, release binder, etc. in various companies) outlines the results of the planning process at overall project level so that a report can be submitted to the project customer or relevant steering commit-tee. Moreover, it forms the basis for consistent project documentation. Its creation must therefore be included even in the documentation plan mentioned above.

> *What does the planning documentation contain?*

The planning documentation may contain the following elements:

- The work breakdown structure
- Network plans for the individual subprocesses as well as the high-level network plan of the total project

- Target-cost-oriented product planning
- Quality plans for the project and its subprocesses
- Risk analyses
- Additional documents such as the project organization plan, the documentation plan, etc.
- Modified estimates of the business data
- Results of the bottom-up expenditure estimation (expert session).

4.2 CONTINUED PLANNING IN THE FURTHER COURSE OF THE PROJECT

> *When is project planning finally completed?*

Project planning is by no means completed at the end of the initialization phase. Indeed, it continues over the entire course of the project in parallel with the implementation of the product (cf. Figure 4.37). The high-level plans of the overall project issued in the initialization phase and the low-level plans for the first phases of the implementation are

Figure 4.37   Subprocesses after initialization that are relevant for project planning

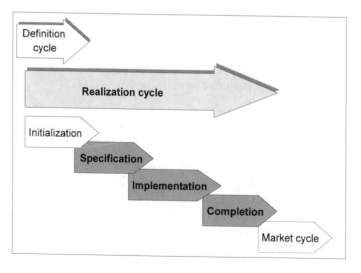

updated, supplemented and detailed as the project proceeds. Thus the product components are detailed during the specification process on the basis of the objectives and documents of the preceding processes. The project teams in coordination then create all additionally required plans with the project managers. These may include manufacturing and service plans as well as any logistics and tooling plans or even training plans for employees of the sales and service departments or of external customers.

In a similar way, the necessary testing and integration activities are planned in detail in the later stages of the project in order to merge the subcomponents into the final product.

> *Why must the project completion be planned?*

The completion of a project must also be planned at an early stage. Thus the hand over of the end product to the external customer or its introduction onto the market (make and market process) must be thought through in good time. Therefore all relevant technical sectors such as sales/marketing or manufacturing are involved in the project from the outset (cf. the high-level network diagrams). In order not to undermine the motivation of the project teams, arrangements should also be made for the continued activities of all employees after the current project has been successfully concluded. In view of the importance of the project completion phase, a special chapter will be devoted to this topic (see Chapter 6 below).

4.3   FROM PLANS TO ACTION: MOTIVATION AND BEHAVIOURAL CONTROL IN THE PROJECT

> *Why is motivation and behavioural control necessary?*

Creating plans does not necessarily ensure that they will be implemented. One of the most important tasks of a project leader is to motivate the team to act in accordance with the plans and to adhere to them. This makes great demands on his/her social skills. The key to the successful implementation of project plans lies in guiding the behaviour of the employees in an appropriate way. Numerous *hard* and *soft* tools are available for this purpose. They may be used by the project managers wherever the structure of the company offers the required scope (cf. Part III, Chapter 10):

- Tools for motivation and behavioural control are designed to ensure that the employees wish to adhere to the set plans **on the basis of their own personal convictions**.

> *What tools are available for guiding behaviour?*

The ways in which employees can be motivated to implement and follow plans varies significantly between individuals (see Figure 4.38).[23]

> *Should all employees be guided in the same way?*

The effect and success of motivational tools as the ones shown in Figure 4.38 will depend on the personality of the individual team

Figure 4.38   Tools for the motivation and guidance of project employees

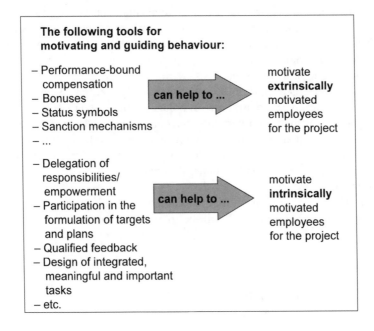

members. Extrinsically motivated employees can be encouraged by bonuses, performance-indexed salaries and other positive or negative sanctions linked to the attainment of project goals. In contrast, intrinsically motivated persons can be motivated to perform tasks, which comply with the targets by making the work itself as attractive as possible. This may involve the fixing of individual goals with the participation of the team members. Here, care should be taken that the agreed goals actually have a motivating effect.

> *What are motivating goals?*

Such goals:

- are **operational** – i.e. the employees must understand them, and they
- must be capable of being both **altered** and **reached**: goals should lie just above the employee's own aspiration level; unattainable goals are as demoralizing as goals that are set too low.[24]

> *What does this mean for the project leaders?*

It has become clear that project management tasks require project leaders to be in direct contact with the members of the project team at all times so that these can be individually motivated. Unsurprisingly, studies show that the success of a project is strongly correlated with the management skills of its leaders.[25]

However, it is important to note that management skills are not the same as employee orientation or policies aimed at creating a good project atmosphere and avoiding personal conflicts. Indeed, there are times in which a hard management style may well be successful.[26] However, the reasons for such an approach, which is very likely to be merely temporary, must be made abundantly clear to the employees concerned.

Motivation in a project-oriented company is the object of Part III, Chapter 10, where this topic will be treated in more detail.

NOTES

1   Cf. Litke (1995), p. 76 f.
2   Cf. Blazek (1990), p. 155

3   Cf. Litke (1995), p. 75 f.
4   Cf. e.g. Blazek (1990), p. 156 or Litke (1995), p. 78 f.
5   Larson and Gobeli (1988), p. 181, make a distinction based on the distribution of responsibilities for the project activities between a **functional matrix** (responsibility lies with the technical supervisor), a **balanced matrix** and a **project matrix** (responsibility is concentrated with the project leader).
6   The *effectiveness* of an organizational form refers to its general suitability to reach a given goal. In contrast, its *efficiency* is the quantitative degree of attaining the goal. This means that the more efficient an organizational form is, the better can its targets be attained with the same expenditures. Cf. Küpper and Weber (1995), p. 96 f.
7   Cf. Frese (1995), pp. 24 ff. as well as pp. 495 ff. for a general overview of coordination and motivation efficiency.
8   Cf. on this point Picot, Reichwald and Wigand (1998), p. 171 f.
9   The spiral model was developed by Boehm (1988).
10 Cf. for the following Litke (1995), p. 98, or Turner (1993), p. 102 ff.
11 A comprehensive treatment of this set of problems can be found in Globerson (1994).
12 Schelle (1996), p. 94.
13 A detailed description of the following tools and additional examples can be found in Turner (1993), pp. 217 ff. as well as in Meredith and Mantel (1989), p. 267 ff.
14 The interested reader is referred to works such as Altrogge (1994), as well as Küpper, Lüder and Streidtferdt (1975), which also handle the approaches described here.
15 In the first planning runs, the recursive calculation of the buffer times may yield negative values. These activities are thus extremely critical and require immediate adjustments to the plan: negative buffer values mean that the final deadline for the whole project cannot be maintained on the basis of the current plan!
16 An explanatory example of this is found in Meredith and Mantel (1989), pp. 271 ff. The ground rules that must be observed in setting up CPM plans are presented in detail in Küpper, Lüder and Streidtferdt (1975), pp. 79 ff.
17 In the case of particularly complex development programmes involving several independent products whose interaction is vital to the planned end product (e.g. the development of a large communications system and parallel development of its equipment) it is recommended that **top-level network diagrams** which reflect the schedule relationships between all corresponding projects are included.
18 Some tools offer the option of coupling high-level and low-level networks electronically. This may appear to be useful at first sight but has the drawback that every small change in the LLN can affect the final deadline, even if this is in fact not the case in reality. It may be better not to perform this electronic coupling but instead to update the high-level network diagram at regular intervals, a task best entrusted to a subproject leader. This strengthens his/her responsibility and also improves communications in the event of deadline changes in the project.

19 More recent project management software attempts to handle this problem by means of integrated contouring functions. Although it makes theoretical sense to define a capacity requirement which changes during the runtime of an activity within a tool, in practice it merely tends to complicate the planning process and above all the control of the project. The results obtained soon cease to reflect any reality, particularly when a change occurs in the project, so their correctness must often be regarded as doubtful.

20 In the literature, the task of planning and monitoring the technical configuration of a product is known as **configuration management**, which forms a part of the management of projects. A presentation of this topic can be found in Kolks (1986).

21 Cf. Madauss (1994), pp. 322 ff.

22 Madauss (1994), p. 328.

23 These statements are based on the motivation theories described in Part III, p. 256.

24 This was shown by a series of behavioural-scientific studies, such as those dealing with behavioural accounting (e.g. Von Stedry and Kay, 1996). A good overview of this topic is given in Schweitzer and Küpper (1998), pp. 550 ff.

25 Cf. Anderson (1992), for example.

26 A detailed description of various studies on successful management in groups can be found in v. Rosenstiel (1992), pp. 306 ff.

5 Monitoring and control of projects

Why is project control needed?

Planning obviously plays a decisive role in projects of all kinds. It defines both the time frame and the execution of a project as well as the resulting products together with their features and properties. Ultimately, however, project planning does no more than formulate plans – i.e. situations to be achieved in the future (targets), and possible ways of reaching them.

In itself, formulating plans is insufficient to ensure successful implementation of the results to be achieved. There are many reasons for this:

- Project plans can never cover all the details of the task in hand. Each member of the project team has a certain freedom of action, which he can and must exercise on the basis of his own knowledge and experience. This is particularly evident in the case of product-innovation projects in which the creative freedom granted to the developers is a necessary condition for the success of the project.
- Projects may run over several months, in some cases even over several years. During this time changes may take place in the company or its environment, which have a positive or negative effect on the project. It is necessary to respond to such changes in a coordinated way.
- Technical or social problems may occur during the execution of the project, which were not foreseen in the original plans. Here too it is important to develop suitable responses in good time.

Successful project management requires not only well prepared planning procedures but also a sophisticated approach to monitor and control the progress of the project in a continuous way (henceforth simply called **project control**):

> *What is the aim of project control?*

- The aim of project control is to ensure that the project targets are achieved in an efficient way.

The minimum aim of project control is to verify that all the formulated plans (schedule plans, cost plans, quality assurance plans, documentation plans, etc.) have in fact been implemented. However, the significance of project control goes far beyond the process of verifying that the project plans are correctly followed.

In fact, project control proceeds in such a way that all information relevant to the control process (control information) is used and evaluated against the background of the existing plan information and other specifications. Suitable countermeasures are taken in the event of any deviations or other disturbances and behavioural guidance is used to ensure successful implementation of the project. This process is shown graphically in Figure 5.1.

Figure 5.1   Typical project-control process

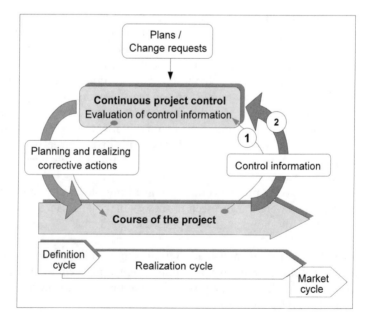

> *When is project control initiated?*

In order to perform these functions successfully, project control must accompany the course of the project over all its subprocesses. This means that the control process outlined above runs continuously (cf. Figure 5.2).

> *What elements does it contain?*

Figure 5.1 already indicates that effective project control requires more comprehensive activities and tools than tend to be implied in the usual sources dealing with project management. These will be discussed in detail in order to do full justice to the importance of each subaspect by traversing a typical process of project control – i.e. starting from the input of the control information (cf. Figure 5.3) via its evaluation up to making suitable adjustments. It will quickly become apparent that although *hard facts* ① are important, effective project control depends to at least the same extent on *soft facts* ②.

> *Who carries out the project control?*

Project-control functions need not necessarily be concentrated in a single agent or department, such as a project leader. Important project-control tasks can also be assigned to other members of the project team, such as group leaders or heads of technical sectors.

Figure 5.2   Continuous project control

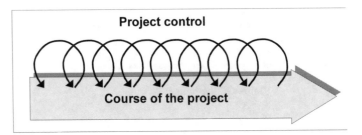

5.1 OBTAINING INFORMATION RELEVANT TO PROJECT CONTROL

> *Why is control information required?*

Control information represents the very basis of every project-control task. All information, which helps to verify the scheduled progress of the project or to initiate suitable adjustments where these are necessary, is relevant to this task. Indeed, it is indispensable if the project is to be coordinated in line with its targets. Without this information, the control procedures would peter out or degenerate to an undesirable groping in the dark. The following sections will show:

- which control information can be obtained and how
- how this information reaches the agencies responsible for project control in the company, and
- what options are available to configure the subprocess of information acquisition as efficiently as possible.

Figure 5.3   Obtaining control information in the course of the project

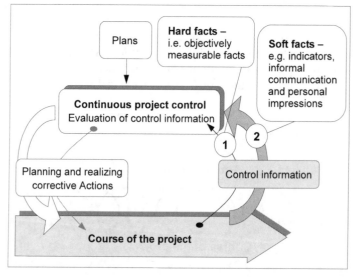

5.1.1 Measuring the progress of a project within project management

> *When can one be sure that the targets have been reached?*

In simplified terms, the project objectives consist of schedule and cost targets as well as targets oriented to the scope of performance and the quality of the end product. In project planning, these targets are converted into corresponding plans, above all into the work breakdown structure and the various scheduling and execution plans. A problem frequently faced in project control is that the attainment of the targets cannot be objectively assessed until the completion of the project or even afterwards. This is particularly evident for technical quality targets. The attainment of the product quality desired by the customer cannot be finally verified until all mutually dependent sub-components have been integrated. The same applies to keeping within the planned product costs.

Despite these difficulties, project control requires information about the progress of the project:

> *What information is relevant for project control?*

- Is the project on schedule? What proportion of the final project performance has already been completed?
- Can the planned deadlines be met?
- Will the product to be manufactured meet the quality criteria and satisfy all planned requirements?
- Will the product be available at the planned costs or keep within the planned manufacturing costs at a later stage (see Target costing, p. 62)?
- Is the project within budget?
- Can unexpected events, perturbations or other problems occur that might jeopardize the progress of the project?

> *Why is it difficult to measure this data?*

It is clear that project control requires up-to-date information about the progress of the project in terms of schedule, quality and cost targets. Such information can be provided by **continuously measuring the performance** of the project. In contrast to other corporate procedures, however, measuring the progress of a project is by no means easy. Because production processes can often be standardized, they allow the current progress of the work done on a product as well as the time and resources still required for its completion to be precisely measured. This is not the case for projects. So how can the progress of a project be measured despite these difficulties?

Measuring the progress of a project

> *What are result checks?*

The completion of the results of a project can be checked by verifying the **attainment of the planned milestones**. It was shown in Section 4.1.4 how the individual elements of the work breakdown structure are scheduled by means of network diagram techniques. It is thus possible to check whether the different tasks of the project have in fact been completed at the respective milestones. Such **result checks** have the advantage that the attainment of the set targets can be objectively verified – i.e. it can be unequivocally determined whether the planned results were achieved or not (cf. Figure 5.4).

> *Why are behaviour or process checks needed?*

Although it is necessary to check the scheduled completion of the individual elements of the work breakdown structure, this is not a sufficient source of information to control the project. As later sections will show, project control must receive information at certain points in the course of the project as to how far the tasks currently in hand have already progressed. In addition to the result checks, therefore, also **behaviour and process checks** have to be carried out. These do not check whether a result has been *attained*, but merely measure the *path traversed so far* towards reaching the target. It will be shown in the following that this is an important but difficult task of project control.[1]

> *What parameters are used in process control?*

A necessary basic item of information required to determine the current progress of work is the **manpower already booked** for the project, for example the man-hours allocated up to that point. Suitable

Figure 5.4   Delays as shown in a bar chart

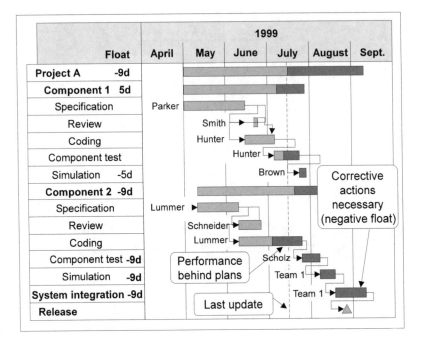

computer programmes (see Resource allocation planning system, p. 97) offer easy ways of comparing the planned and actual manpower deployment at various aggregation stages of the project (cf. Figure 5.5).

Particularly at the beginning of a project, it is important to check whether the allocated resources really are available for the project or are perhaps already tied up in another project. If significant deviations are noted, relevant countermeasures must be taken immediately (cf. Section 5.3).

> *When can work units be measured?*

Another interesting variant of assessing the progress of a project is to measure the accomplished work units, such as the number of lines of code written in software development. However, this variant can be used only in specific exceptional situations, such as in programming.

Figure 5.5   Comparison of planned and actual manpower usage

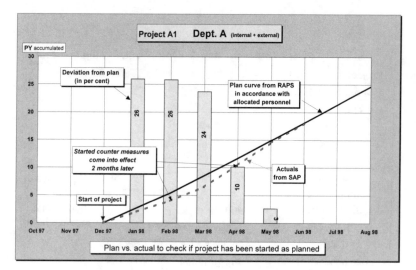

Why is the percentage of completion needed?

A mere measurement of the input (work deployment, quantitative performance) is not sufficient to estimate the performance level of a project, as it does not yet provide any information about the output achieved. For example, information about the number of work hours expended says nothing about the work results which were achieved as a result. Therefore, information is required about the current degree of implementation of the subactivities within the project – i.e. about the **percentage of completion (PoC)** of the specific processes. This information is particularly important, for instance for determining the earned value, as will be shown in Chapter 5.2.4.

How reliable are employees' estimates?

In practice, the most usual way of assessing the degree of completion of a project subactivity is simply to ask the employees involved. After all, those who have to deal with a task have the best-detailed knowledge about the actual progress made. Nevertheless, it is not wise to

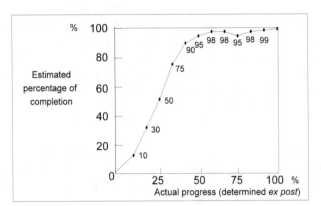

Figure 5.6   The 90 per cent syndrome

place too much faith in the accuracy of subjective estimates of the progress made toward reaching a target. This is because whenever questions are asked about the degree of implementation of a task, a problem known as the **90 per cent syndrome** (Figure 5.6)[2] is frequently encountered.

Figure 5.6 shows the results of a regular survey by a software developer of the degree of completion of the work package assigned to him. After as little as about 50 per cent of the time that ultimately turned out to be necessary for this task, this developer subjectively estimated the progress he had made as 90 per cent. We see a typical phenomenon here: namely that the time required for the final completion of a task is underestimated by a considerable margin. This need not happen intentionally. Unexpected problems often occur at the end of a task or subsequent improvements become necessary. All this requires additional effort.

For project monitoring, the 90 per cent syndrome means that the progress of work cannot be assessed solely on the basis of an estimate by the person responsible for achieving the result in question.

Can the 90 per cent syndrome be circumvented?

One way of getting round the 90 per cent syndrome is to use **estimates of the remaining effort** – i.e. asking what remains to be done rather than what has already been achieved. It is based on the assumption that estimates of the effort still required to complete a work package are usually tackled much more realistically than estimates of the degree of completion already attained. This is due to the different characters of the two estimations. When estimating the degree of completion of work, the employee must directly justify the effort he has already expended. In contrast, an estimation of the remaining effort resembles a planning situation. The employee is aware that his performance will ultimately be measured on the basis of the statements he now makes.

A limiting factor, which cannot be ignored is that the effect of the remaining estimate of expenditure also depends significantly on the information flows and climate prevailing in the project. This question will be examined more closely in Section 5.12.

> *How is the PoC calculated?*

When the remaining effort per work package has been estimated, the percentage of completion is calculated via the following formula:[3]

$$PoC = 100 * (\text{Planned Effort} - \text{Remaining Effort})/\text{Planned Effort} \tag{5.1}$$

The remaining effort is subtracted from the originally planned effort. If this difference is expressed as a ratio of the planned effort, the result is the estimated percentage of completion actually reached so far.

> *What are the consequences in practice?*

It has so far become apparent that it is difficult to measure the progress achieved in a project by means of **behaviour** or **process checks**. Although the subresults achieved in a project can be verified in objective terms (**result checks**), this is often insufficient for assessing the degree of performance of the project. In practice, therefore, the following procedure has proved effective.

The low-level network diagrams are intentionally planned in such detail that check points whose attainment can be verified by result checks are placed at sufficiently short intervals. Regular updating of the network diagrams then includes all procedures which:

- should have been started at the updating point
- should have been finished at the updating point, but are not yet designated as completed, and
- are currently still being processed.

> *How is the PoC measured in practice?*

A check is made to determine whether the process was started at the planned time and whether the planned final deadline, and thus the planned result of the process, has been reached or can still be reached from the present perspective. After the deadlines of each process have been updated, which may involve changing the initial and final deadlines, the percentage of completion is calculated automatically by the software tool. The PoC parameter is then set equal to the percentage of completion that should have been reached up to the update time.

Measuring product quality during the project

Information about the quality level of both the **project processes** and the **products** to be implemented in them is already needed during project execution so that corrective action may be taken where necessary.

> *How is product quality measured?*

Depending on the type of project and the product in question (construction of an installation, software development, etc.), various ways of **measuring the product quality** are conceivable, some of which may be supported by sophisticated testing procedures. The tools used for measuring product quality therefore cannot and will not be examined in detail at this point. However, in order to detect errors as early as possible, tests must already be run at relatively low aggregation levels, such as the level of individual subcomponents. This accords with the philosophy of **total quality management** (TQM), which states that every subprocess should be regarded as an internal client relationship. A sub-component should not be implemented and handed over to the *client* until it has verifiably satisfied the previously defined quality targets.[4]

> *Why must the total future costs be checked?*

The quality of a product is also a factor in determining its costs. Especially in the sector of product innovation, therefore, it is important to ascertain the **total future costs** associated with the product as early as the development stage. Any errors made at this point can lead to profitability losses, which are almost impossible to correct in the further market cycle of the product. A target costing programme must thus be applied throughout the course of the project in order to ensure that the product quality complies with the requirements of the market (see Target costing, p. 62).

> *What is process-referred quality measurement?*

Many quality defects resulting in serious consequences have their origin in basic planning errors. So it is a good idea to run quality tests **as part of the quality measurement process** right from the early phases of a project. For example, a check should be made to ensure that the persons originally assigned these tasks in the quality plans correctly issued critical specifications or planning documents. The *measurement* of the process quality extends as far as verifying the correct performance of reviews, tests, inspections as well as all other quality-control measures laid down in the PQA and QA plans (cf. the treatment of quality planning in Section 4.1.4 p. 121).

Measuring project costs

> *Is cost measurement difficult?*

Compared with measuring the progress and quality of a project, measuring the project costs represents a relatively minor problem. However, this applies only where a number of necessary framework conditions are in place within the company. These will now be examined in somewhat more detail.

Project-referred recording of personnel costs

> *Whose working hours should be booked on a project?*

In personnel-intensive sectors such as research and development, the personnel costs represent a significant part of the total project costs. In order to compare actual personnel costs with the planned costs, a differentiated collection and structuring must initially be made of the manpower needed to implement the project. The tool applied for this purpose is **time recording**. All those involved in a specific project must show how much time they have expended on it with the aid of suitable recording tools. This procedure excludes only those categories of staff (top management, secretaries, etc.) whose exact time allocation would be neither possible nor make much sense in view of the diversity of projects in which they are involved. Their costs are allocated indirectly by means of surcharges on the hourly cost rates. External subcontractors, trainees, etc. are also excluded from the time allocation procedures if their costs are recorded elsewhere (direct booking of costs to project cost units).

> *How detailed should the time allocations be?*

The **degree of detail** of the time allocations is of critical importance for the accuracy of the later comparisons between the planned and actual results. It can vary in the different levels of the work breakdown structure. If the planned costs were estimated at work-package level, their attainment can be effectively verified only if the actual costs are recorded at this same level of detail. A cost allocation system should consequently be designed around targets to be reached on the basis of the actual recorded data. Various degrees of detail will be appropriate depending on what kinds of analyses are to be performed.

> *An example of a time allocation system*

Figure 5.7 shows an example of a **time allocation system**. In addition to evaluations at project level, it enables analyses of individual subprocesses such as collection, evaluation, packaging, initialization, etc. which may be used as internal and external benchmarks. In principle,

Figure 5.7   Example of a time-recording system

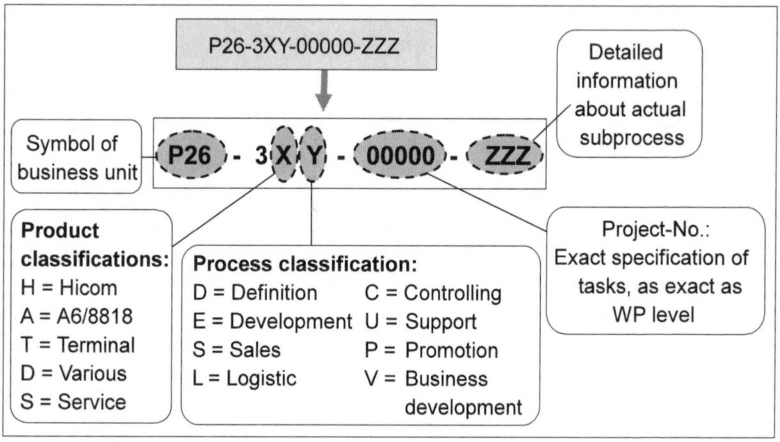

therefore, this time allocation system can support all the analyses to be examined in the following discussions. It can also provide quantitative information across the entire project in order to ensure continuous improvement.

> *How are such systems implemented?*

In practice, a time allocation system of this kind is implemented by means of **user-friendly dialogue systems.** The user can thus ignore the complex number systems operating in the background (cf. Figure 5.8). The recorded data flows directly into the relevant controlling systems – i.e. into SAP R/3 in this example.

> *What recording cycle is appropriate?*

The question as to how frequently members of the project teams should record their time allocations cannot be answered across the board. Because the effort this procedure involves is significantly minimized by a simple user interface, a short **recording cycle** (daily, weekly) is an optimum choice. Longer cycles can reduce the accuracy of the time allocation data.

Figure 5.8 User interface of a time-recording system (example)

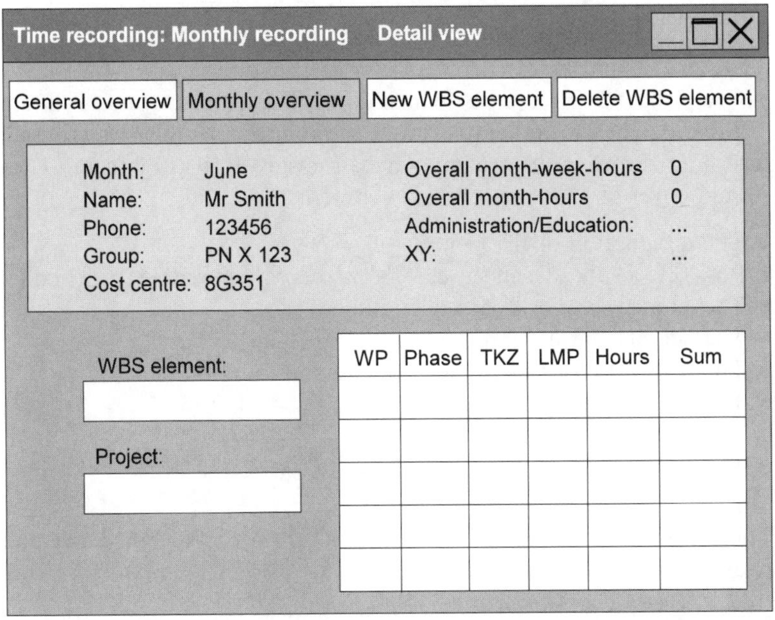

| Time recording: Monthly recording | Detail view | | | | | | |

General overview | **Monthly overview** | **New WBS element** | **Delete WBS element**

Month:	June	Overall month-week-hours 0
Name:	Mr Smith	Overall month-hours 0
Phone:	123456	Administration/Education: ...
Group:	PN X 123	XY: ...
Cost centre: 8G351		

WBS element:	WP	Phase	TKZ	LMP	Hours	Sum
Project:						

What are hourly cost rates?

To calculate the personnel costs of a project, the number of allocated hours are multiplied by **hourly cost rates**. These rates are calculated by dividing the annual budget of a cost centre by the number of hours of productive work performed in the year. They consequently represent the price, which must be paid to a cost centre for utilizing its capacities per man-hour:

$$\text{Hourly cost rate} = \frac{\text{Annual budget of cost centre}}{\text{productive hours performed}} \qquad (5.2)$$

Because it is as a rule not up to the leader of an individual project to define the internal hourly cost rate, this calculation will not be pursued in any more detail at this point.[5]

Project-referred recording of other cost types

> ## What contents should the records cover?

Those project-referred costs, which go beyond personnel costs should also be assigned to individual projects as far as possible. Entering all incoming records into a computer can ensure this assignment. They should cover at least the following contents:[6]

- The designation of the project
- Possibly, a suborder in the case of an external purchase (order code)
- The subtask or work-package number
- The activity in question
- The relevant cost type in terms of quantity and/or value
- The job number and date.

> ## Which costs are recorded?

The following are examples of costs, which are distributed over all relevant projects:

- **Production factors** originating from within the company
- Travel expenses, consulting expenses, insurance expenses (known as **interface costs**[7])
- Other **external expenditures**
- **Depreciation**: sometimes a distinction is made between time- and usage-related depreciation[8]
- **Imputed interest**: this may be applied because uncharged order costs tie up necessary operating capital
- **Other**: such as transport or energy costs (water, power, heating, etc.)

This procedure allows the project managers and controllers to obtain the information they need to control the **actual costs** of a project. These can then be compared with the originally planned costs recorded in the base line – i.e. the initial fixed planning data.

Some of the ways available for determining the actual status of a project in terms of its schedule, cost and quality targets have so far been explained. These procedures show up any deviations from the initial plans, which may occur in an insidious way during the course of the project or as a result of acute interim events. The following section will show how relevant control information can be provided to agents who can intervene by making appropriate adjustments.

Case study 5.1 Stakeholder-oriented management of projects

A project touches on the interests of numerous groups within and outside the company in which it is run. Known as **stakeholders** of the project, they can either promote or impair its success. Quite apart from the customers of the project, employees from other projects or from the line may have an interest in the project if it affects their functions or area of responsibility. The project managers should therefore identify such stakeholders at an early stage and attempt to estimate their influence on the project and its results.

One of the first steps a new project leader should take is thus to **analyze the environment of the project** and the stakeholders present within it so that he can apply suitable pressure to ensure the successful implementation of the project. Such a stakeholder orientation may usefully include the following three components:[9]

(1) *Identify the stakeholders*
    Stakeholders of the project may be found in the following groups:

- Groups directly affected by the project such as team members, suppliers, project customers and other contractors.
- People who can affect the framework conditions impinging on the project – i.e. its necessary infrastructure, the available financial and material resources as well as employees or corporate policy factors.
- People and institutions whose positions of authority give them power to affect the project. Apart from top management, these may also include governments and unions at local, regional or county level.
- People and institutions in whose interests the success or failure of the project lies.

(2) *Categorize the stakeholders*
Not all stakeholders are equally critical for the project. It is thus useful to subdivide them into categories, such as:

- Stakeholders who can be controlled
- Stakeholders who can be influenced
- Stakeholders who can hardly be influenced (Figure 5.9).

Figure 5.9   Categorization of stakeholders

Stakeholders who	have little influence on project progress	have moderate influence on project progress	have great influence on project progress
can be controlled			
can be influenced			
can hardly be influenced			

Within these categories, the individual stakeholders can additionally be classified on the basis of their power to affect the success of the project. This classification offers a particularly good basis for creating a public relations plan for the project at a later stage by revealing the controllability of individual stakeholders as well as their potential impact on the project:

(3) *Set up and implement a public relations (PR) plan*
The PR plan should include strategies for addressing the stakeholder groups in a pro-active way. The aim must be to promote any positive influences and to counteract any negative ones from the beginning. As in other planning procedures applied in the project, resources must be allocated to specific measures and their correct implementation must be monitored.

An open information policy is particularly important to ensure an effective stakeholder orientation in project management. Any stakeholder queries must be regarded as urgent and be handled with circumspection. Although this may initially consume resources, it can promote the progress of the project in the mid-term in a sustained way.

An example of the need for marketing a project actively *vis-à-vis* its stakeholders can be seen in the case of the company's executive management. Although support by top management is obviously critical for the success of a project, their commitment to a project often declines significantly after its release. Unless the relevant PR activities are given an additional boost, this commitment will not increase again until shortly before the completion of the project or unless major problems occur during its execution. A pro-active information policy aimed at these echelons can increase their interest in the project and thus ensure their support for any critical situations, which might arise.

5.1.2 Reporting procedures in the project

What is the purpose of reporting procedures?

Reporting procedures regulate the flow of information in the project and thus represent one of the most significant sets of project management tools. They regulate a flow of control information, which takes place principally along the vertical path (e.g. from the teams via the project management to the steering committee and the customer), but also along the horizontal path (e.g. between subproject leaders or from one project leader to another):

- Project reporting procedures must be designed to ensure that the **relevant** information is conveyed to the **correct recipients at the right time**.

Is it important to receive information early on?

Figure 5.10 shows how important it is to respond to any problems arising during the project by making suitable adjustments as early as possible. Because of the limited duration of a project, it is frequently not enough to **react** to disturbances once they have occurred. Often, there is no time left after the problems have been identified to tackle the

Figure 5.10 Importance of early corrective actions

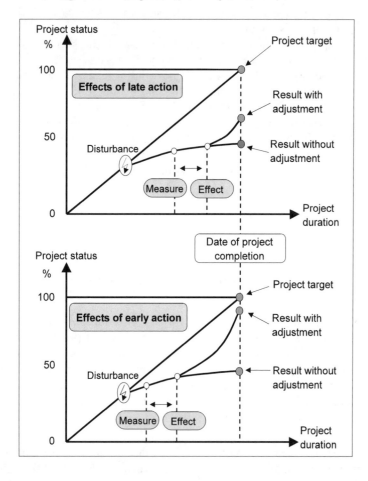

resulting deviations. Impending disturbances must therefore be identified as early as possible so that adjustments can be made before the
damage has reached its full extent. Effective project control means
anticipating possible disturbances pro-actively in order to **act** before
the resulting problems have reached their full dimensions:

- Project controllers should **act rather than react**. They must at all
  times endeavour to identify potential disturbances before they
  actually occur.

> *What do the reporting procedures contribute?*

The reporting procedures must therefore be designed in an appropriate way to ensure such a response capability. In particular, the types of report must be defined together with their relevant contents and the reporting cycle. A distinction can be made between **standard reports** and **ad hoc** or **contingency reports**.[10] Whereas standard reports are issued regularly, ad hoc reports are designed to inform the recipient flexibly about particularly important events occurring in the project.

Standard reports

> *Do the contents of reports depend on their recipients?*

The starting point for defining the contents of standard reports must be to determine the kind of information actually needed by their various recipients. In order to avoid an information overload, the contents of the reports must be strictly relevant to their particular recipients and must be correspondingly individualized. The groups who commissioned the project in the first place (steering committee, decision-making group, customer) are less interested in detailed technical data than in information about the status of the project with respect to the overall objectives. In contrast, (sub)project leaders require more precise information about the development of individual critical activities so that they can quickly initiate countermeasures for anticipated problems in good time:

- The contents of the reports must be limited to information relevant to the control of the project.

> *Is this requirement currently met?*

Although it is obvious, the requirement to limit reports to information relevant to project control is nevertheless frequently ignored. This is shown by the loads of lists and reports, which constantly confront many managers. One reason for this undesirable development is the ease with which information of all kinds can be distributed via electronic media. An unnecessary flood of information then burdens staff and blocks capacities. They are obliged to sort out the relevant information instead of being employed productively in the project. One of the most important tasks of project control is therefore to coordinate the information requirement of the project managers with the sources of this information (cf. Part III, Chapter 12).

> *What information must a report contain?*

The recipient of the report will in general require the following information, which usually is the next-highest agency in the project:

- A compact overview of the **current project situation** – i.e.:
  - Key activities performed since the last report
  - Information about the situation with respect to scheduling, cost and quality targets
  - An analysis of current risks (see Risk-aware project management, p. 47),
  - A current profitability analysis of the project
  - Information about any **acute problems** including solutions which have already been implemented or are planned (**action items**)
  - Information about sectors and problems which still **require a decision** from the recipient of the report
- **The need for support** by the report recipient, as well as
- **Information** specially **requested** by the report recipient – this last point is particularly important in customer-order projects where the external customer may stipulate regular reporting of specific contents.

> *What is an early warning system?*

The contents of the reports should not be limited to measurable facts of the kind outlined in the preceding section. It is a good idea for them to include an **early warning system** (EWS)[11] which points out impending disturbances in good time. Its basic idea is to develop indicators for potential problems and defective developments at an early stage in the course of the project. The introduction of a project EWS therefore is closely allied to the concept of **risk-aware project management** (see Risk-aware project management, p. 47). It allows project control to be oriented to previously identified risk factors, which can then be closely monitored in the course of the project.

> *How helpful is a stakeholder orientation?*

Another useful way of identifying potential disturbances and their effects on the project at an early stage is in a consistent **stakeholder orientation** by the project leaders. From the start of the project they should analyze those agencies and persons who have an interest in the project or the power to affect it. Any changes occurring in the stakeholder situation must be included in the reports. Suitable measures can then be applied to channel the effects of these stakeholders in a positive sense (more details on this point see Stakeholder-oriented management of projects, p. 151).

> *Are standard formats helpful?*

To ensure that the persons and agencies dealing with these procedures do not omit any important factors, a standardized reporting format should be established in project-oriented companies. The **traffic-light forms** shown in the Figures 5.11, 5.12 and 5.13 represent a transparent format of this kind. They immediately show up the project status assigned by the project management as a green circle, a yellow square or a red lozenge. The symbols indicate whether a project is expected to run according to schedule. The principal milestones are also displayed in the form of a table or milestone trend analysis.

The reports on the status of the overall project shown in Figure 5.1 and Figure 5.12 can be usefully supplemented by more detailed reports from all the technical sectors involved in the project or subprojects (Figure 5.13). These reports cover the current status in each subsector, any problems that have arisen as well as possible solutions. A special section is devoted to post-processing the reports. This includes the results of meetings and other feedback, which is thus recorded in a binding way.

> *How can IT help?*

Such standard formats are particularly efficient if they are transformed into user interfaces in suitable **groupware systems**. This is because systems such as TopInfo offer the supplementary functions to make information rapidly available to potential recipients in paper-less form (see TopInfo, p. 268). They can then obtain the necessary information about the current status of the project in advance. This allows them to approach problems and devise solutions more effectively in the project meetings, which are usually announced at this point, or else request further details on individual points.

Figure 5.11   Traffic-light report on overall project level (p. 1)

For internal use only   **BETA-A Rel. 1**

Monthly Project Report

- Page 1 -

Project Name: BETA-A Release 1   **Total Assessment:**

Project Leader: Realization Team 1

Report Period: 01 May 2000 **to** 31 May 2000   **As-of-Date:** 02 Jun 2000

A. Milestones

Milestone	Original Date	Last report (if changed)	New (if changed)
M1	31 Jan 2000		
M2	31 Mar 2000	30 May 2000	23 Jun 2000
M3	30 May 2000	29 Aug 2000	19 Sep 2000
M4	30 Jun 2000	30 Sep 2000	31 Oct 2000
M5	31 Oct 2000		21 Nov 2000

Assessment of Participating Function Units:

◆ SW Development

◆ HW Development

● Business Administration

▢ Logistics

▢ Manufacturing

● Sales/Marketing

● Service

● No problems   ▢ Might become a problem   ◆ There is a problem

Figure 5.12   Traffic-light report on overall project level (p. 2)

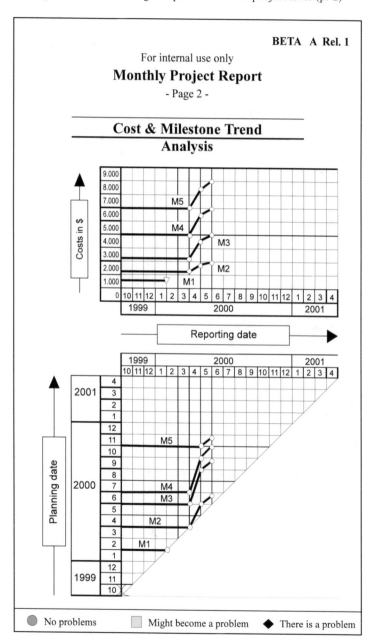

Figure 5.13   Reports of individual functional units

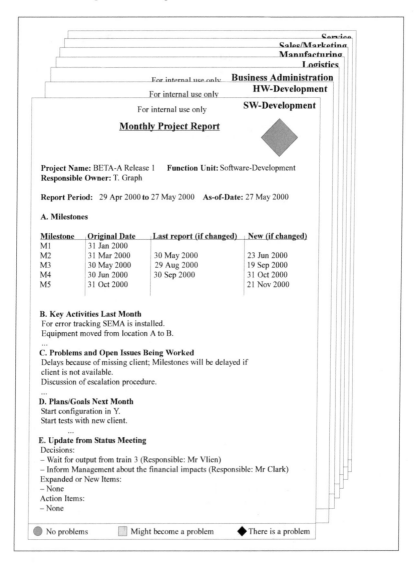

Service
Sales/Marketing
Manufacturing
Logistics
Business Administration
HW-Development
SW-Development

For internal use only
For internal use only
For internal use only

Monthly Project Report

Project Name: BETA-A Release 1   **Function Unit:** Software-Development
Responsible Owner: T. Graph

Report Period: 29 Apr 2000 to 27 May 2000   **As-of-Date:** 27 May 2000

A. Milestones

Milestone	Original Date	Last report (if changed)	New (if changed)
M1	31 Jan 2000		
M2	31 Mar 2000	30 May 2000	23 Jun 2000
M3	30 May 2000	29 Aug 2000	19 Sep 2000
M4	30 Jun 2000	30 Sep 2000	31 Oct 2000
M5	31 Oct 2000		21 Nov 2000

B. Key Activities Last Month
For error tracking SEMA is installed.
Equipment moved from location A to B.
...

C. Problems and Open Issues Being Worked
Delays because of missing client; Milestones will be delayed if
client is not available.
Discussion of escalation procedure.
...

D. Plans/Goals Next Month
Start configuration in Y.
Start tests with new client.
...

E. Update from Status Meeting
Decisions:
– Wait for output from train 3 (Responsible: Mr Vlien)
– Inform Management about the financial impacts (Responsible: Mr Clark)
Expanded or New Items:
– None
Action Items:
– None

⬤ No problems   ▢ Might become a problem   ◆ There is a problem

Ad hoc reports

> Should ad hoc reports be regulated?

Despite the scope granted to employees in performing individual project tasks, higher-level agencies (project leaders, project controllers, etc.) and the sectors involved must always be notified whenever changes occur which might jeopardize more comprehensive targets. In other words, everyone affected must be informed as soon as disturbances occur in a work group which may endanger the scheduling, quality or cost targets of the higher-level project components.

Because efficient project control relies on obtaining relevant information as early as possible (cf. Figure 5.10 again), the regular reporting procedures should be supplemented by an explicit procedure dealing with such **ad hoc reports**. Special **escalation rules** may specify that the higher-level agency must be informed immediately when a situation arises in which major project targets will be jeopardized unless countermeasures are taken by this agency.

> Should the contents be prescribed?

The contents of ad hoc reports can also be suitably prescribed. For example, the causes and potential impact on the project targets of any problems, which occur should always be analyzed to give the decision-makers a rapid overview of the urgency of the problem. Conceivable solutions should be presented in addition to a description of the acute problem. This enhances the efficiency of the reports and the relevant project meetings because it allows decisions on suitable adjustments to be made more quickly.

Planning and convening project meetings

> How frequently should meetings be held?

Project meetings have proved to be the most effective communications platform for project reporting. Thus project-oriented companies have found it useful to specify that meetings be convened at specific intervals at least for the higher echelons of the project. A common approach is to introduce **monthly status meetings** in which the project leaders or managing teams of all current major projects report to the sector or corporate management or to relevant committees.

> *What are project rounds?*

In addition to the monthly status meetings, it is useful to introduce **project rounds,** which monitor the current status of the project in a shorter cycle of some 14 days on the basis of reports from the subproject leaders and employees assigned to specific performance features. Such meetings go beyond individual subsectors and are particularly important for the uncertain dynamic projects associated with the development of new products where changes and developments in one sector often have an impact on activities in other subsectors.

> *When should internal meetings take place?*

Within individual subprojects and work groups, each subproject or group leader decides how frequently to convene the members of his team to status meetings. But here too it makes sense as early as the start of the project to designate a regular schedule of meetings in order to motivate the employees by means of these deadlines.

> *What situational factors must be observed?*

The frequency of reports and meetings depends not only on their recipients/participants but also on the prevailing project situation. Depending on the **urgency** and **strategic importance** of a project, its customer may require more frequent and more detailed progress updates.

The same applies in the case of acute crisis situations. In addition to the regular meetings, **ad hoc meetings** may be convened at all project levels in order to discuss acute problems and possible solutions to them.

In addition to the factors already mentioned, the selection of the reporting cycle will in some cases also be subject to certain **framework conditions**. Thus a cost report will tend to be tied to the account period of the corporate accounting department, which is as a rule monthly.

> *Are there success factors for project meetings?*

The following success factors can be identified for convening project meetings of all types:

- Documents should be distributed before the meeting at least in a brief version so that all participants can make any **necessary preparations**. Groupware systems such as TopInfo offer a suitable distribution platform.
- The preparations and overview of the participants can be facilitated if the reports, which are discussed and presented in advance are based on an **established standard** (such as the traffic-lights sheets mentioned earlier).
- The project leader or facilitator should urge that any problems submitted be fully examined and suitably presented: What are the potential reasons for the problem? Who might be affected? Have solutions already been proposed? Who should do what to eliminate the problem? Once it is established in the project and company, a **meeting culture** of this kind contributes to convening meetings more efficiently. Groupware systems can help by defining entry fields, which are mandatory for the release of a report. Even entry of a simple *None* in some fields (cf. the question on the actions decided in Figure 5.13) gives the recipient more information than a blank.
- The reports on the status and problems of the (sub)project should be contributed in bottom-up mode. If the **project leader's report is placed at the end** of the list of speakers, his statements will not affect the reports of the other participants.
- Wherever possible, **discussions** about details of individual reports should wait until **after** all the speakers have made their contributions. This prevents unnecessary discussions about points, which may well be cast in a different light by a subsequent report. Moreover the prospect that the meeting will shortly end also enhances its efficiency by curtailing debates that diverge too far from the issue at hand.
- Meetings frequently result in decisions being made with serious consequences. These must be suitably **documented** just like all other project plans and adjustments. Groupware systems provide useful support here too. A mere filing of the documents is not sufficient. Care must be taken that all project team members always have access to the latest documentation and project plans. Many Groupware systems offer a data dictionary, a status overview and links between contents.

Informal reporting in the project

> ### What is informal reporting?

In addition to the formal forms of reporting, which largely take place in official meetings, *informal reporting* also invariably occurs within a project. Two of its components may be summarized as follows:

- The unstructured transfer of status or problem information to the affected agencies in the project – e.g. via chats in the corridor or canteen.
- The information transmitted *between the lines* in project meetings.

> ### Is informal reporting desirable?

This aspect should be looked at from two angles. First a project leader should urge that any information conveyed to him and other project managers be prepared and structured with the recipient in mind. Important information must thus be exchanged along the official channels, inclusive of the relevant documentation. An employee who briefly informs the project leader verbally about a problem cannot be absolved of his duty to provide information in more formal ways (in the sense of 'But I told you about it at the time'.). On the other hand, such informal information channels also represent an important source of **early warning signals**. In this sense, a project leader should always have an ear open for incipient problems in the project. Mastering this dilemma is one of the skills that a project leader is called upon to practise on a daily basis.

> ### How should employee statements be interpreted?

In contrast, the second aspect of informal reporting must be regarded as absolutely essential. It demands a high level of social competence from the project leader – i.e. he must be able to correctly interpret the statements made by his various team members. Different personality types tend to react differently to crisis situations. Whereas some employees will overestimate the problems involved in a situation or respond with exaggerated alarm, others tend to play down difficulties occurring in their sector. The statement 'there may be a problem there' can thus be interpreted in very different ways. In order to do this, the project leader must know his team members well and maintain regular personal contacts with them.

The information and communications culture as a factor in successful reporting

> *Which 'soft factors' are important for reporting?*

The efficiency of the information flows in a project depends significantly on the prevailing **information and communications culture**. It is one of the most important tasks of a project leader and all the employees involved to promote this culture. How is a positive information and communications culture characterized?

- **Avoid fear of negative information**
  If employees fear an unpleasant reception as *bringers of bad news*, they will intuitively delay such information or play down its negative character. This is a sure way of not identifying information relevant to project control until it is too late. The recipient of negative news should rather express his gratitude for the early notification rather than vent his displeasure about the situation on the messenger.
- **Maintain an internal customer orientation**
  Every transmitter of information in the project should be aware of the purpose of this process. This is the only way of ensuring that the information is always prepared in a way that complies with the needs of the recipient.
- **Keep the hierarchy loose**
  When problems arise, employees frequently tend to seek a solution exclusively by reporting to the next highest echelon in the hierarchy. But a good project leader should rather seek to encourage direct communication between individual members of the project team. Thus in cases of doubt he may refer one employee directly to another. Communal break facilities and canteens as well as a closer spatial configuration of the teams are all important ways of promoting direct communication – i.e. not going via the superior.
- **Avoid casting blame**
  If negative developments are detected in the project it is important to know *how* the situation arose. This can help to solve the problem. It

is usually only of secondary importance to identify the employee *who* actually caused the situation. The best way of demotivating an employee for a protracted period is to censure him in public. This is also an unfruitful approach because the person causing the problem frequently possesses the detailed knowledge required to solve it (with appropriate support).

- **Don't** *sacrifice* **employees**
  Another tactic sometimes applied must be regarded as highly dubious: namely to seek and publicly sacrifice a scapegoat as a way out of a serious crisis in order to remotivate the team. This may help in the short term but will frequently poison the overall atmosphere of the project.

5.1.3 Project audits as a source of valuable control information

> *Why might reporting procedures be insufficient?*

Project leaders and their teams possess the insight into and detailed knowledge of the project that are needed to make corrective interventions. Nevertheless, their exclusive perspective from within the project can limit their horizons. A *naive* view of the project processes which is less distorted by extensive detailed knowledge can prove most helpful: specific crises can be defused and valuable information and indications can be obtained for making improvements and identifying potential sources of danger. **Project audits** are carried out in order to achieve this end.

Audits can be performed at various stages of the project (overall project, individual subprojects etc.). They have the following typical objectives:[12]

> *What objectives are pursued by audits?*

- To check the correctness of the project definitions (project targets, initial planning procedures aiming to reach particular goals, etc.).
- To assure the quality of the management processes.
- To include experience from previous projects more fully in the current project and to identify potential error sources, risks and opportunities.
- To check identified project risks and the correct ways of handling them (**Risk audit** see Risk-aware project management, p. 47).

> *Who should act as the auditors?*

It is recommended that teams of **in-house specialists** who are external to the project should be called in to carry out a project audit. They have the necessary distance to the details of the project execution. Also, the team members are not unnecessarily perturbed by the presence of external consultants. To be most effective, the audit team should comprise specialists from various technical departments relevant to the project (technology, IT, commercial sector, etc.). In order to be acceptable in terms of their position and qualifications, the auditors should be appointed at least at the same hierarchical and technical level as the members of the project team. They should also be sufficiently well informed of the company's global goals and the strategies pursued by the sector in question.

> *Do audits contribute to personnel development?*

Because participation in audits is in itself a way of training future project leaders and team members in project management, it is a good idea to include employees with little project experience in the audit teams. It also makes good sense for project-oriented companies to set up a **pool of specialists** from which the auditors are regularly recruited. This allows the relevant experience and know-how to be concentrated in the company.

> *What does a typical audit look like?*

The following sequence represents a useful way of **performing** a project audit:[13]

1. **Interview** the project leader, but particularly the project teams: it may make sense to work from *bottom to top* to avoid assuming the perspective of the project leader in advance by hearing his version first.
2. **Analyze the data** used in the project; plans and data collected are checked for their completion and consistency: were sufficient quality assurance measures planned and was their implementation verified? Were any additional tasks carried out correctly and punctually?

3. **Check project reports** for the relevance of their contents to controlling.
4. Compare the observed actual situation with **best practices** – i.e. with particularly successful projects. The members of expert teams can do this implicitly on the basis of their past experience. It should, however, be performed and documented systematically.
5. If any questions arise, **steps 1–4 are repeated**.
6. **Identify strengths and weaknesses** of the project management procedure.
7. **Identify possible improvements** and discuss them with the members of the project team.

> *How is implementation of the audit results assured?*

Close cooperation between the members of the project examined and the auditors is highly desirable to ensure a successful audit. Without such cooperation, no learning effect can be expected to enhance the efficiency of the project work. The potential positive effects of an audit must always be weighed up against the manpower capacity which is temporarily tied up by it.

> *What basic rules help in auditing?*

A number of useful ground rules should be observed when performing audits and reviews:

- The **size of the individual work groups.** The auditors plus project team members should comprise between 6 and 12 members. This is the optimal size determined by behavioural psychologists for efficient group work. If the number is larger, there is too great a risk of team members not pulling their weight by hiding in the shadow of their colleagues.
- To make sure that the results of the audit flow into the future execution of the project, the project team members participating in the audit should act as **promoters**. Their technical or hierarchical position should give them the natural authority to influence other members of the project team. The popular practice of delegating dispensable employees to an audit team is thus highly questionable.
- There should be an absolutely **open exchange of information** between the auditors and the project.

- Audits are useful only if the project team members can learn something from them. The project teams are the customers of the auditors, who should regard themselves as **service providers**. A climate of control is obstructive to the effectiveness of an audit.
- If it is to have a positive effect on the project, the audit must be performed at the correct **time**. Data and process routines must already be available for reviewing but there must still be enough scope for adjustments. It is therefore recommended that the audits be performed after between a third and a half of the total project term has elapsed.

5.2 ANALYZING CONTROL INFORMATION

> *Why is the information analyzed?*

After the information relevant to controlling has been made available by the reporting procedures at the earliest possible time, the next main task of project control is to process this information (cf. Figure 5.14). The type and significance of the deviations must initially be determined

Figure 5.14   Analyzing control information

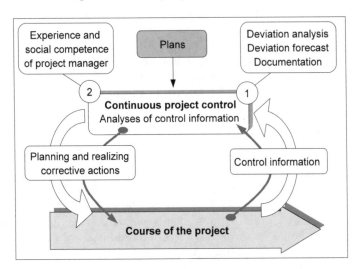

to allow suitable adjustments to be made in the event of any problems. To ensure that the learning effect is sustained for the current and subsequent projects, it may also be useful to analyze the causes of some of these deviations more closely.

5.2.1 Selecting deviations for analysis

> *Is it useful to analyze as many deviations as possible?*

Not all deviations actually detected between the planned and actual progress of a project require corrective intervention. An essential task of every employee involved in project control is to sort the available data and to take corrective action only in the event of major deviations. Equally, it makes little sense from the standpoint of efficiency to subject every reported deviation to a more precise analysis:

- Every evaluation costs time and money without necessarily improving the performance of the project. In selecting which deviations must be examined more closely, it is thus important to ascertain whether the resulting information permits *successful intervention* in the project. The answer is also decisive for the type of deviation analysis to be selected.
- *Analyses of deviations generate information.* If the members of the project team are bombarded with superfluous information, they will find it correspondingly difficult to extract what is of relevance to them (information overload). Large amounts of unnecessary information lead to a commensurate decline in the effectiveness and efficiency of handling the information which really is relevant.

> *Who decides what should be analyzed?*

It is up to the employee who is entrusted with monitoring the project at the relevant level to decide which deviations should be examined more closely in a given case. This may be a team leader or a subproject leader, a project leader or more highly placed manager. The project controllers should be involved in the deviation analysis because they have the necessary expertise. A number of rules of thumb can be applied to selecting those deviations, which can be usefully analyzed:

> *Which deviations should be analyzed more closely?*

- Deviations which jeopardize the attainment of higher-order targets are particularly problematic and thus of obvious interest to an analysis. An example is a delayed deadline at a low level, which will have an impact at the next highest level.
- Deviations which, if allowed to continue, could delay the overall project should also be examined more closely in order to prepare suitable corrective action.
- In a project-oriented company, an attempt must be made to learn from current deviations for the benefit of subsequent projects. A closer analysis of deviations, which are unlikely to be corrected in the current project may nevertheless yield useful data for later projects and is therefore worthwhile. The causes of both negative and positive deviations should be examined. However, capacity problems may well defer the analysis until after the project has been completed.

5.2.2 Determining and analyzing schedule deviations

> *Do schedule delays present problems?*

In the overwhelming majority of cases, a delay in the final deadlines represents the most serious conceivable threat to the project. A newly developed product will then miss a planned market window or because penalty clauses and loss of image *vis-à-vis* important customers would result. A project delay usually also has a negative effect on the project costs and thus on the ability to keep within the project budget. So careful monitoring of project deadlines is usually the most urgent task for the project managers.

Determining schedule delays

> *Why are low-level plans aggregated?*

The first step toward this goal is to update the project schedules on the basis of the information obtained on the progress of the project. In this process, the network plan subdivision shown in Section 4.1.4 is reversed as the current **low-level plans** are aggregated to produce an updated **high-level plan**. In the case of complex projects, which are subdivided into several complementary subprojects, this aggregation is continued right up to the **top-level plans**.

The method of aggregation from low-level to high-level plans must be selected at an early stage and with due consideration:

> *When is an automatic aggregation recommended?*

- In small projects with no more than a few hundred low-level activities, automatic data aggregation by means of a project management tool (such as TimeLine, Primavera) has proved worthwhile.

As a result of automatic data aggregation, every change in a deviations, which are unlikely to be corrected in the current project, becomes immediately visible in the latter. However, care must be taken when selecting the aggregation method that the high-level plan can continue to operate autonomously. It must remain possible to calculate and record the critical path of the project at the high level too:

- In large projects with up to several thousand low-level activities, automatic data aggregation has not proved of much value.

> *When does automatic aggregation create problems?*

The automatic aggregation of low-level plans requires considerable programme servicing where a large number of activities are involved. In particular, salient points such as milestones, which provide the basis for the aggregation of the individual plans must be continuously checked for consistency.

On the whole, the complex configuration of low-level and high-level plans is no longer sufficiently flexible to react quickly in the event of any disturbances at a low level. This is because even minor and possibly transient changes are recorded on the high level. As a result, the high-level plans frequently no longer reflect the reality of the project. This leads to acceptance problems and makes time-consuming improvements necessary:

- In very complex processes, decoupling to the low-level plans from the high-level plans is recommended.

> *How does high-level updating take place?*

The high-level plans provide the basis for the schedule reporting procedures. They designate a scheduling agent who is responsible for high-level reporting at the time of updating (such as a subproject leader). The high-level plans are subsequently updated at regular intervals in conjunction with the project controllers.

> *What are the advantages of decoupling?*

Decoupling has the advantage that a delay at a low level does not automatically lead to deferment of the deadlines at a high level. The scheduling agent can then determine whether a low-level delay is really so critical that it will affect the entire project. Such discretion in making decisions not only promotes flexibility in planning but is also an effective motivator.

> *A useful hybrid form*

It was shown in Section 4.1.4 that separate high-level plans whose scheduling data is nevertheless interlinked are issued for all the functional units involved in complex projects. At this high level of aggregation, the automatic data-aggregation functions offered by software tools can also be used if the low-level plans are decoupled from the high-level plans. These tools then generate the high-level plan for the overall project from the high-level plans of each functional unit.

Analyzing schedule deviations

> *How should the aggregated plans be interpreted?*

The aggregation of the current low-level plans reveals the consequences for the project deadlines of uncorrected deviations that have occurred up to the time of monitoring. Figure 5.15 shows that a deadline for the development of an element for a subassembly was delayed at the monitoring time. The relevant low-level plan for the development

Figure 5.15　　Aggregating low-level plans

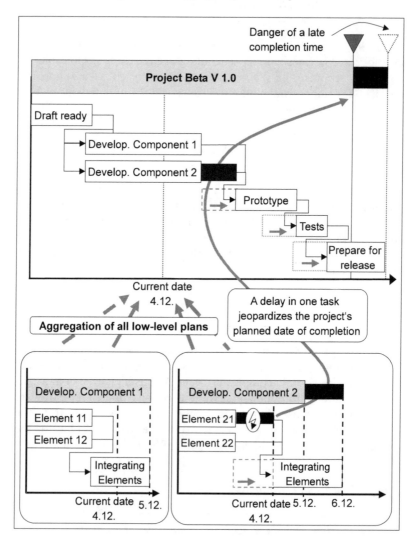

process was consequently revised. However, it is too late to meet the original deadline. Because this subassembly is located on the critical path of the overall project, the overall project would suffer a corresponding delay unless suitable adjustments were made. In such a case, corrective intervention is absolutely essential. As will become apparent later, this may take the form of shifting capacities between processes, adding new capacities or running processes in parallel (e.g. tests and the preparation for release).

> *What is the follow-on effect of delays?*

The full significance of a deviation becomes clear only when its more far-reaching side effects are also considered. A delay in individual activities or in entire subprojects will tend to reschedule the capacity requirements of the project. Figure 5.16 shows how delays in the development of a subassembly tie up an employee longer than expected, which in turn leads to conflicts with a project y to which the employee had already been assigned.

Figure 5.16   Effect of a delay on the capacity requirements of the project

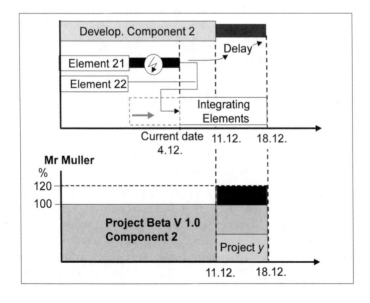

> *What does this mean for resource planning?*

If the delay also leads to the postponement of subsequent activities (Figure 5.15), additional problems will occur. The capacities planned for these activities will then be required at different times than originally planned. Usually project-oriented companies plan their resources very tightly so that they are fully utilized at all times. Delays in the use of a resource can thus lead to conflicts with other processes. Valuable support for displaying capacity conflicts and deriving suitable adjustments may be provided by applying a tool for resource allocation planning to the entire project (see Resource allocation planning system, p. 97).

> *Is profitability affected?*

Situations with resource conflicts because of time delays are not untypical. They cause costs either by tying employees up in the project for longer than originally planned, or by utilizing capacities more intensively – for instance in the form of overtime or increased work-loads. In the event of a delay, the profitability of a project will be additionally affected by deferred capital returns (sales) which can have a particularly negative effect on project profitability. Ways of dealing with deviations in project costs or profitability will be described in more detail later on. Before that, however, it is useful to take a look at the analysis of quality deviations.

5.2.3 Determination and analysis of deviations in the quality targets of the project

> *How are quality problems analyzed?*

The exact analysis of the causes and consequences of quality defects in a product is a technical problem that differs from project to project and product to product. However, it is still useful to describe some early indicators of likely failure to reach the quality targets of a project. Indeed, this aspect is of particular importance in a customer-oriented project where the quality of the product stipulated by the customer must be a major objective.

What are key elements of quality control?

In the section on quality planning (see p. 121), it was shown how a **configuration basis** is defined at the start of the project and then frozen in stages, thus fixing the technical product features required by the customer. These are summarized together with other quality targets in the Product Quality Agreements (PQAs). The product managers must compare the information they receive about the progress of the quality parameters with the current configuration basis and the PQAs. This tells them whether the project is currently on schedule to achieve the quality targets specified by the customer. The significance of any deviations that occur must be interpreted and their urgency must be estimated so that decisions on possible corrective action can be taken in good time. The *hard* data from quality routines in previous comparative projects are thus supplemented by the *soft* experience of the project leader, which allows him to assess the gravity of the situation.

Why are detailed quality plans helpful?

The greater the detail in which the quality targets and the corresponding quality plans are specified, the easier it is for the project managers to analyze and correct the progress of the quality parameters in the sense of a **configuration management**.[14]

An example of detailed quality planning was seen in the treatment of software development errors described in the section on quality planning. Because of its transparent structure, this sector is well suited to highlighting the principles involved in forecasting the consequences of deviations.

An example of determining quality deviations

Every product (including the software used in nuclear power stations or space travel) still contains a number of undiscovered residual errors at every point of its development and life cycle. Empirical values obtained from previous projects as well as from existing products and product components can be used to make forecasts about the number of errors that will occur in a planned system made up of newly developed components. Sophisticated algorithms, which are continu-

Figure 5.17   Number of actually found versus forecasted errors

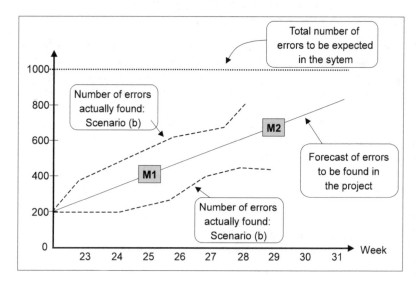

ously updated are applied to this end. The number of errors remaining to be detected in each subprocess by means of tests can be estimated in a similar way (e.g. Figure 5.17). By comparing these forecasts with the actual number of errors found, quality deviations can be determined and quality criteria derived for the project:

> *How are quality developments interpreted?*

- The tests defined in the QA plan must have been performed precisely in line with these specifications.
- The specified number of errors must have been found and eliminated.
- If fewer errors are found than forecast (scenario (b)), this may indicate either particularly good performance or insufficient testing.
- If more errors are found than forecast (scenario (a)), this may indicate low product quality or particularly effective tests.
- The slope of the error curve can be interpreted as an early warning signal. If the curve diverges significantly from the forecast line, appropriate adjustments will have to be made (e.g. additional tests).

Figure 5.18 Planned and forecast progress of product quality in a
software-development project

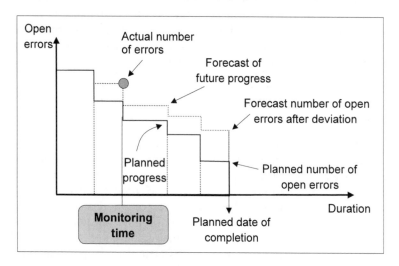

Are simpler methods available?

This method is difficult to apply in practice because a great deal of
experience is required to determine the initial parameters. However, its
underlying idea also provides the basis for the following method, which
is simpler to apply.

The number of errors, which have been found and were not yet
eliminated as well as the number of outstanding high-priority errors is
agreed as the minimum quality criterion for reaching particular milestones. A comparison of the detected errors with the planned progress
(cf. Figure 5.18) allows an estimate to be made of how seriously the
future course of the project will be affected if this number of errors is
exceeded at the monitoring time.

Is a project database useful?

Another early warning signal for jeopardized product quality is
the accumulation of a **waiting queue of uncorrected quality defects**.

To measure this indicator, the quality defects which have occurred (e.g. errors) must first be accurately **recorded**. This may be done in a centrally administered project database. The number of observed defects is entered regularly into this database on the basis of priorities (from 1 = usability of the overall product jeopardized to 4 = defect with no further importance for the subcomponents).

What does a build-up of uncorrected quality defects mean?

Figure 5.19 shows various evaluation modes which may be applied with the aid of a project database. The build-up of the waiting queue mentioned above is a particularly important indicator. Experience shows that as more uncorrected errors accumulate in the queue, the error elimination process becomes correspondingly slower.[15] So it is important to examine not only the total number of quality defects or errors occurring at any time, but also their pattern of development. The significance of individual new errors will vary, depending on the acuteness of the relevant situation. In the example shown in Figure 5.19, the number of outstanding errors increased by four in the week in question. Twelve new errors occurred. During this period, three outstanding errors were classified as not significant, five outstanding errors were eliminated and the effects of three eliminated errors could be finally cleared from the system (including documentation etc.).

What role does target costing play?

The importance of the quality feature *future total costs of the product* in product-innovation projects has already been pointed out. The significance of any deviations in this parameter can be examined with the aid of a **value control chart** (see Target costing, p. 62 for details). Deviations in less vital components are obviously less critical than in components which have a greater effect on the way the customer perceives the product.

- To summarize: a continuous check of product quality as well as the timely application of suitable adjustments in the event of quality deviations is a basic condition for the development of a product that is optimally oriented to the customer requirements.

Figure 5.19   Evaluations of a project database

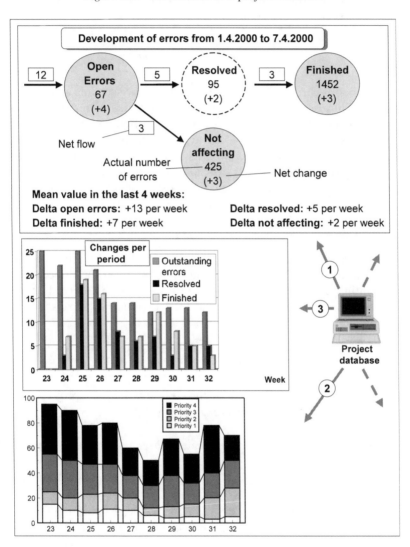

5.2.4 Determination and analysis of deviations in the project cost targets

> *Are cost targets important?*

A continuous check must be made not only of the schedule and quality targets, but also to ensure that the project remains within budget. In product-innovation projects, this cost target often has a significantly lower priority than the schedule target. In contrast, it is of great importance in customer-order projects because the profits to be derived from the project often directly depend on it. The degree of detail of the project-control activities oriented to costs and efficiency must be matched to the respective weighting of the cost targets.

Isolated determination of the cost variance

The project management obtains information about the project costs, which have already been incurred and booked from the project cost accounting. Depending on the degree of detail of these records, they can be assigned down to the level of the individual work packages as subcost units.

> *How is the isolated cost variance calculated?*

The simplest way of looking at the cost situation of a project is to measure the **isolated cost variance** (Figure 5.20):[16]

Total variance = Actual costs − Planned costs　　　　　　　(5.3)

At each checkpoint, the actual costs incurred are compared with the costs planned for that deadline.

In principle, the isolated cost variance can be calculated at all levels of the work breakdown structure to assess the cost situation either in the overall project or in individual work packages. The fundamental prerequisite is merely that the actual costs must be recorded with at least the same level of detail as the original cost plans. Thus cost planning at work-package level is of little use without a correspondingly exact allocation of the actual costs incurred at a later stage: it then becomes impossible to exhaustively verify the realization of the plans at work package level.

Figure 5.20   Isolated cost variance

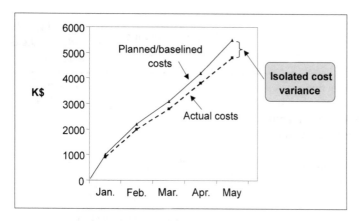

Why must the results be adjusted?

In order to assess the share of the total cost deviation caused by the department responsible for the task, all relevant disturbance variables must first be isolated. In particular, this will include unexpected salary increases or currency fluctuations but also change-order costs – i.e. the cost increases due to plan adjustments already approved by the customer. This step is important in order not to demotivate employees by making them responsible for exceeding costs over which they have no control.

What are the benefits of this analysis?

The **benefit** of an isolated calculation of cost deviations is questionable:

- The analysis of the isolated cost variance takes the calendar time as the only parameter affecting the project costs. This assumes that the project performance is always developing according to the original plans. However, this is often not the case in reality.
- The cost variance gives no indication at all as to whether its cause should be sought in deviations from the planned efficiency or from the planned output. So if the actual costs fall behind the planned costs (cf. Figure 5.21), this can mean one of two things: either that the planned output was in fact reached much more efficiently than

Figure 5.21   Actual and scheduled costs, earned value

	Output/performance considered	Costs with which the performance is evaluated
Actual costs	Actual	Actual
Scheduled/planned/ baselined costs	Plan	Plan
Earned value	**Actual**	**Plan**

anticipated, or simply that too little work was done on the project and the booked costs were correspondingly low. In extreme cases the actual costs could be zero if the scheduled project work had not even been started.

> *Why must efficiency factors be included?*

The measurement of an isolated cost variance is clearly insufficient to assess the real cost situation of a project. And yet the latter is needed in order to derive the necessary adjustments. That is why an isolated cost consideration must be extended to a comprehensive analysis of the **project efficiency**.

Key data for analyzing the efficiency of a project

In order to analyze the efficiency of a project, its output and cost development must be assessed in an integrated way. A number of key figures with more extensive application are helpful for this task. In particular the **earned value** (planned cost of work complete) is a needed information, which can be calculated with the aid of a number of commercial software tools:[17]

> *How is the earned value calculated?*

The **percentage of completion** of the project or its individual work packages must first be measured to provide a basis for further processing this key figure. A number of ways of doing this have already been presented together with their limitations in Section 5.1.1. The **earned value** represents those costs which should have been incurred for the output actually realized by the project so far on the basis of the original plan (cf. Figure 5.21). The completed output (such as a work package) together with the costs initially planned to achieve it is thus evaluated.

Depending on the way of determining the percentage of completion, the earned value is calculated as follows:

$$\text{Earned value} = \sum (PoC_i * BC_i) \tag{5.4a}$$

In other words, the percentage of completion (*PoC*) of each sub-component *i* (such as a work package) is multiplied by its baselined costs (*BC*) and then summed over all the subcomponents involved. Another way of calculating the earned value is as follows:

$$\text{Earned value} = \text{Total Budget} - \text{Residual Costs} \tag{5.4b}$$

i.e. the costs originally baselined for the relevant components minus the still expected residual costs.

> *What is the planned percentage of completion?*

The **planned percentage of completion** expresses the proportion of the output that should have been realized with the resources already booked. It is therefore calculated as follows:

$$\text{Planned percentage of completion} =$$
$$\frac{100 * (\text{Resources booked so far})}{(\text{Resources budgeted for the whole project})} \tag{5.5}$$

> *What is the percentage spent?*

The **percentage spent** is calculated in a similar way as the ratio of the actual and planned costs. It indicates how much of the budgeted costs have already been consumed up to that time:

$$\text{Percentage spent} = 100 * (\text{Actual costs})/(\text{Planned costs}) \tag{5.6}$$

> *What indicators can be derived here?*

This initial data allows **indicators** to be derived for assessing the efficiency of the project work done so far (see An example of estimating the efficiency with the aid of key figures, p. 191):[18]

The cost performance is represented by a **cost-performance indicator (CPI).** This is calculated as follows:

$$\text{CPI} = \text{(Percentage of Completion)/Percentage Spent)} \qquad (5.7)$$

The **schedule performance indicator (SPI)** is useful in assessing the performance of a project in terms of its output or scheduling:

$$\text{SPI} = \frac{\text{(Percentage of Completion)}}{\text{(Planned Percentage of Completion)}} \qquad (5.8)$$

> *What are SPI and CPI used for?*

If these **indicators** are plotted in a time-performance diagram, project *temperature charts* (cf. Figure 5.22) are obtained which provide useful support for deciding on the time and intensity of any corrective action.[19] They also offer a basis for organizational learning because a comparison of the curves of several projects allows potential problems in the processes and structures of a project-oriented company to be identified.

Figure 5.22   Project temperature chart

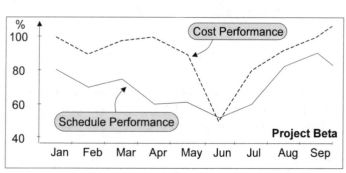

Case study 5.2   An example of estimating efficiency with the aid of key figures

A short numerical example will illustrate the significance and application of the key figures described above. It is based on a sample project whose total budget is set at $65 million. The planned resource allocation is 260 PY.

At the time of reporting, the remaining effort is estimated as 78 PY. On the basis of (5.1) a percentage of completion can be determined as follows:

$$PoC = (260PY - 78PY)/260PY = 70\%$$

Currently, 200 PY are booked for the project, and the actual costs are $48 million. This yields the following relationships:

$$\text{Planned percentage of completion} = 200PY/260PY$$
$$= 77\% \qquad (5.5)$$
$$\text{Percentage spent} = \$48\,m/\$65\,m = 74\% \qquad (5.6)$$

This means that 74 per cent of the project budget has already been spent. The resources utilized so far should have resulted in completion of 77 per cent of the output, whereas in reality this figure is only 70 per cent. The scheduling performance is consequently:

$$SPI = 70\%/77\% = 91\%$$
and thus behind the target figure (100%) $\qquad (5.8)$

The same applies for the cost performance where:

$$CPI = 70\%/74\% = 95\% \qquad (5.7)$$

Integrated cost and performance analyses (earned-value analyses)

What does an earned value analysis include?

The previously calculated planned costs allow an **integrated cost and performance analysis** (cf. Figure 5.23) to be performed. It can be used to derive more accurate information about the current status of the project and the causes of any deviations from the schedule and cost targets. (see Example of an earned-value analysis, p. 191.[20] The earned value is compared with the actual costs from the project cost accounting and the baselined costs from the original project plans. The earned value represent those costs which should have been expended thus far to achieve the *actual* output according to the project *plan*. As against this, the actual costs are the costs *actually* incurred for the *actual* output and the planned costs represent the costs *planned* for reaching the output at the time at which the estimate was made. By including the output achieved at the point of monitoring, therefore, the total cost deviation can be split up as follows:

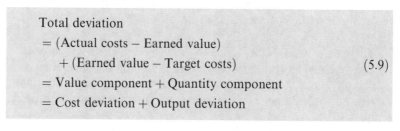

Total deviation

$$= \text{(Actual costs} - \text{Earned value)}$$
$$+ \text{(Earned value} - \text{Target costs)} \qquad (5.9)$$
$$= \text{Value component} + \text{Quantity component}$$
$$= \text{Cost deviation} + \text{Output deviation}$$

Figure 5.23   Earned-value analysis

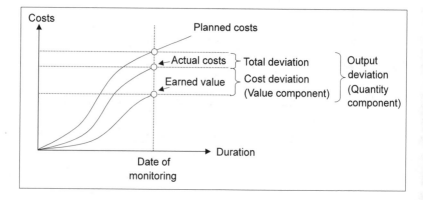

> *What do the sub-deviations mean?*

The **output deviation** (quantity component) determined in this way shows whether the project has deviated from the plan – i.e. whether the output reported at the point of monitoring has fallen behind schedule (negative deviation) or is ahead of the plan (positive deviation).

In contrast, the **cost deviation** (value component) reveals whether the profitability of the project corresponds to the plan. A positive cost deviation would mean that the output so far was realized at too high a cost, possibly because more or costlier resources had been utilized than was originally planned.

The graphical representation of the integrated cost and performance analysis yields illustrative *s*-curves that provide a good overview of the current project situation (cf. Figure 5.24).[21]

Figure 5.24   Cost-*s*-curves in the earned-value analysis

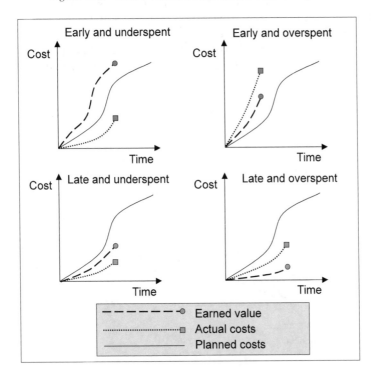

How urgent are interventions?

Appropriate adjustments can be made in order to correct deviations in cost and performance. To assess the urgency of these interventions, not only the magnitude of the deviation but also its likely consequences for the progress of the project must be borne in mind. The basic approach is similar to that used to deal with the consequences of individual schedule delays for the overall project schedule as described in Chapter 4.

How might cost deviations evolve?

Cost deviations can occur **in isolation** without having any impact on the further course of the project (cf. Figure 5.25). An example of this would be a non-recurring increase in the contract sum for a project supplier. In contrast to this, it is characteristic of **progressive** cost deviations that they lead to more far-reaching excess costs in the course of the project than those occurring at the estimating time. Thus if the efficiency of the project performance turns out to be below par, the danger exists that the absolute cost deviation would progressively increase as the project proceeds. Adjustments are particularly urgent in such a case.

Figure 5.25   Future consequences of current deviations

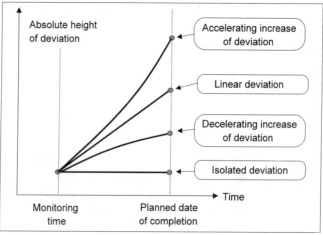

Case study 5.3 An example of an earned-value analysis

An example will now illustrate the principle of an integrated cost and performance analysis, also known as an earned value analysis. It is based on a sample project that has already run for 10 of its planned 36 months (Table 5.1).

Table 5.1   Initial data for the earned-value analysis

Month	Total Project budget	Remaining costs (*costs left after the current plan*)	Earned value cumulated (*budget less remaining costs*)	Planned costs (*costs originally planned for this period*)	Planned costs cumulated	Actual costs (*from reports*)	Actual costs cumulated
1	20 000	19 500	500	510	510	500	500
2	20 000	19 000	1 000	620	1 130	600	1 100
3	20 000	18 200	1 800	790	1 920	750	1 850
4	20 000	17 700	2 300	620	2 540	600	2 450
5	20 000	17 350	2 650	430	2 970	400	2 850
6	20 000	17 000	3 000	530	3 500	480	3 330
7	20 000	16 500	3 500	550	4 030	500	3 830
8	20 000	16 200	3 800	610	4 660	550	4 380
9	20 000	15 800	4 200	730	5 390	650	5 030
10	20 000	19 500	500	510	510	500	500

(*Values in K$*)

Table 5.1 records the results of the reports received up to month 10. In addition to the budget available for the overall project, it shows the residual costs laid down in the plan for the outstanding work packages. The (culminated) earned values are then calculated from the difference between the budget and the residual costs. Table 5.1 also lists the planned costs from the baseline as well as the actual costs reported from project cost accounting.

A graphical display makes the cost patterns stand out in bold relief. Whereas the actual costs, planned costs and the earned value still follow approximately the same pattern in the first three months, greater divergences become apparent from the fourth month onwards. It can be seen from Figure 5.24 that this curve indicates a project with delayed schedules and simultaneously overrun costs.

Figure 5.26   Cost progressions in an earned-value analysis

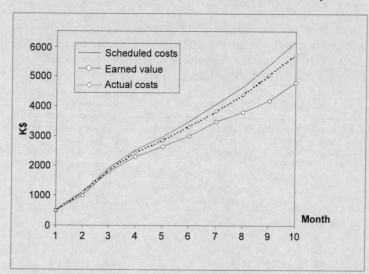

What advantages does the integrated cost and performance analysis offer in this case? An isolated cost approach would merely compare the actual and planned costs at every point. However, the resulting cost divergence would yield very little useful information. It may indicate either that the project performance has fallen behind schedule or that the planned output was attained at particularly low cost. It can therefore show the project in either a positive or negative light.

A more precise interpretation of the reasons for this divergence will require the earned value to be calculated by the integrated cost and performance method (Table 5.2). It is apparent that while part of the total budget divergence is due to poor performance (negative performance deviation), another part was accounted for by excessive costs per unit of output compared with the planned costs (positive cost deviation). A more detailed knowledge of the causes of the deviation would allow project control to intervene more effectively in the project. When applied with the required accuracy, it also prevents the project leader getting blamed for causes of deviations that lie outside his power, such as salary increases or currency fluctuations contained in the cost divergence.

Table 5.2   Deviation analysis

	Isolated cost consideration	Integrated costs and performance consideration		
Month	**Isolated cost deviation** (cumulated) (*Actual costs − Planned costs*)	**Cumulated cost deviation** (*Actual costs − Earned value*)	**Cumulated performance deviation** (*Earned value − Planned costs*)	**Total budget deviation** (*Actual costs − Planned costs*)
1	−10	0	−10	−10
2	−30	100	−130	−30
3	−70	50	−120	−70
4	−90	150	−240	−90
5	−120	200	−320	−120
6	−170	330	−500	−170
7	−220	330	−550	−220
8	−280	580	−860	−280
9	−360	830	−1190	−360
10	−440	930	−1370	−440
				(*Values in K$*)

Figure 5.27   Deviations

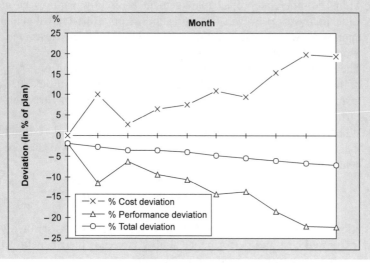

In the sample project, an isolated cost approach (the total deviation in Figure 5.27) would give a picture that is far too positive compared with the actual progress of the project. In reality, the deviation between the actual and planned costs is relatively low over a period of months and is in any case negative. However, this is due essentially to the project performance running far behind schedule. In fact, there is a significant delay in producing the planned output. At the same time, the output realized so far has greatly exceeded the cost target.

Selecting the right method to use

> *What criterion should be used for selection?*

At the beginning of this section it was pointed out that the methods of analyzing cost deviations must be selected with great care. The benefit, which can be achieved with a particular method must justify the effort, which it involves. In personnel-intensive projects in which the cost targets have a significantly lower priority than the schedule and quality targets, earned-value analyses run into problems.

> *What restricts the suitability of earned-value analyses?*

- Many commercial project management tools now support earned-value analyses. However, these presuppose an **effort-related planning approach** whose disadvantages have already been described in Section 4.1.4 *Issuing low-level plans*.
- The estimation of the correct percentage of completion of a project or individual functions is **difficult** and **complex**. Without this information, however, project management tools cannot carry out an earned-value analysis either.
- Where the percentage of completion cannot be correctly estimated, the results derived from the earned-value analysis will also be **of doubtful value**.

> *When does an isolated cost analysis suffice?*

Particularly in complex and matrix-based projects, the effort involved in integrated cost and performance analyses exceeds their benefit if the cost targets are not assigned the highest priority.

In such projects, an isolated cost analysis together with a comparison of the planned and actual personnel deployment is usually sufficient to track the costs. However, the project plans must define sufficiently short individual processes in order to ensure that the schedule and quality targets can be monitored continuously and objectively by means of results checks.

5.2.5 Assessing the significance of deviations for project profitability

The first analyses of a project's profitability have already been made in its definition cycle in order to assess the basic success prospects for a project and the resulting product (cf. Section 3.2.2. in Part I). The initial data is still uncertain, but it gradually acquires firmer outlines as the project proceeds. Regular profitability analyses must therefore accompany the entire term of the project. They make use of the following information:

> *What information are used?*

- **Actual current information**: above all the project costs already incurred.
- **Current plan data**: this will reveal both the deviations in the quality and schedule targets described in the preceding chapters as well as the revised cost plans for the outstanding project sections.

> *What impact do budget overruns have?*

A profitability analysis applied to a product-innovation project based on the profitability comparisons widely used in practice is shown in Figure 5.28 (see Profitability analysis, p. 40). It shows a case in which the project costs exceeded the baseline by about 25 per cent at the point of monitoring. The project is still scheduled to be completed at the end of the year 2000. It is apparent that the cost increase shows up in a lower **return on sales** of 5.72 per cent (as against a previously planned figure of 7.67 per cent) over the period under consideration. More than that the expected **break even** – i.e. the time at which the sales of the end product recover the costs incurred – is deferred to the year 2003.

Figure 5.28   Profitability analysis after a cost overrun by 25 per cent

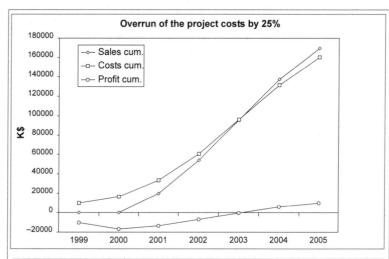

(T $)	Proj. progress 1999	2000	Market cycle 2001	2002	2003	2004	2005	Total
Sales vol.	0	0	3.500	6.000	7.300	7.300	5.700	29.800
Revenue	0	0	19.950	34.200	41.610	41.610	32.490	169.860
Direct costs	0	0	11.760	20.160	24.528	24.528	19.152	100.128
R&G overhead	7.845 ~~6.276~~	4.165 ~~3.332~~	500	500	500	500	300	14.310 ~~11.908~~
Sales overhead	1.375 ~~1.100~~	1.205 ~~964~~	2.600	3.800	5.300	5.800	5.200	25.280 ~~24.764~~
Other costs	875 ~~700~~	1.045 836	1.800	3.200	4.800	4.600	4.100	20.420 ~~20.036~~
Sum of costs	10.095 ~~8.076~~	6.415 ~~5.132~~	16.660	27.660	35.128	35.428	28.752	160.138 ~~156.836~~
Profit	-10.095 ~~8.076~~	-6.415 ~~5.132~~	3.290	6.540	6.482	6.182	3.738	9.722 ~~13.024~~
Revenues cum.	0	0	19.950	54.150	95.760	137.370	169.860	169.860
Costs cum.	10.095 ~~8.076~~	16.510 ~~13.208~~	33.170 ~~29.868~~	60.830 ~~57.528~~	95.959 ~~92.656~~	131.386 ~~128.084~~	160.138 ~~156.836~~	160.138 ~~156.836~~
Profit cum.	-10.095 ~~8.076~~	-16.510 ~~13.208~~	-13.220 ~~9.918~~	-6.680 ~~3.378~~	-198 ~~3.104~~	5.984 ~~9.286~~	9.722 ~~13.024~~	9.722 ~~13.024~~
in % of revenue	–	–	-66,27 ~~49,71~~	-12,34 ~~6,24~~	-0,21 ~~3,24~~	4,36 ~~6,76~~	5,72 ~~7,67~~	5,72% ~~7,67~~

> *What effect do delayed schedules have?*

This example is limited to showing the consequences of cost overruns. Delayed schedules would have an even more pernicious effect, especially in the product innovation sector. This is because the negative effects of a delayed entry to the market would then compound the additional costs of a longer project. The result can be a significantly later break-even point and a significantly reduced project profitability. Figure 5.29[22] shows relevant empirical values.

Figure 5.29   Consequences of missing the set targets

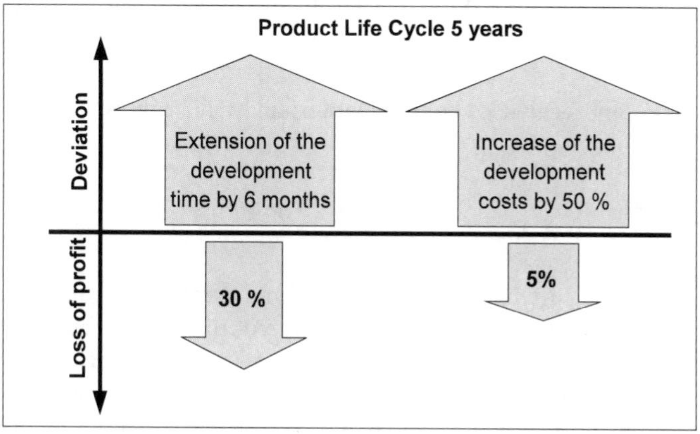

> *Do schedule targets always have priority?*

The situation can appear somewhat different in customer-order projects. Overrunning the project deadline may have less negative consequences there than failing to keep within budget. Especially in fixed-price projects, every overrun of the planned costs will eat into the profits to be realized by the project.

> *Why are profitability analyses made?*

The point of applying a profitability analysis throughout a project is to obtain a new overview of the project's profitability on the basis of current data. It thus helps to assess the consequences of any deviations which have arisen for the project's profitability.

> *So what affects the profitability?*

In summary, the profitability of a project is affected by:

- Changes in the final **project deadline** and the associated higher project costs, later and possibly lower sales, contract penalties, etc.
- Deviations in **product quality** and the associated losses in attainable sales revenues, as well as
- Inefficiencies in the project itself which manifest in increased **project costs**.

5.2.6 Getting feedback about deviations and their causes

> *Why is feedback important?*

Before adjustments can be worked out and applied to correct deviations which have been detected and analyzed, the employees and teams involved should be appraised of their gravity. **Cooperative and constructive discussions** are a good way of making them aware of the reasons for the problems, which have occurred so that they can be avoided in the future.

> *How are the underlying reasons for deviations found?*

It is helpful at this point to borrow the concept of the '**five whys**' from the field of lean production. Every problem which occurs should be traced all the way back to its original causes and a solution worked out with the aid of the information obtained in this way (Figure 5.30).[23]

The idea behind the 'five whys' is not to be too ready to accept a simple reason for deviations but to seek out the underlying originating factors in order to assure a learning effect for future projects. Figure 5.30 illustrates this principle on the basis of a concrete example.

Figure 5.30   The 'five whys'

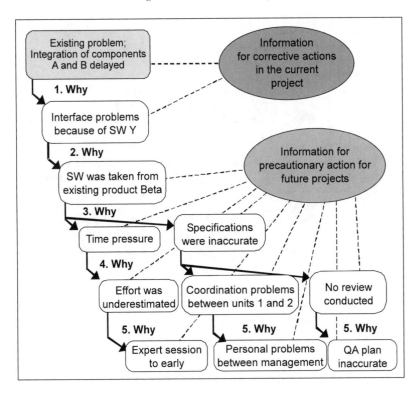

5.3   DEVELOPING ADJUSTMENTS AND APPLYING THEM SUCCESSFULLY TO THE PROJECT

What is the point of this subprocess?

After project deviations have been analyzed, appropriate corrective actions should be developed to adjust the course of the project (Figure 5.31). Various measures may be selected depending on the actual or anticipated deviation. An obvious first step is to eliminate the causes of a concrete problem such as a technical defect or organizational hitch. But a number of more general ways of dealing with perturbations along the path to project targets are also available.

Figure 5.31   Taking corrective actions in the course of the project

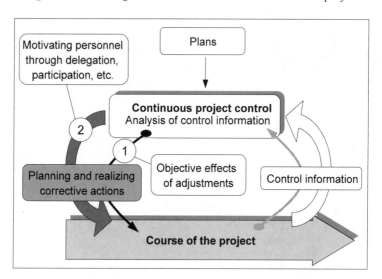

Why must the measures be carefully apportioned?

Most of the adjustments listed in Table 5.3 incur costs, either directly in their application or indirectly in the form of reduced sales or a delayed completion of the final product. They must therefore be apportioned with care so that the targets are achieved without excessive control. The adjustments should be selected to optimize their effect on the highest-priority targets, which often are the schedule targets, without jeopardizing the other targets.

The final and most drastic control measure is to **abort the project**. The complexity of a decision to abort becomes clear from the various factors, which must be considered before taking it:

What must be considered before aborting a project?

- The costs expended so far for already completed and initiated activities must be compared with the expected sales revenues. If the latter do not cover these costs, this would indicate the advisability of aborting the project.

> *Which measures suit which problems?*

Table 5.3   Effect of various countermeasures

Type of action:	Points to be noted for this action:	Effect on:		
		Schedule situation	Product quality	Project costs
Enhance employee motivation	Very soft tool, cost-effective, also desirable from employee side	☺	☺	☺
Increase personnel	Works in the mid-term, as short-term capacities for on-the-job training of new employees are blocked. ⇒ May have a contrary effect in the short term!	☺	😐	☹
Replace project personnel	Can reduce the efficiency of teamwork in the short term. Effects depend on costs and qualification of the new personnel	☺ / 😐 / ☹	☺ / 😐 / ☹	☺ / 😐 / ☹
Re-assign personnel within projects to critical processes	Should be performed in conjunction with project controlling to estimate consequences for other activities	☺	😐	😐
Assign activities to external staff	Specifically in R&D sector a danger of brain drain ⇒ longer-term consequences to be considered	☺	☺ / 😐 / ☹	☺ / 😐 / ☹
Overtime	Short-term only, as it increases stress and jeopardizes motivation	☺	😐	☹
Use less expensive resources (materials)		😐	😐 / ☹	☺
Extend reviews and technical checks	Ties up capacities and incurs costs ⇒ importance of cost-benefit considerations	☺ / 😐 / ☹	☺ / 😐 / ☹	☺ / 😐 / ☹
Reduce technical complexity (e.g. leave out components)	Effects on quality perceived by customer and associated sales expectations must be examined; coordination with project customer may be required	☺	😐 / ☹	☺
Revise schedule or cost targets	Last alternative! Profitability comparison with other actions required. May be impossible for strategic or customer reasons	😐	😐	😐

- The expected residual costs as well as any contract penalties due in the event of a project abort must also be included in the calculation.
- Equally important are opportunity cost considerations: how much sales volume will be lost if the project is continued because no other projects can then be run? After all, the current project ties up resources from which other projects could benefit.
- In addition to the profitability considerations for an individual project, the consequences for business strategy of aborting it (image, product policy, business development, competitive situation, etc.) must be considered. On the other hand, of course, these considerations may themselves be the very trigger inducing the decision to abort.
- Finally, side effects must be anticipated within the company due to the discontinuation of complex processes: Will employee motivation suffer? Will there be consequences in industrial/labour law? Are direct follow-on activities available for all employees, etc.?

> *Why should aborted projects be celebrated?*

In view of its complexity, any decision to abort a project must be carefully considered. And yet, this option may be necessary in order not to jeopardize the productivity of the overall company. The project termination itself must then be regarded as a positive step for the company and be appropriately performed. Demotivating consequences for the members of the project teams must be avoided at all costs. Failure to take this into account may have the following undesired consequences:

- It will be difficult to persuade employees to be involved in innovative and thus more risky projects in future
- the open transfer of information about negative project developments will be undermined in the future, and
- decisions to abort a project in future will be postponed for as long as possible, with the associated negative consequences for the company.

> *How can the success of adjustments be secured?*

When suitable adjustments have been selected, the project control process is not yet completed. Only when it has become clear that the project and its products have been adjusted as required is this process finally rounded off. In project control, no less than in project planning, **motivation** and **behavioural control** is the crucial link between planned and applied measures (cf. Section 4.3).

The success of corrective intervention can be increased by considering a number of relevant factors:

> *Who selects the actions to be taken?*

- A **solution** to a problem must be selected in close cooperation with the project teams. The project managers must be willing to accept responsibility for an action suggested by a member of their project team.

Project crises tend to weaken the motivation of the project teams. And yet it is precisely in critical situations that increased motivation is needed in order to improve matters quickly, especially as the individual team members are likely to have the know-how required to eliminate deviations and problems. The project leader must therefore do all she can to increase the commitment of his team still further in such situations. In Western cultures, **delegation** of decisions about the solutions to be applied as well as **participation** in centrally taken decisions can prove effective.[24] Employees should also be given solid **feedback** on any solutions they suggest or decisions they may make. In this way, the project leader secures the commitment of the teams in the future too:

> *Who applies the adjustments?*

- The **implementation of the solution** should be delegated to the project teams. The project leader and his staff then act in a coaching capacity and coordinate the implementation.

> *How is employee know-how utilized in crises?*

Project teams are motivated both by being included in selecting appropriate adjustments to eliminate a problem and by sharing the responsibility for implementing them. But this approach does more than increasing their motivation and commitment; it can also activate their know-how for the progress of the project. This in turn represents a success factor for effective intervention in the project.

The effective implementation of the adjustments terminates a typical process of project control. However, another substep must be performed in parallel with this and must under no circumstances be neglected: as soon as adjustments are decided or project targets changed, the **project documentation** must be correspondingly updated.

5.4 UPDATING THE PROJECT DOCUMENTATION

> *Why is it important to update documents?*

The corrective actions taken at various levels (team leader, subproject leader, project leader, etc.) may have far-reaching consequences for the progress of the project: by shifting capacities, deferring processes or even by changing entire subtargets of a project.

All those involved in the project must be kept appraised of its status at all times. After all, it would be undesirable if some employees continued to act on the basis of old plans, which had in the meantime been replaced by new ones. The updating of the project documentation therefore represents a project management task in its own right. All documents contained in the documentation plan must be updated in the event of any changes (cf. the documentation planning in Section 4.1.4). Especially in complex projects, this should be done with the aid of state-of-the-art software tools in order to minimize expenditures. Groupware and documentation management systems have now become indispensable helpers in this task (see TopInfo, p. 268). They are used to process the entire documentation and to administer documents in current use.

> *How does this process help organizational learning?*

Updating the project documentation also has another purpose, namely to supply inputs for **organizational learning**. Two project documentation tools will now be examined more closely: **milestone** and **cost-milestone trend** analyses. Their principal use in a project is to facilitate progress reports to the next-highest project echelon. They display the development of the entire project graphically and allow it to be easily compared with other projects. Weak points in current processes can then be identified.

> *What are MTA and CMTA?*

Milestone trend analysis (MTA) and cost-milestone trend analysis (CMTA) are certainly the best known documentation tools for projects. Both are well suited to give a compact overview of the progress of the project up to the time of reporting. They can in principle be applied to all levels of the project at which separate schedule plans exist – i.e. from individual work packages to the overall project level.

> *How should an MTA be read?*

An MTA comprises a planning axis and a reporting axis (Figure 5.32). Both axes represent identical linear calendars suitably subdivided into sections of days, weeks or months. The current **planning dates** of all milestones relevant to each project section can be entered into the resulting grid at every reporting date. The resulting overview shows how frequently the initial plans had already been changed up to the current reporting date. An MTA is read from left to right. A horizontal line means that the scheduling has remained unchanged for the milestone in question. Ascending (descending) lines show that the scheduling (row) for that particular milestone was revised backwards (forwards) at a particular reporting date (column).

> *How should the example be interpreted?*

Figure 5.32 shows the status of a project in August 2000. The baseline established in January 1999 stipulated that milestone M2 should be reached at the end of February 2000 (read off in the first column of the MTA). This date can be derived from the intersection of the M2 line with the planning time axis. If the curve is traced further, the following can be observed: up to June 1999 it was reported at every

Figure 5.32 Milestone trend analysis at reporting date: end of July 2000

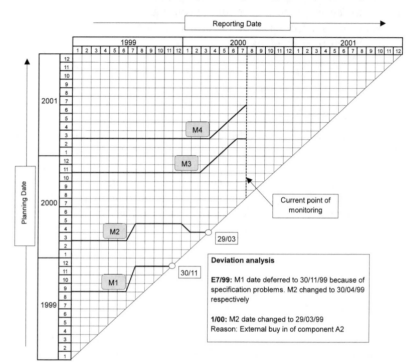

monitoring point (the columns of the MTA) that the originally planned deadline for M2 could be reached (horizontal part of the curve). However, the project seems to have run into a number of more serious problems in July 1999, as the M2 deadline was revised forwards by two months to the end of April 2000 (see the reporting point in column 7/ 1999). The time alteration for M1 is even more clearly apparent: this milestone was simultaneously deferred by three months to 30 November 1999 (ascending curve). Finally, in January 2000, the planned deadline for M2 was brought forward by a month to 29 March 2000 (descending curve) where it was ultimately concluded (intersect with the diagonal).

An MTA is designed to be supplemented by additional information about acute problems occurring in the project and the **action items** applied to deal with them.

The curve trajectories in an MTA provide useful information for managing the relevant subsectors of the project:

> *How are MTA curves interpreted?*

- Steeply ascending curve sections may be due to unexpected changes caused by technical hitches, problems with suppliers or with the customer. But they are often a sign that excessively optimistic estimates were made over a long period of time and that the gravity of the situation was not recognized at an early stage.
- Steeply descending curves can occur in the case of technical innovations or a reduction of the size of a work package. If this happens more frequently, it may indicate excessively conservative initial planning which included too many security reserves. This is as equally undesirable as excessively tight planning, as it leads to at least temporary withholding of unnecessary capacities for the project and thus increases costs.
- A strong divergence or convergence of the curves of individual milestones for the same work package or project section can indicate forecast errors. Thus if the curve of M3 were to ascend continuously while the curve of M4 remained constant, this would be a reason to review the entire plans. An example of this can be seen in the MTA shown in Figure 5.12.

> *What is a CMTA?*

Cost-milestone trend analyses (CMTAs, cf. Figure 5.33) offer a similarly convenient way of displaying the progress of a project as MTAs. They differ from the latter by including the cost trajectory of the project.

To create a CMTA, another diagram with an identical time axis is superposed onto the MTA. The development of the planned costs for the various milestones is then plotted onto it. A comparison of the development of the schedule and cost targets helps to detect inconsistencies at an early stage, as delayed schedules tend to mean increased costs. If it shows that the scheduling has been significantly revised but the cost plans remain unchanged, this is a good reason to check the consistency of the plans.

Figure 5.33   Cost-milestone trend analysis

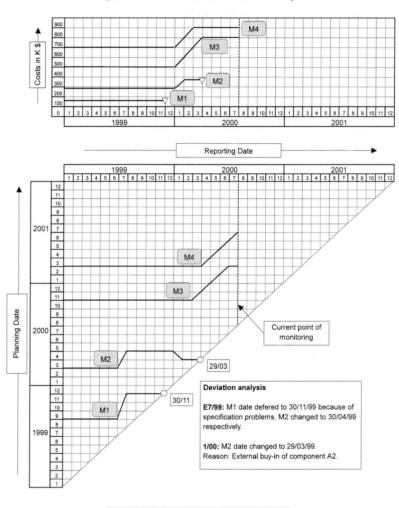

How is a CMTA interpreted?

In the example shown in Figure 5.33, the planned costs of the individual milestones are increased in steps. At the current reporting time (end of July 2000, cf. the broken line) the cumulated costs required up to M3 are estimated to be $700 000, and those up to M4 to be $800 000. Milestones M1 and M2 were realized with costs of $80 000 and $280 000 at 30 November 1999 and 29 March 2000, respectively.

> *Which other plans must be updated?*

Another minimum requirement on updating project documentation is to prepare a current **profitability plan**. If the product specifications have been modified or supplemented, the **configuration basis** must also be updated and all the **quality planning** elements based on it must be adjusted accordingly. More details on this point are given in previous sections of this book.

> *What is the new documentation used for?*

The updating of the project documentation closes the circle of project control. This documentation can be used at any time to report any changes or problems at a particular level to the next-highest agency in the project. Thus if a subproject leader realizes that a milestone which is important for the overall project cannot be reached at his level, he can raise it to the next-highest level. The project leader then uses this control information to initiate a new project control process which in turn results in updated documentation.

5.5 CHANGE MANAGEMENT – HANDLING CHANGES IN PROJECT TARGETS

> *Why is change management required?*

So far it has been assumed that the targets are *set in stone* or *frozen* from the outset as the very foundations of the project. And indeed, the project targets should not be subsequently changed in the course of the project. However, in the real world of project management, requests for changes are repeatedly made in the course of the project whose acceptance would in fact have the effect of modifying the project targets. Because they involve measures, which were not agreed internally as part of the project control process, such **change requests** should be treated like external inputs, even if members of the project team submit them (Figure 5.34).

Figure 5.34   Handling change requests

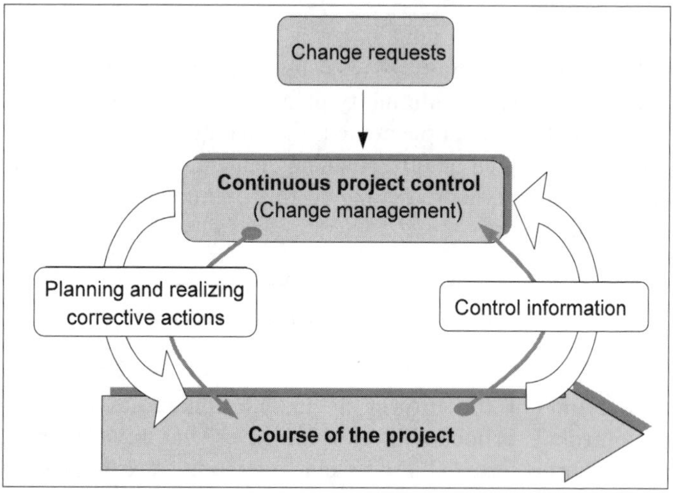

5.5.1   Sources of change requests

Changes in individual project targets may become necessary for a number of reasons:

> *How are changes triggered?*

- **Changes initiated by the project customer**: This is a frequent source of change requests, particularly in the customer-order sector. However, the internal client of a product-innovation project may also request changes, for instance to reach an earlier market window or to add new technical features, which he regards as profitable.
- **Technical problems**: The increasing level of detail accumulated as the project proceeds can lead to problems which were not yet discernible at a higher level. It is vital to detect serious problems in good time and to forward them to the relevant departments in order to minimize troubleshooting expenditures.
- **Changes in the business environment**: Especially in the field of product innovation, it may become necessary to adapt the configuration of the planned product to the dynamics of the competition as the project progresses. New competitor products may reduce the

maximum permissible sales price of the planned product or new market trends can change the weighting of particular product features from the customer's viewpoint. If the new product is to become a market success, sufficient flexibility must be built into the procedures to allow individual specifications to be changed and product features to be added or removed from the overall package as required. Major changes can have such serious repercussions that it may be necessary to initiate a separate project for a new product variant at an early stage in order not to jeopardize the current project.

An institution, which continuously coordinates the individual projects from a market standpoint is required to monitor relevant changes in the business environment around the project. This function may be assigned to the definition team, which already exists.

- **Creativity of the members of the project team**: This factor can be both positive and negative. Because of their special expertise, the employees assigned to individual tasks can submit specific suggestions for improvement which increase the overall efficiency of the project. However, their creativity can have a negative effect if the discretionary scope available within the project is misused to realize personal ideas going beyond the specification. The well known phenomenon of over-engineering is due in part to this problem.

As soon as change requests are made, the question arises as to how they should be handled.

5.5.2   The change management process

> *Which change requests are accepted?*

The routine of handling change requests illustrated in Figure 5.35 resembles the definition process used to select product ideas for inclusion in the project.

In the first place it must be ensured that *only* those changes are considered which are submitted in the form of a **change request**. This requirement, which may appear somewhat bureaucratic at first sight, is of great importance because it prevents changes flowing into the project from unreported sources. Thus changes may be made in

Figure 5.35   Change-management process

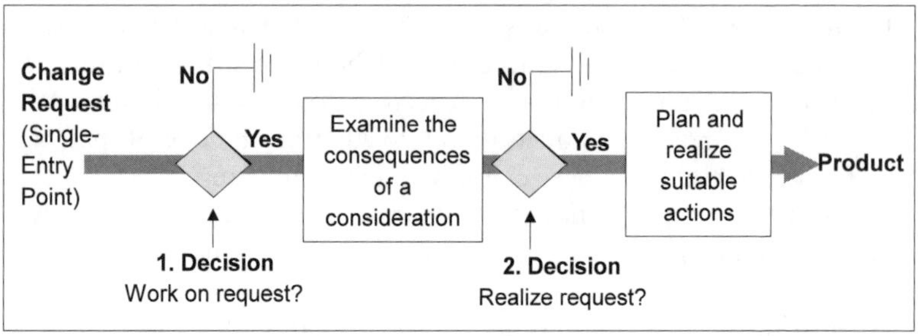

particular specifications as a result of a verbal agreement between a development engineer and an employee of the customer's company. These can have serious consequences for the overall project unless they are coordinated over all the sectors, which are affected by them (cf. Figure 5.36 as an illustration).

> *Who is responsible for change management?*

Creating single-entry points for receiving the change requests and processing them further can ensure this coordination. In smaller projects, the project leader may exercise this function, whereas in more complex ones it is a good idea to convene a **change control board**. This should comprise not only the project leader but also representatives from the development, quality control, sales and commercial sectors, as well as additional technical representatives where required.

> *How are change requests evaluated?*

After being submitted, change requests are **evaluated** for their importance. Necessary changes that have no impact on higher-level task complexes or the project targets can be implemented without too much difficulty. However, as soon as a change request could imply more fundamental alterations in product specifications, routines, deadlines or costs, it must be scrutinized more closely. The process is similar to that used for evaluating customer requirements when selecting projects: specifications are issued for the change requests, which

Figure 5.36   Effect of coordinated change management

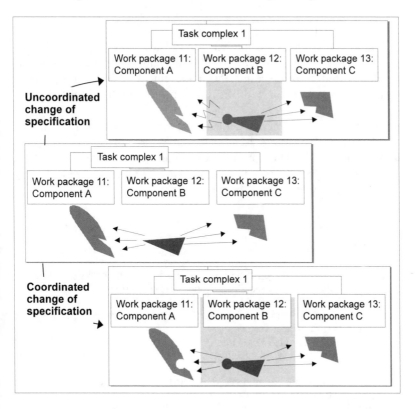

examine their implications for the profitability of the project. They must explicitly include aspects such as the costs incurred by a delayed completion of the project, dependencies to other projects as well as the capacity and budget situations.

Who releases the requests?

It is up to the project managers in coordination with the project customer to make the required changes in the current project on the basis of this evaluation. Change requests in customer-order projects are subject to an **external release.** This specifies the changes requested by the customer and clarifies the distribution of the costs incurred as well as other consequences.

> *How are changes implemented?*

The agreed changes are implemented in the same way as a specific subproject. The necessary activities are planned together with their deadlines and resources and the achievement of the set targets is continuously monitored with the aid of project control tools:

- In view of their potential effects on the principal project targets, subsequent changes represent an extremely critical aspect in projects.
- An important aim of project control must therefore be to avoid subsequent changes or to minimize their consequences by identifying their necessity as early as possible.

NOTES

1   The distinction between behavior, process and result checks goes back to Frese (1968), p. 61 f.; see also Küpper (1997), p. 169.
2   Taken in slightly modified form from Boehm (1986), p. 536. The diagram shows a typical example indicating the progress reports of a programmer in a software project.
3   Based on Turner (1993), p. 199.
4   Cf. on total quality management Ahsen (1996) and Oakland (1994) for example.
5   More details on calculating the hourly cost rate can be found in Burghardt (1995), p. 298 f.
6   For the following treatment, see Studt (1983), p. 178.
7   Studt (1983), p. 176.
8   A more detailed treatment of this topic may be found in Studt (1983), pp. 148 ff.
9   Cf. on the following: Wideman (1990), p. 62.
10 Cf. Küpper (1997), p. 149.
11 An extensive treatment of the topic of early warning in a company is given in Krystek and Müller-Stewens (1993). Special reference to projects may be found in Krystek and Zur (1991), pp. 304 ff.
12 Cf. Turner (1993), pp. 372 ff. on the following.
13 Cf. Turner (1993), pp. 375 ff.
14 Cf. Kolks (1986), pp. 289 ff.
15 The phenomenon in which an increasing length of wait queue increases the traversal time of a process is originally known from the manufacturing sector. A good illustration is offered by a funnel that gets clogged when too much material is put into it. Cf. on this point Wiendahl (1987), p. 57 f.
16 Cf. Coenenberg and Raffel (1988), as well as Seiler (1985) for the following.

17 Cf. Seiler (1985) for the following.
18 The designation *indicator* instead of *index* emphasizes that these values provide indications about the project output. However, they by no means suffice on their own for an assessment of the project performance! Cf. Seiler (1985) for a dissenting view.
19 These key figures are used to compare the planned progress of the project on the basis of the actual values recorded at a review time. It is up to the project manager to decide which of these comparative parameters are in fact measured. The various key figures will be of varying usefulness for different projects. The more difficult it is to determine the degree of realization of individual subelements of the work breakdown structure, the more unreliable will the resulting indicators be. Moreover, the measurement of the key figures and the information it requires involves a certain effort. In practical applications, the benefit to be expected from these key figures must justify the effort of determining them.
20 Cf. Coenenberg and Raffel (1988), p. 200.
21 Adapted from Turner (1993), p. 204.
22 Taken over from Schmelzer (1982), p. 50.
23 On the problem-solving approach of the 'five whys', cf. Womack, Jones and Roos (1994), p. 62.
24 These are countries with a *minimum authority distance* between superiors and employees, cf. Hofstede (1993), p. 92 ff. Examples are the countries of northern and central Europe with the exception of France. In countries with a greater authority distance between superiors and employees in contrast, a more **dominant approach by the project leader** is likely to be successful. In this case, the project leader should select the solutions and present them to the project teams as a decision which may not be questioned.

6 Successful completion of a project

> *What must be avoided when concluding a project?*

A project does not simply stop with the end of the realization process – i.e. with the completion of the product. The project's completion itself is a significant subprocess of project management (Figure 6.1). It should help to avoid any potential dangers, which would result if the project were simply left hanging at this point. These include:

- Non-attainment of the project targets
- Unnecessary delays in concluding the project and additional costs incurred owing to:
  (a) Over-engineering
  (b) Subsequent stipulations by the customer

Figure 6.1   Completion in the course of a project

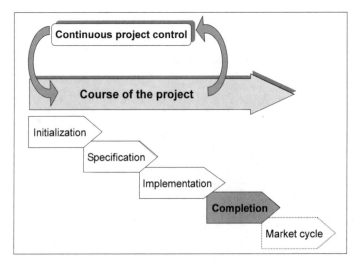

216

(c) The performance of tasks (services or products) which could equally well have been performed or supplied by units external to the project,

(d) Weakened motivation of the employees owing to a lack of clear follow-on activities

- Insufficient securing of the accumulated know-how
- Delayed release of important resources for follow-on projects.

Which subprocesses are involved in concluding the project?

To ensure that these problems do not occur, the activities and subprocesses shown in Figure 6.2 form part of the project-completion process. It has proved most efficient to include these activities, like all other important project activities, in the project plans and to check their implementation in line with the set targets. In addition to planning elements, the completion process also comprises some of the project control aspects described previously. It will now be treated separately.

Figure 6.2   Project-completion process

	Project completion		
Decision to conclude	Hand-over of the project results	Demobilize resources	Project evaluation

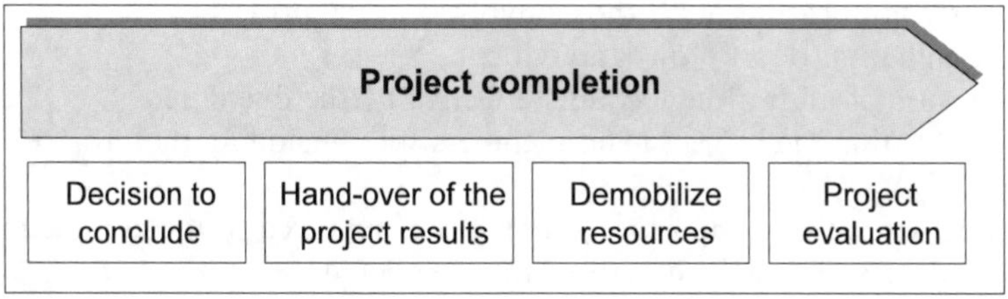

6.1   CONCLUDING THE PROJECT

The initial step in concluding a project is a respective request of the project managers to the project's customer. This is usually done in a special status meeting. The information about the current status of the project presented there provides the starting point for taking the decision to bring the project to a conclusion.

> *What does the completion decision involve?*

If the project targets have been reached, the completion and transfer activities can be immediately initiated. The decision to conclude the project then presents no problems. It is not quite as simple if some of the project targets were not reached. Even if not all subtargets were reached to 100 per cent, the project should still be concluded as early as possible. To this end, all outstanding activities must be listed in coordination with the customer as well as internal and external experts. In particular, possible alternative ways of reaching a satisfactory end result should be examined. The outstanding tasks are then planned in a similar way to the original project – i.e. their cost and schedule effects are determined, they are assigned to areas of responsibility and their implementation is agreed in the project completion process.

> *How is the decision implemented?*

After the elements of this decision have been finalized, they must be implemented. This process covers the following steps:

- early notification of all those involved in the project
- termination of all project activities
- closure of all project accounts effective by the due date
- motivating the project team members for concluding the project.

Three particularly important subprocesses involved in the completion procedure will now be described in more detail.

6.2　HAND-OVER OF THE PROJECT OUTPUT

A project is initiated with the explicit aim of producing an agreed output, which may be a bridge, a new product or the installation and successful operation of a software system. After the end product has been completed, it must be handed over to the customer so that he can check its compliance with the targets. Specifically, the following points must be taken into account:

> *What must the considered for the hand-over?*

- The **hand-over** process should be **planned** and **scheduled**.
- A **hand-over protocol** should be prepared. It documents the attainment of the targets as well as any deviations and outstanding points and specifies ways of dealing with them.
- Suitable structures must be set up for transferring the **end-product** and all supplementary components required for its use (documentation, know-how, etc.) to the customer. For example, the customer's employees may need to be involved and suitably trained even before the hand-over.
- In the case of external customers, the project managers should be particularly **sensitive** to the customer's perception of the degree of target fulfilment. Ultimately, the handed-over result will largely determine his satisfaction with the overall project. Active **marketing of the project results** must therefore ensure that this potential is not lost by the project slowly petering out (see Stakeholder-oriented management of projects, p. 151).
- However, the results should also be **actively marketed** in the company which implements the project. Especially the top management and the rest of the company's employees should be notified of the successful completion of a major project. Such success announcements also have a positive impact on employee motivation in other corporate sectors.
- Not only for the customer does the hand-over of the results represent the most critical substep of a project. The members of the project team have worked consistently to achieve these results. The successful hand-over of the these results should therefore be adequately celebrated. Appropriate bonuses can enhance the positive experience gained by the team members in working on projects.

6.3 DEMOBILIZING PROJECT RESOURCES

> *Why is this task a responsibility of project management?*

A project is designed to run for a limited period of time. Its existence should not be prolonged beyond that point, as it would then tie up corporate resources for activities which could be more usefully invested in other tasks. Provision should therefore be made in the project completion phase to **pass on** the resources linked to the project as **efficiently** as possible. Like the project results themselves, its resources must not be left hanging at the end of the project and ignored thereafter. During the project, responsibility for the required resources was entrusted to the project management. They must now also fulfil their obligation at the end of the project:

- **Utilization plans** should be drawn up for all the assets linked to the project such as offices, test installations, etc. These plans are then used to organize the hand-over or disposal of the resources.
- It is particularly important to prepare **transfer plans** for the project employees at an early stage. This involves detailed discussions about the performance of the individual employees, issuing appropriate testimonials as well as granting incentive bonuses and commendations. The assignment of follow-on activities has the effect of increasing the motivation of the employees for completing the project efficiently. But it also guarantees that the know-how accumulated in the project continues to be available to the company.

> *When should the hand-over take place?*

It is vital that the project resources are handed over at precisely the right time. A delayed release can lead to unnecessary capital tie-ups and squandering of resources. But if hand-over of assets and project employees is started too early, the efficient completion of the project could well be jeopardized.

6.4 PROJECT EVALUATION AS A CONTRIBUTION TO ORGANIZATIONAL LEARNING

> *What can be learned from past projects?*

In project-oriented companies, every single project represents a source of valuable experience for subsequent projects. If useful lessons are to be learned from the current project, it is helpful to prepare a **critique of manoeuvres, post mortems** or **experience reports** in the *concluding project rounds*. The deeper-lying causes of any deviations and problems that occurred during the project should be discussed and documented in an atmosphere free from acute project pressures.

> *How is an effective post mortem created?*

It has proved of value to organize the **concluding project rounds** in the form of one or more team meetings based on the meta-plan method. After the project activities have been completed and the results have been handed over to the customer, the project team members meet in a more relaxed atmosphere to discuss the project. A neutral facilitator who was not involved in the project should chair the meetings. Positive and negative elements of the completed project should be discussed in the concluding project rounds and possible improvements immediately formulated. The principle of the *five whys* already mentioned (Figure 5.30, p. 199) could be most helpful in this task.

> *Should the external customer be involved?*

Particularly interesting results are obtained when the customer of the completed project is directly involved in the critique of manoeuvres. Ways of achieving an improved customer orientation in the way the company manages its projects can then be examined.

> *How are the results post-processed?*

The results are post-processed in the concluding project rounds on the basis of the documentation from the critique of manoeuvres. Experience reports from different projects may also be collected at a central point and published, for instance in the form of a special Intranet page. This can then help designated project leaders to avoid potential problems in future.

The suggestions for improvement should also be converted into concrete action plans. These should designate named persons to super-vise specific improvements.

Part III Project-Oriented Corporate Management System

Parts I and II showed how a company could focus its resources optimally to its customers by selecting appropriate projects and implementing them efficiently. We have seen that a **project-oriented company** is characterized by adopting this approach as a matter of corporate policy and by running its operational business primarily in the form of projects. However, it is not sufficient for such a company merely to develop the capacity to run individual projects, as described in Part II. *Project orientation* implies that project management is not used only as a tool but is implemented across the board as a distinct corporate philosophy.

> *What elements go into the management system?*

Successful corporate management is based on the use of a series of tools, which can be subsumed under the term '**corporate management system**'. Such a system of tools, techniques and structures is designed specifically to support corporate management in fulfilling its tasks. In reading the following chapters, it is important to note that the different elements of a management system do not presume the existence of certain institutions in a company, but merely describe necessary functions and tools. This means they can be performed by disparate employees and departments as required in any given case. At this stage, nothing is yet said about their assignment to any particular

Figure III.1   Management system of a project-oriented company

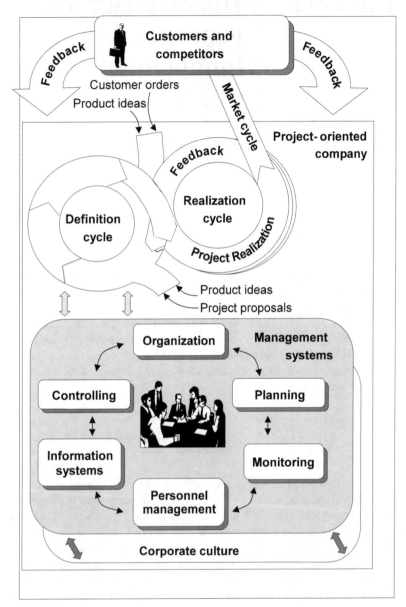

organizational unit. The most important elements of a **corporate management system** are shown in Figure III.1. These are:[1]

- To **organize** and allocate tasks appropriately in the corporate organization in order to ensure that they can be performed effectively and efficiently.
- To **plan** for decisions about future activities of the company such as setting targets, analyzing problems and identifying suitable modes of action.
- To **monitor** parameters by comparing them with each other and evaluating their differences. A typical example is to verify whether a plan was in fact duly implemented. Another form of monitoring is to compare the performance of different companies – for example, as a part of a benchmarking process.
- To **motivate** employees to act in accordance with the objectives set by the corporate management. This is a particularly important task: all the tools and processes that can help to achieve this end are made available within the scope of **personnel management**.
- To **provide** tools for the acquisition, storage, processing and distribution of the necessary information via an appropriate **information system**.
- Finally, to support the corporate management in **coordinating** the various management tools. This is the task of the **controlling**, which ensures the mutual coordination of the tools deployed for planning, monitoring, personnel management, organization and information management.

> *What does project-oriented corporate management mean?*

Seen as a **management concept**, project management must be reflected in the entire management system of the company. In contrast to conventional companies, a project-oriented company must therefore ensure that this system satisfies **two additional requirements**:

1. The management system of a project-oriented company must ensure that corporate executives receive optimal support in managing *with* projects.
2. The management system of a project-oriented company must ensure that the project leaders who act as entrepreneurs within the company receive optimal support in their management *of* projects.

Figure III.2   Elements of a corporate management system to support project
management

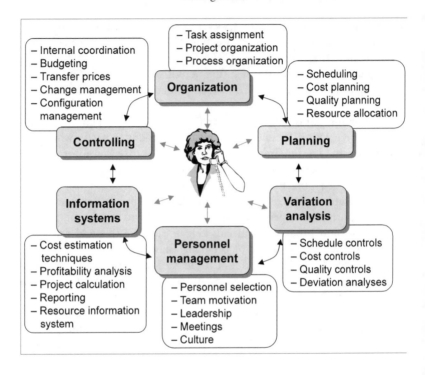

- Internal coordination
- Budgeting
- Transfer prices
- Change management
- Configuration
  management

- Task assignment
- Project organization
- Process organization

Organization

- Scheduling
- Cost planning
- Quality planning
- Resource allocation

Controlling

Planning

**Information
systems**

**Variation
analysis**

- Cost estimation
  techniques
- Profitability analysis
- Project calculation
- Reporting
- Resource information
  system

**Personnel
management**

- Schedule controls
- Cost controls
- Quality controls
- Deviation analyses

- Personnel selection
- Team motivation
- Leadership
- Meetings
- Culture

What tools are available?

Important aspects of this second requirement were already discussed
in detail in Part II. Figure III.2 once more summarizes some of the
tools and methods, which support project managers in their tasks.

How do the tasks of project and corporate management differ?

The principal task of *corporate management* differs from that of
project management: unlike the latter, it is not focused on the successful
implementation of a single project. Its brief is to satisfy fundamental
corporate objectives such as making a profit, ensuring growth, maximizing shareholder value and ensuring solvency. Project-oriented

companies regard project management as a way of reaching these objectives by means of projects and the customer orientation which this entails.

Managers of project-oriented companies must thus endeavour to administer their **project portfolio** – i.e. all projects, which are planned or currently in process – in order to satisfy the corporate goals in an optimal way. They must base their decisions on these goals even if these may at first sight appear to have negative consequences for an individual project and the resources tied to it:

- Employees of project-oriented companies must be aware of the difference in the tasks and responsibilities of project and corporate management in order to have an insight into the decisions taken in this context.
- The corporate management must consequently identify, define and communicate the various functions in the company.

> *What is the aim of Part III?*

The aim of Part III of the book is to show what the management system of a project-oriented company must **additionally** ensure in order to support the corporate management in an optimal way. The next chapters will not attempt to describe all aspects of a company's management functions. Rather, they will focus on specific features arising from a project-oriented approach. Their structure is based on a systematic presentation of a corporate management system as originally proposed by Küpper for discussing the controlling functions of corporate management.[2]

> *How should the management system be weighted?*

However, before the elements of a project-oriented management system can be described, a fundamental aspect should first be addressed:

- The actual value added in a project-oriented company is generated within individual projects. The management system should do no more than support this process. This fact must always be borne in mind when configuring and weighting the system in order to avoid creating any unnecessary sources of overheads.

NOTES

1   Cf. Küpper (1997), p. 15.
2   Cf. Küpper (1997), pp. 13 ff.

7 Project-oriented organization

> *Project versus process management?*

Conventional companies tend to be organized in order to perform standard recurrent tasks as efficiently as possible. A number of methodologies have been developed to redesign existing organizational structures for performing these tasks. As an example, **business re-engineering** focuses on developing integrated business processes. A *process owner* is made responsible for a complete customer-to-customer process, whose implementation he monitors from beginning to end.[1] Such process organization philosophies are best applied to transparent tasks whose basic structure is not subject to significant fluctuations. Examples are order processing in an insurance company or the administrative activities commonly performed in the business world and public authorities. However, such standardized business processes fail when they are faced with unique, complex and innovative tasks

Figure 7.1   Organization in project-oriented companies

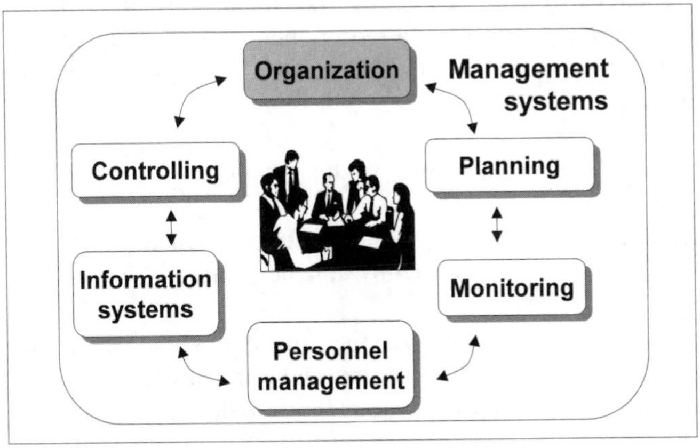

such as the flexible manufacture of a product to individual customer requirements.

A project-oriented corporate organization closes this gap by transferring the basic idea of universal processes to complex tasks. A company operating on this basis thus pursues a more flexible form of **process organization**.

> *How must a project-oriented organization operate?*

This approach makes the following demands on the organization of a project-oriented company:

- The importance of the projects must be reflected in the organizational development of the company.
- Suitable operations planning must ensure that the projects are implemented as efficiently as possible.

7.1   PROJECT-ORIENTED COMPANY HIERARCHY

> *What blocks entrepreneurs within a company?*

Project-oriented corporate management implies that the projects are integrated into the company hierarchy at a suitably high level.[2] Figure 7.2 illustrates this idea. The project leaders are required to act as entrepreneurs within the company. To do so, they must be equipped with the necessary authority, a requirement that is frequently ignored. Thus the project leader's entrepreneurial actions are often made unnecessary difficult if:

- she has little or no influence on the selection of the members of the project team, or
- is granted no disciplinary or at least technical authority over her team members during the course of the project.[3]

As a result, projects are not given their due importance in the corporate organization. Matrix structures dominate and projects are treated as special cases to be fitted in around the functional hierarchy as far as possible.

Figure 7.2   Project-oriented hierarchy

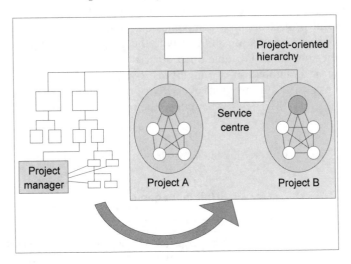

> *What is a project-oriented matrix?*

In contrast, a consistently project-oriented corporate organization turns this matrix structure on its head (cf. Figure 7.3). Projects are shifted into the very centre of the corporate hierarchy. The various departments (such as human resources, purchasing, controlling, accounting etc.) become **service sectors** whose main task is to support the projects running in the company.

> *What is required for its implementation?*

However, simply renaming existing organizational units will hardly suffice to impress a project structure onto the corporate organization. Project orientation must be lived by the employees; it must become an integral part of the corporate culture. We will return to this point in more detail in Part IV.

> *How should workplaces be arranged?*

A good way of encouraging this process is to arrange for the project teams to be **accommodated in the same location**. The regular workplaces of at least the core teams should be located together to allow close cooperation and engender a feeling of group solidarity. Particularly successful project-oriented companies are characterized by extending such a project orientation all the way to the design and configuration of the office buildings. Portable office structures (partitions, etc.) support flexible accommodation of employees. Symmetrical floor and office divisions ensure a transparent overview of the functions of the employees who work there (e.g. Where does the project controller sit?).

Figure 7.3   Reversing the matrix in a project-oriented company

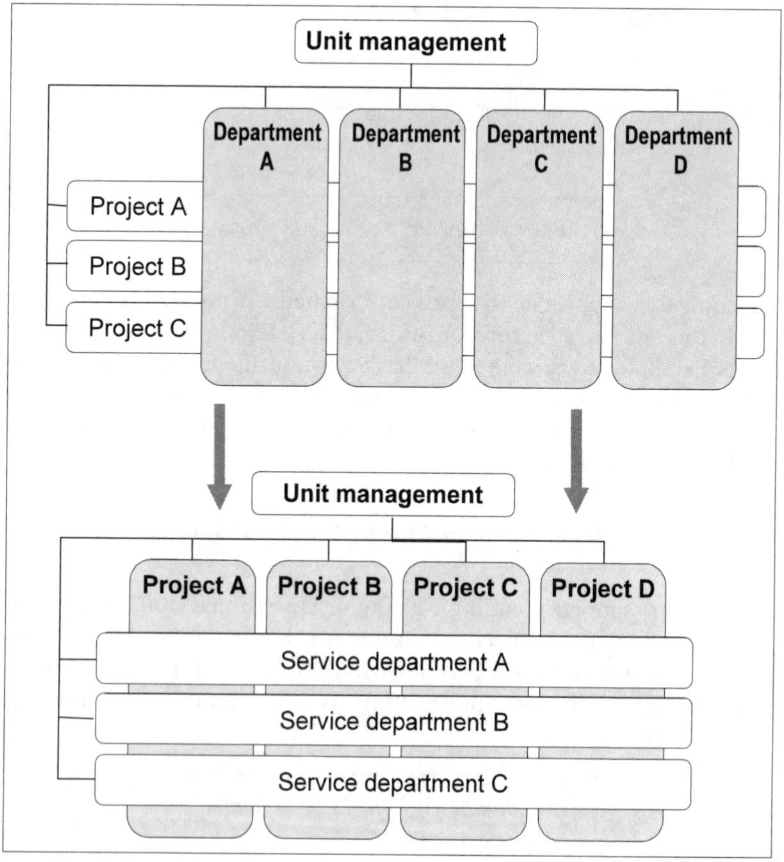

7.2 PROJECT-ORIENTED PROCESS ORGANIZATION

> *What is the aim of process organization?*

The quality and speed of business procedures play a particularly important part in project-oriented companies. Project orientation has already been equated with flexible process structures. The aim of process organization is thus to configure the processes involved in project management as efficiently as possible.

> *Are process guidelines useful?*

Parts I and II of this book described the execution of a possible project from its selection to its ultimate conclusion. It is useful to identify **project processes** – i.e. project-referred business procedures – within a company and to describe them in institutional form in order to facilitate the work of individual process leaders in their capacity as **process users**. The resulting **process guidelines** can then be supplemented and improved in steps as a result of the experience gained in the individual projects (see EFQM, p. 235). As Figure 7.4 shows, this involves traversing the following stages:

> *How is continuous improvement of the processes assured?*

- **Process managers** should be appointed at every level (corporate, business, function, etc.). Their job is to implement suitable processes for the projects in their sector and to continue working on their improvement.
- **Improvement teams** (CIP teams) ensure that know-how about possible process improvements is exchanged between and across all levels.
- Suitable metrics (cf. Section 12.2.1) are used to continuously measure the efficiency and effectiveness of existing processes. In addition, 'soft' experience reports and opinions of the project team members are used as a basis for identifying possible problems in processes.
- After the process measurement procedures have been evaluated, suitable ways of improving them are identified and implemented.

Figure 7.4   Continuous improvement process

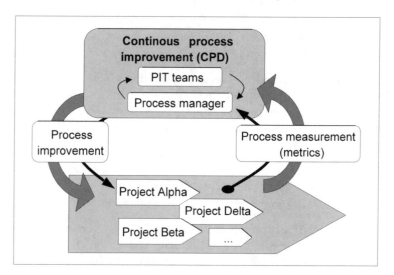

Does project-orientation facilitate organizational learning?

It is clear that a project-oriented company can improve its organizational development more quickly than conventional companies. This is because the conclusion of every project represents a breathing space for the company, which can be used to implement changes. Organizations without this specific orientation must seek out such upheavals or even intentionally create them. This is also indicated by the fact that re-engineering measures can often be very successful. In project-oriented companies, modified processes can be made immediately available to each new project without intervening in existing activities in a disruptive way.

What are the benefits of process guidelines?

The implementation of project processes and the corresponding process guidelines have the following benefits:

- A new project leader can benefit from the experience gained in past projects and can avoid any errors made there. This increases project efficiency by minimizing start-up problems.

- A standardized project language develops in the company. This facilitates the comparison and exchange of know-how across projects.
- Once process guidelines have been established, the need for coordination in and between projects is reduced.
- Established project processes offer a good basis for responding flexibly to the requirements of external customers. Thus processes required by customers can be translated into corporate routines. This makes the projects less unfamiliar and this way facilitates the work of project leaders and team members.

> *How can red tape be avoided?*

Despite the advantages of process guidelines, care should be taken not to lose the flexibility and entrepreneurial scope offered by projects. The guidelines should be regarded purely as recommendations, never as detailed directives for action. Otherwise, despite a project orientation, it can be all too easy to fall into the trap of bureaucratic **red tape,** which can be a major problem in rigid corporate structures. This can be avoided by observing the following points:

- The descriptions of the subprocesses to be traversed should be kept at a relatively abstract level, and
- The guidelines should include only the results aimed at by the individual subprocesses, but no instructions for achieving them. This gives the project leaders plenty of scope to organize their work in an individual way.

Case study 7.1　EFQM (European Foundation of Quality Management)

The EFQM has developed a model to ensure a comprehensive level of quality management. It may also be used in project-oriented companies as a basis for making gradual improvements.[4]

In a self-evaluation process, companies can assess their quality performance on the basis of nine criteria (Figure 7.5). These cover firstly the measures and methods that are specified and/or used in the company for improving quality (*enabler*). In addition, the results obtained by the company are analyzed on the basis of these quality criteria and included in the evaluation (*results*). Each of the nine evaluation criteria is further broken down into subpoints, which focus the assessor's attention onto particularly important subaspects of the relevant components.

Figure 7.5   EFQM criteria

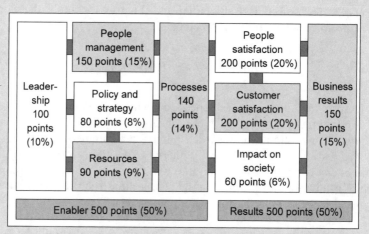

The selection of evaluation criteria reflects the stakeholder orientation that a successful company must strive for. The model covers customer orientation, employee orientation and corporate responsibility to society. But it also takes into account the quality development of corporate processes and resources as well as the commitment of corporate management to enhancing quality in the company. The EFQM model thus offers a suitable framework for evaluating all quality-relevant features and results of a company and for examining them in order to identify potential improvements.

Teams specifically set up for this purpose should perform the self-assessment. The involvement of additional employees helps to disseminate the quality philosophy throughout the company and thus helps the corporate culture to evolve over the long term. The EFQM also provides various process suggestions and back-up resources such as standard forms and evaluation tables for facilitating the self-evaluation.

The results of the self-evaluation can yield valuable suggestions for making improvements in the company. These should be converted into specific action plans and project suggestions and forwarded to the relevant single-entry points. The most important suggestions can then be transferred directly to the process of defining new projects. Moreover, the EFQM assessment also forms a suitable comparative basis for benchmarking projects because a large number of international companies already participate in this initiative.

The EFQM awards the *European Quality Prize* to companies whom have achieved outstanding performance by means of a continuous process of improvement. The best of these prize-winners is distinguished with the annual *European Quality Award*.

NOTES

1 The best known source on this topic is certainly Hammer and Champy (1993).
2 Cf. also Gareis (1991) and well as Gareis (1992) on this point.
3 The positive effects of project team members being subject to the authority of the project management have been shown by authors such as Rickert (1995), p. 187. However, it should also be noted that companies tend to be very hesitant in introducing such arrangements in practice (cf. Rickert 1995, p. 92).
4 More information on self-evaluation based on EFQM as well as contact addresses can be found in: NN (1995).

8 Project-oriented planning

Significant parts of the planning activities of project-oriented companies have already been covered in Parts I and II and will merely be briefly summarized and supplemented at this point.

In a project-oriented company, planning takes place at two different levels (Figure 8.1):

> *What are the aims of project-oriented planning?*

- **Project planning** deals with the implementation of an individual project. Its aim is to ensure that the schedule, quality and cost targets can be achieved with the resources available to the project. The various steps and tools required to do this were described in detail in Part II.
- **Multi-project planning** ensures that a balanced portfolio of projects is created in line with corporate strategies. Its aim is to plan a project portfolio on a continuous basis in which corporate resources are

Figure 8.1   Planning in a project-oriented company

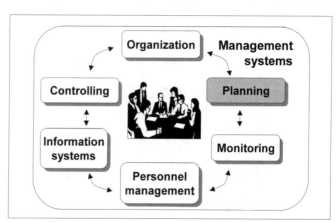

optimally deployed in order to satisfy the company's strategic and operative goals. In addition, the project leaders must be provided with all the tools and expertise which they require for planning their projects.

> *Who is responsible for planning?*

Whereas individual project planning is essentially the responsibility of the project managers and controllers, multi-project planning is usually administered by agents whose purview covers all corporate projects. These may be members of the corporate management or specifically formed *project balance teams*.

Two main functions of multi-project planning which are of particular relevance in a project-oriented company will now be described.

8.1 PLANNING A BALANCED PROJECT PORTFOLIO

> *What tools are available for multi-project planning?*

The first step in creating a balanced project portfolio – i.e. one that is oriented to the strategic objectives of the company – is to select suitable projects. A number of useful tools for **multi-project planning** have already been described in Part I. These are:

- Strategic planning methods such as portfolio presentations or strategic gap analyses
- Methods for analyzing the operational consequences of planned projects (profitability analyses, cost estimation techniques, etc.)
- Processes for the stepwise selection of product ideas and project suggestions
- Scoring methods and ranking models.

> *What does multi-project planning determine?*

Among the main tasks of multi-project planning is to secure a balanced project portfolio by distributing corporate resources in an appropriate way among the projects. The tools mentioned above support the planning of the activities this involves. Accordingly, the following elements are determined within the scope of multi-project planning:

- the **budget** released for the individual projects
- the **employees** allocated to the various projects, as well as
- other **resources** assigned to the individual projects.

> *Is resource allocation of strategic relevance?*

Every project ties up resources in order to focus the company's activities in a specific direction. This applies not only to product-innovation projects but also to internal projects and external customer projects. As a result, every project is of strategic significance. This clearly implies that strategic considerations must always be borne in mind when distributing resources among the projects (cf. Part I).

> *How are corporate resources distributed among the projects?*

In some cases, corporate resources are assigned **directly** to individual projects. A typical example is that of project budgets which supply the necessary funds to projects. These may either be derived from a corporate budget or be based on a fixed price (less a margin) arranged with the customer.

Because decision-making responsibility is delegated to the individual projects, it may be possible to have only an **indirect** influence on the allocation of corporate resources to these projects. It was described in Part I how project priorities are set within the scope of multi-project planning. Depending on how such priorities are defined, there are various ways in which projects can autonomously gain access to resources. Another means of exercising an indirect influence is to define transfer prices for internal services or products. This will be covered in the section on project controlling.

> *Dealing with disturbances in the portfolio*

The continuous planning of the project portfolio also involves preparing and initiating suitable adjustments as early as possible in the event of any disturbances. For example, a particular project may run into a critical situation, which jeopardizes the balance of the entire portfolio. The failure of a product-innovation project of great strategic importance could well have negative effects on the long-term development of the company.

Multi-project planning also involves the need to analyze any problems occurring in the portfolio (see the section on project-oriented monitoring, p. 244), to prepare suitable countermeasures and plan their implementation. Typical countermeasures, which may be required in this context, are:

- Increasing the budget of individual projects
- Changing the priorities of individual projects
- Shifting resources between projects.

> *How are such measures planned?*

Planning such countermeasures is in principle similar to dealing with change requests in individual projects. Here too, the adjustments must be checked for their effects on the schedule, quality and cost targets of the projects in the portfolio as well as for any consequences for the corporate targets. The project is not finally released until all these effects have been examined, their consequences revealed and clearance granted by the management.

8.2 STRATEGIC RESOURCE PLANNING

> *Why is strategic resource planning needed?*

In project-oriented companies, the available resources must be distributed over all the projects in accordance with strategic considerations. In parallel with this, however, an appropriate long-term development of the company's resources must be ensured, too. A company must coordinate its resources so that they can be used to satisfy the requirements of its future customers in an optimal way. Strategic resource planning (Figure 8.2) thus forms an important supplement to planning a balanced project portfolio.

Figure 8.2   Role of strategic resource planning

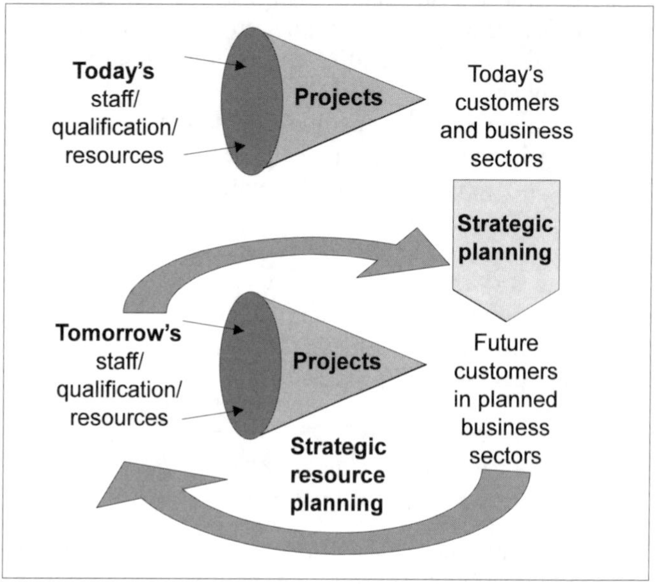

How is it oriented?

The decision about which markets and target groups to aim at in future is made within the scope of strategic business planning. This is where the basic orientation is set as to which business fields and products should be targeted in the long term. The company must be able to implement customer-oriented projects in those future fields of activity. As human resources are a key success factor for any kind of future project, it is essential to derive a **resource planning strategy** from the strategic business plans. This strategy ensures that the company will develop the know-how and experience necessary for an effective project orientation in the long run.

How is a resource planning strategy implemented?

Suitable **human resource plans** are applied within the framework of a resource planning strategy to ensure that the business targets can be successfully implemented over the long term. The various measures, which are appropriate to achieve this end will be treated in detail in Chapter 10. They range from personnel selection over personnel development to the wide and important field of culture management described in Part IV.

In the sector of material resources, attention must be paid to acquiring the necessary capital as well as the technologies and corresponding investments. This includes participating in decisions about the acquisition or sale of entire corporate units.

> *Does resource planning determine corporate strategy?*

It is shown in Figure 8.2 that strategic resource planning simultaneously yields important information for strategic business planning. In particular, it provides indications as to which core skills can be achieved in the future by applying suitable techniques of human resources management. Business strategies are meaningful and realistic only if they can also be supported by appropriate core skills in the company.

9 Project-oriented monitoring

The processes applied in project-oriented companies must be checked to verify that they lead to the attainment of the corporate goals. Monitoring is therefore another important tool of corporate management. However, the scope of monitoring tasks in project-oriented companies goes considerably beyond the mere verification that strategic plans have been realized:

- It must check whether the portfolio – i.e. the totality of currently planned and implemented projects, is running according to plan.
- It must check the planning of individual projects to ensure that they provide the necessary support to the corporate goals.
- It must ensure that the individual projects run on schedule.
- It must create the basis for ongoing organizational learning. This is because monitoring is critical for ensuring continuous improvement in project-oriented companies.

In project-oriented companies, monitoring plays an important supporting role for the individual projects (Figure 9.1). It helps the relevant employees achieve the project goals in the best possible way. It also ensures that the overall corporate goals are actually attained.

Figure 9.1   Monitoring in a project-oriented company

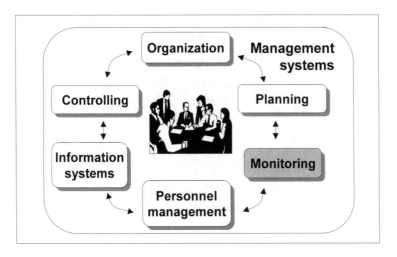

What tools are used in monitoring?

To satisfy these requirements, the monitoring process must cover the three components shown in Figure 9.2 and be well established within the company, as far as possible with the aid of suitable tools.[1] These components are:

- Regular checks of the premises on which the plans are based (**premise checks**).
- Continuous checking of the progress of current activities in the company (**progress checks**).
- Checking the results obtained (**realization checks**).

Who monitors whom?

At this stage, there is no indication about who should perform the tasks and elements involved in the monitoring process. Such functions must under no circumstances be seen as supervision. Quite the opposite in fact: autonomy is an important feature of well-functioning teams and project groups.

Figure 9.2   Forms of control in a project-oriented company

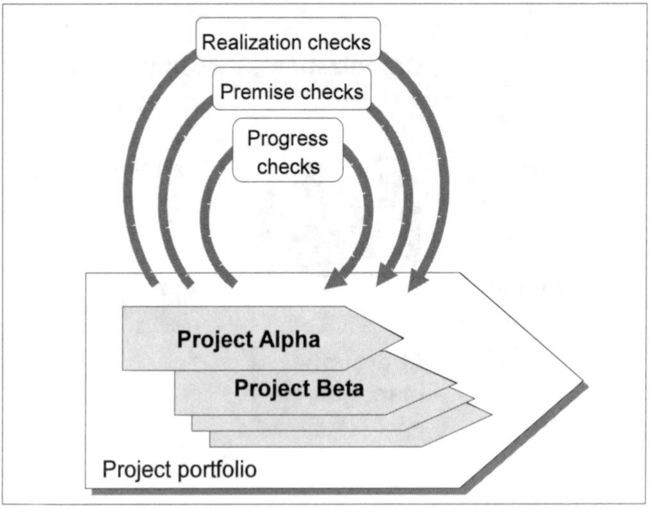

9.1   CONTINUOUS PROGRESS CHECKS

> *How is the progress of individual projects monitored?*

The process of monitoring **individual projects** has already been dealt with in Part II. It includes the regular acquisition of information of relevance to control and its use at an early stage to identify any deviations from the plan. The following were among the aspects, which were discussed:

- Tracking the degree of realization of individual work packages or subprojects
- Tracking the development of the product quality required by the customer, for example by quantifying error rates or other technical product features
- Checking that the project budget has not been overrun during the realization of the project.

| *What tools are required?* |

An important aspect of management *with* projects – i.e. managing a project-oriented company is to provide the project leaders with suitable tools for monitoring the progress of their project. Among these are the information tools examined more closely in Chapter 11. Some of these monitoring functions are also covered by commercial project planning and control tools such as Primavera, MS Project and TimeLine.

| *Why are overall progress checks required?* |

At **trans-project level**, it is important to ensure that the progress of the various projects in the portfolio is on schedule. After all, the projects were released in order to reach overall corporate goals. Information about any problems, which may occur is needed in order to make the necessary corrections at the right time. These include:

- The short-term redistribution of resources to acutely critical and important projects, and
- Changing the targets of individual projects.

To allow the corporate management to perform these tasks, the relevant information must be made available by a suitable information system (cf. Chapter 11).

9.2 CHECKING THE PREMISES OF THE PLANNING PROCEDURES

| *What are planning premises?* |

The whole point of a project is to make a specific contribution to attaining the company's strategic and operative objectives. Their innovative character and the risks involved, some of which may be considerable, characterize projects. As a consequence, the course and consequences of a project cannot be precisely forecast at its definition stage. At the same time, project-oriented companies tend to assign priorities to projects on the basis of their importance. One of the factors affected by this prioritization is the allocation of scarce resources such as employees or budget. In order to set priorities despite the uncertainty of the projects, the corporate management makes fundamental assumptions, known as *premises*. Examples of such premises are:

- the future development of the market and the competitive situation
- the market window for a new product
- the anticipated project costs
- the availability of preliminary products, tools etc. at the right time
- successful cooperation with external suppliers, and
- the containment of other previously identified project risks.

The more uncertain a project is at the time of its release, the more assumptions must be made when making the release decision. This point is particularly relevant in the product-innovation sector.

> *Why must the premises be monitored?*

Because projects usually run over several months, changes are likely to occur in some of the premises as the project progresses. Thus the market window – i.e. the planned completion date for a current product-innovation project – may have to be brought forward as a result of market changes. The aim of monitoring the premises is precisely to detect such changes. Premise checks determine whether the fundamental assumptions on the basis of which the project plans were issued still apply.

> *How are premise checks performed?*

To allow such checks to be performed, the assumptions made must already have been documented during the definition cycle. They must therefore be specified by the corporate management as mandatory contents of the project documents on whose basis the release decision is taken (cf. Section 3.4 in Part I). During the reporting procedures accompanying the project, the individual premises must be regularly checked for their continued validity. If changes do occur, corrective interventions can be made in the project portfolio. Examples of these are:

- changes in setting priorities for individual projects, or
- changes in specific project targets.

> *What effects must be considered?*

When such changes are made, it must always be borne in mind that they may have significant consequences for the project portfolio. After all, a project cannot usually be assigned a higher priority without at the same time relegating other projects to a lower one. So this is where the planning circle for the project portfolio closes in the way described in Chapter 8.

9.3   REALIZATION CHECKS

> *Why are realization checks necessary?*

Realization checks are applied to the results attained by a project. This makes them unsuitable as a source of information for correcting projects currently in progress. However, they are of particular importance as a basis for organizational learning in project-oriented companies. They ascertain whether the company is able to satisfy the requirements of its stakeholders (see EFQM, p. 235). These are above all:

- The requirements of the project client or customer
- The goals of the company
- The requirements of the employees.

> *How can customer satisfaction be verified?*

The first step in determining whether the **customer requirements** were satisfied by the project after its conclusion is to compare the final deadline, achieved quality and incurred costs with the targets specified in the project order. In the event of any deviations, the principle of the 'five whys' can be applied in order to determine the deeper reasons for their occurrence (cf. Section 5.2.6 in Part II).

However, realization checks should go further than this minimum requirement. In particular, they must examine the long-term impact of the projects on the customer. Were customer requirements which were not explicitly specified in the project order also satisfied? Examples are the planned utilization period of a manufactured product or an x per cent reduction in overheads as a result of a reorganization project.

> *When are such checks prepared?*

The foundation stone for such realization checks in the market process is laid as early as the definition cycle, even if some of these checks are not carried out until long after the end of the project. Suitable check criteria and times should be explicitly specified and cleared with the customer. Although this may mean more effort at the outset, it does give the customer a clear signal that the company is committed to satisfying his requirements in the best possible way.

> *What is learned from realization checks?*

Customer-oriented realization checks give a project-oriented company valuable feedback for defining future projects. It might, for example, become clear if the company has succeeded in this early phase of the project in identifying the customer's requirements and evaluating them correctly. If the customer is involved in the manoeuvre critique after the conclusion of the project (cf. Section 6.4 in Part II), information may be obtained about any weak points in one's own project management. This in turn represents an important input for a continuous improvement process and thus for organizational learning in a project-oriented company.

> *How is the attainment of corporate goals checked?*

Projects are not released for realization unless they can make an appropriate contribution to the **corporate goals**. It is part of the definition cycle to determine whether they look likely to do so. Profitability analyses are also carried out, strategic considerations examined and the projects arranged on the basis of a number of key criteria. To ensure that no systematic errors are committed in these early phases of the project, a check should be made after the conclusion of the project whether the forecasts made at the project release really did materialize at a later stage. This avoids, for example, regular overestimation of the attainable sales figures of new products or underestimation of the subsequent costs of customer-order projects.

> *How is employee satisfaction measured?*

Motivated and satisfied **employees** are the most important resource available to project-oriented companies. Employees have certain expectations and hopes as regards their project activities. The realization checks performed after the conclusion of the individual projects must therefore be systematically extended by respective aspects (see EFQM, p. 235). Employees also represent one of the best sources of suggestions for improving structures and processes in project-oriented companies. Realization checks can therefore provide a basis for:

- Structuring the project organization by revealing weak points and problems in current processes, in the hierarchy of individual projects as well as in the integration of projects into the corporate hierarchy and processes
- Structuring personnel management by revealing the need for development and training in technical and social skills by all the individuals involved in the project.

Employee surveys (cf. the manoeuvre critique in Section 6.4 in Part II), project evaluations and discussion rounds should be established within the organization on the basis of the *meta plan* method in order to determine the deeper causes of positive or negative events. Especially when held after project completion and moderated by a neutral and respected employee of the company, they are a valuable tool for realization checks. Here too, suitable checklists support the speedy collection of all information relevant to a continuous process of improvement.

NOTE

1 Cf. for the following Küpper (1997), pp. 169 ff.

10 Project-oriented personnel management

What is the function of human resources management?

Employees represent a critical success factor for any company. In its own interest, therefore, the company must provide appropriate encouragement to its employees, who are after all important stakeholders. **Personnel management** provides all the tools and processes which support the corporate management in this task (Figure 10.1). A well-qualified programme of managing human resources helps to motivate and encourage employees and to guide their behaviour with respect to the corporate goals.[1]

Figure 10.1   Personnel management in a project-oriented company

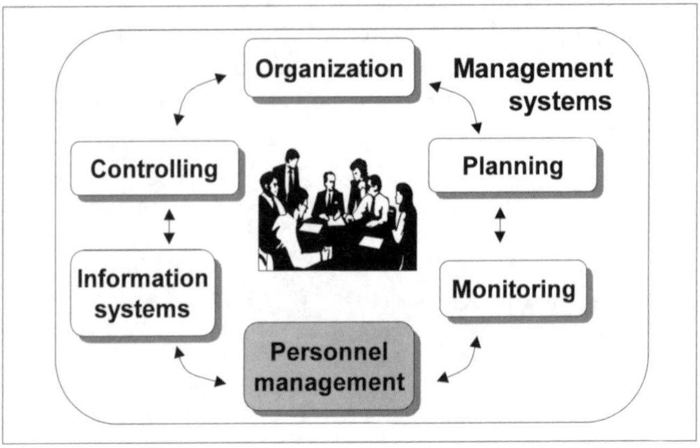

Who is responsible for personnel management?

The functions of human resources management are performed by all agents in the organization whose job it is to manage employees in the short- mid- or long-term. This refers primarily to managers but also to specifically designated human resources (HR) departments.

The requirements of project-oriented HR management can be summarized as follows:

What are the aims?

- Employees must be motivated *for* projects
- Employees must be motivated *in* projects
- Employees must be trained to use project management tools correctly, using these tools must become a natural way of dealing with day-to-day tasks
- Employees must be trained to deal with their social environment in order to enhance the efficiency of their assignments in temporary, inter-disciplinary and inter-cultural work groups.

10.1 MOTIVATING EMPLOYEES FOR PROJECTS

In a quarry, all the workers were doing the same work. However, an observer noticed different expressions on their faces. So he asked the workers to tell him what they were doing. The sorrowful worker said: 'I'm breaking up stones.' The satisfied worker replied: 'I'm earning my living.' The joyful worker answered: 'I'm building a cathedral.'[2]

Why motivate for projects?

It is a significant goal for project-oriented companies to arrange project activities and integrate them into the company in such a way so that **qualified** employees **spontaneously** prefer to take part in a project rather than to perform line functions. After all, one source of success in a project is employees who are competent and motivated at the same time.[3]

- For suitable employees, the work in a project must on the whole be more attractive than routine tasks in line departments.

Figure 10.2   Extrinsic and intrinsic motivation through project work

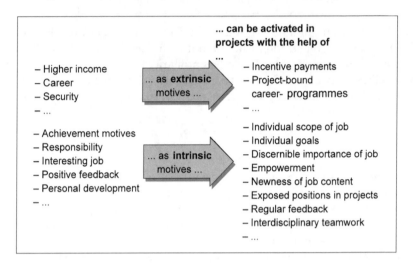

> *How is motivation for projects achieved?*

In order to motivate employees for projects, their individual motives must be appropriately addressed. Here motivation theories teach us that people differ greatly in their motivations (see Motivation theories, p. 256). Some employees may be motivated by the prospect of financial bonuses (**extrinsic motivation**). Others may find a task attractive in itself due to the responsibility it involves or the interesting nature of its contents (**intrinsic motivation**). It is not easy to say which type of employee would be *better suited* for a particular project. The only important thing is to individually motivate competent employees to work in the project.

Project motivation can be achieved by applying a balanced mix of elements, which can appeal to both intrinsic and extrinsic motives. Figure 10.2 shows that project assignments in particular offer a wide range of options in this regard.

> *How are suitable project leaders motivated?*

The management of a project is a very challenging task, which can have a great appeal to intrinsically motivated persons. A project leader is given considerable responsibility in being assigned a project. His work is demanding and varied, it requires not only technical expertise but also above all social skills. At the same time, a project leader who agrees to take on a project finds himself in an exposed position in the company. The success or failure of the project will be critically observed by a series of stakeholder groups. In addition, the successful result of a project will not only affect his remuneration but also the further course of his career. Depending on the importance of the project, the willingness to lead it is thus associated with both career opportunities and risks. Such tasks tend to be taken on by people who not only have the required skills and feel they can deal with such a challenge, but are also prepared to take calculated risks. All these are the qualities of a good project leader.

> *What elements are involved?*

To make sure that suitable employees are motivated to take on the job of a project leader, the following elements must therefore be considered:

- To allow a successful and personally motivating position of project leader to exist at all, suitable **project-oriented structures** must initially be created. After all, it is not a very attractive option to take on a project under unsuitable framework conditions. This book has already pointed out the extensive demands which are made on project-oriented structures.
- The project work must offer the project leader attractive **career prospects**. The individual career goals of the selected employee must be considered with respect to their technical or managerial aspects.
- A project leader is an *entrepreneur within an enterprise*. To attract employees with an entrepreneurial mind-set to this position, **variable remuneration components** must be linked to the success of the project. Examples of these are financial and assets bonuses, opportunities for promotion, additional vacation etc.
- To ensure effective motivation, the variable components must be communicated to the project leader in a **comprehensible** way. He or she must be able to estimate the **risk** associated with the project for him/her.
- In order to stress both the exposed position of a project leader and the attractions of this job in a project-oriented company, the **project must be marketed** to highlight its meaning and significance for the company.

> *How are employees motivated for projects?*

A combination of intrinsic and extrinsic incentives should be applied in order to motivate employees to participate in project teams. **Individual target agreements** can be drawn up to make clear to potential project employees the importance of the project and the tasks they have to perform there. The introductory quote on p. 253 illustrates why it is important to be aware of the objectives of one's work. This has also been confirmed by process theories dealing with motivational research (see Motivation theories, below). **Performance-related bonuses** as well as the prospect of progress along a **technical or managerial career track** are tools for extrinsic motivation of employees.

> *Which personnel management tools can help?*

A project-oriented personnel management policy must ensure that suitable tools are made available for motivating the employees. Some of the main ones are:

- **Flexible systems of remuneration** comprising individually agreed performance-related components in addition to fixed ones.
- **Career paths** whose route in both its technical and managerial branches goes via successful participation in projects.
- Requisite action to create a **project-oriented entrepreneurial culture** in which project activities are regarded as tasks which are eminently worth pursuing (cf. Part IV on this point).

Case study 10.1　Motivation theories

The need to find out more about the causes and possible ways of influencing motivation at work has led to the development of a series of diverse motivation theories. These may be subdivided into two groups:

- *Contents theories* examine the factors which motivate people to work: i.e. *what* motivates employees?
- *Process theories* try to explain *how* the conduct of employees can be influenced in terms of orientation and intensity.

HERZBERG'S TWO-FACTOR THEORY (FIGURE 10.3)

Herzberg's two-factor theory is the best known *contents theory* for employee motivation. It makes the following distinctions:

- *Extrinsic hygiene factors*: These aim at extrinsic motives, which are not satisfied by carrying out the work itself, but by its consequences or accompanying circumstances. Some examples of such extrinsic hygiene factors are:

  (a) Remuneration inclusive of social security benefits
  (b) Job security
  (c) Relationships to colleagues and superiors
  (d) Company policy
  (e) External conditions of work.

- *Intrinsic motivators*: These stimulate intrinsic motives which are satisfied by the work itself. Some examples of intrinsic motivators are:

  (a) Interesting and demanding work
  (b) Possibility of assuming responsibility
  (c) Possibility of personal and professional development
  (d) Recognition on the basis of the work done.

Figure 10.3   Motivators and hygiene factors

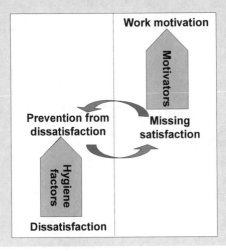

The core statement of the two-factor theory is that real job satisfaction comes only from *intrinsic motivators*. If such motivators are lacking, this may lead to a lack of job satisfaction but does not necessarily mean that the employees are actually *dis*satisfied.

*Dis*satisfaction at work is caused by a lack of extrinsic hygiene factors. These must therefore be present if dissatisfaction is to be avoided. Although hygiene factors can certainly avoid dissatisfaction, they are insufficient to achieve job satisfaction on their own.

For the practical tasks of managing employees, it follows from the two-factor theory that more value must be placed on intrinsic motives, as this is a promising way of enhancing the satisfaction and motivation of the employees. In addition to financial incentives, it is important to create demanding and responsible positions, which offer the employees opportunities for their personal and professional development.

EXPECTANCY THEORIES

Expectancy theories such as those of Vroom or Lawler and Porter are process theories, which explain why employees choose to act in a particular way at work. The basic relationship is expressed by the equation in Figure 10.4:

Figure 10.4　Expectancy theories

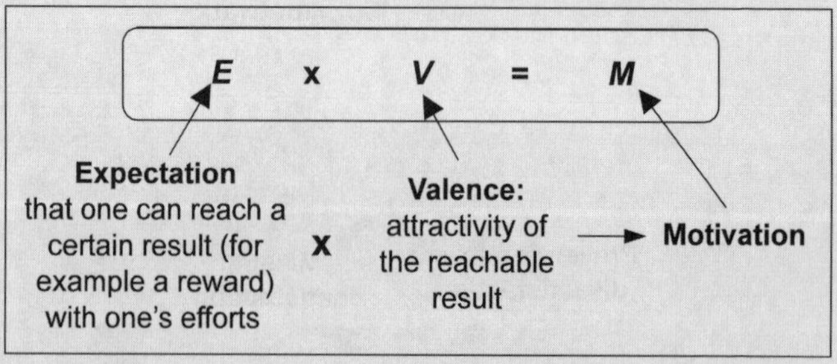

An employee's work motivation is consequently affected by three components:

- The subjective expectation that particular conduct can lead to the achievement of a specific result

- the probability that this result will lead to a desired personal goal, as well as
- the significance of this goal for the individual employee.

This yields a number of interesting aspects, which may be applied to the practice of personnel management:

- Training courses should be 'hands-on' as far as possible. This strengthens the employee's confidence in being able to achieve good performance by means of his own efforts.
- The performance targets should be demanding but reachable. Negative effects will result if the objectives are unclear or are frequently changed.
- Remuneration rules, bonus schemes, etc. must be simple and easy to follow. Otherwise employees will not be clear about the positive consequences of their efforts.
- Rewards must be coupled to performance factors, which the employee can actually influence! Otherwise they will not have a motivating effect.
- Finally, rewards should be individually selected because they are also evaluated on an individual basis. For example, some employees may find financial bonuses less interesting than more leisure time.

However, it becomes particularly clear that more is required to motivate employees than granting them bonuses. The entire configuration of the tasks involved must have an overall motivational effect.

10.2 MOTIVATING EMPLOYEES IN PROJECTS

The ability to motivate employees in projects is one of the most important social skills needed by a project leader. He must try to address the intrinsic and extrinsic motives of the members of his team by a suitable combination of the measures summarized in Figure 10.2. These include the following tools from the arsenal of personnel management:

> *What motivation tools are available?*

- The project leader must be able to impart a **vision** to his team members, which makes clear the long-term significance of their work.
- **Targets** should be agreed individually with the team members. The project leader must assess their primary motivation and match the targets to their capability level.
- The most motivating targets are those which, though attainable, are a little above the **aspiration level** of the employees. Targets, which are too easy to reach are just as demotivating as unattainable ones.[4]
- Once set, targets should not be subsequently **changed**, as this can be demotivating to the employees. The project leader must protect his teams from external changes in the objectives.
- **Variable remuneration components** can be linked to the attainment of the targets. They must also be matched to the individual motives of the employees.[5] Employees with a strong intrinsic motivation can even be demotivated by the granting of financial bonuses.[6]
- **Personal feedback** should give the employee information about the quality of his work. Both praise and constructive criticism are important here.
- **Delegation of responsibility** activates the intrinsic motives of employees. This is particularly important in the event of project crises. A project leader must be able to delegate decisions for solving problems to his team members in a judicious way. After all, they are largely in possession of the specialist know-how needed to solve any problems, which may arise.

> *Why are social skills so important?*

It is clear that close personal contact between the project leader and the members of his project team is needed to motivate employees. Social skills – i.e. the ability to reach targets in cooperation with others – are a critical success factor for project leaders.

10.3 PROMOTING PROJECT-RELEVANT SKILLS

A person's **competence** is always measured by how he or she can deal with a current situation with the aid of his/her skills and capabilities.[7]

Work in projects confronts employees with situations characterized by the following features:

> *What characterizes project tasks?*

- The **novel nature** of the task environment – i.e. **interdisciplinary cooperation** in technical teams formed specifically to implement a particular customer request.
- Increasing **international** and **intercultural** cooperation,
- **Uncertainty** and relatively **loose structuring** of the assignments.
- The long-term **strategic importance** of the tasks, such as in research and development or in the key-customer sector.

> *What skills must project team members have?*

In order to deal with such situations, the members of a project team must clearly possess technical skills in all the disciplines in which the company intends to be competitive. In project-oriented companies, however, these must be supplemented by competence in using the comprehensive set of project management tools described in the preceding chapters.

In addition to **technical skills, social skills** are of fundamental importance to the employees of project-oriented companies. They allow employees to attain their targets in situations characterized by social interaction.[8] They also enhance the efficiency of productive teamwork by helping employees to utilize their abilities optimally in teams or to handle delicate negotiations with others. A project-oriented personnel management policy must ensure that appointments are made on the basis of integrated technical and social skills.

> *What skills must a project leader have?*

Project leaders are *entrepreneurs within the enterprise*. They are key figures in a project-oriented company. Their brief is to plan and organize the project activities so that the project targets are reached. Technical know-how alone is insufficient for this purpose. Project leaders must be **generalists** with a number of diverse skills. Figure 10.5 illustrates that **social skills** play a particularly important role in

Figure 10.5   The project manager as a generalist

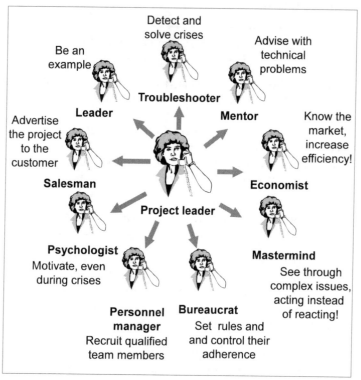

their work. A successful project leader must be able to realize the objectives entrusted to him in cooperation with employees from diverse technical sectors as well as customers, line managers, suppliers and other stakeholders.

Personnel management provides tools for developing such core skills.

> *What tools are suitable for personnel management?*

- When **selecting staff**, emphasis must be placed on social skills in addition to technical expertise.
- A consistent policy of **personnel development** must focus on promoting social skills and training relevant expertise in addition to a knowledge of the project management tools. Training courses,

including those for project leaders, must lay particular emphasis on presentation techniques, spoken manner, management style, motivation techniques, crisis management, negotiating skills etc. Personnel development measures must be set up over the long term in line with the core skills needed in the future for implementing customer-oriented projects in order to support strategic resource management for projects.

- Official participation in **project leader pools** promotes exchanges of views and know-how between project leaders and thus encourages personal and organizational learning.
- **Mentor programmes** prepare budding project leaders in current projects and designate experienced project leaders to act as mentors who familiarize young candidates with their future activities.
- **Career paths** run from simple participation in projects via leadership of subprojects up to responsibility for strategically vital key projects.

NOTES

1   Cf. Küpper (1997), p. 105. The personnel management *system* encompasses not only the tools and processes of employee guidance in conceptual form, but also all guiding and guided employees and managers.
2   Grosse-Oetringhaus (1993), p. 283.
3   A highly recommendable source (in German) on topics relating to motivation of employees for and in projects is Hartmann (1998). It includes a discussion as to how the motive structure, expectations and attitudes of employees affect their motivation as well as specific consequences for the coordination of inter-disciplinary projects.
4   This became clear from a series of scientific studies, such as on the topic of behavioral accounting. Examples are Stedry and Kay (1966). A good overview of this topic is given in Schweitzer and Küpper (1998), pp. 550 ff.
5   Thus Hartmann (1998), pp. 167–71, shows that different types of researchers show differing preferences for various incentive variables.
6   Just think of a private situation in which a good friend shows his appreciation for a particularly enjoyable city tour with you in cash. One should also be aware of the danger that intrinsic motivation can in the long term be displaced by extrinsic rewards. This can be the case if a mentality develops in which services are rendered only in return for extra payment. More details on the relationships between extrinsic and intrinsic motivation may be found in Frey and Osterloh (1997).
7   An exact definition of competence, and particularly social competence, may be found in Böhnisch and Nöbauer (1995), esp. pp. 1945 ff., as well as in König (1992), esp. p. 2046 ff.
8   Cf. Grosse-Oetringhaus (1993), p. 276. He goes into great detail into the strategic significance of social skills for companies.

11 A project-oriented information system

What must the information system (IS) achieve?

A significant part of management work involves the transfer and processing of information. The availability of relevant information is of fundamental importance for planning and monitoring tasks, for personnel management as well as for controlling and organizing functions within a company.

How important is the IS?

In view of this importance of information, the **information system** (IS) represents the basic element of a corporate management system. In corporate practice, the function of the information system is frequently established in the company in the form of an **information management policy**. It encompasses all persons and resources who deal with the

Figure 11.1   Information systems in a project-oriented company

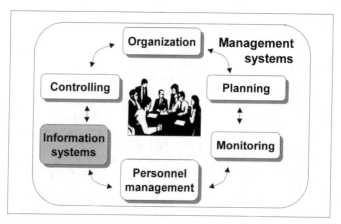

acquisition, storage, processing and transfer of information.[1] Explicit highlighting of the information system as the basic instrument of project-oriented corporate management places emphasis on the target-oriented and integrated configuration of all information tools such as computer programmes, management information systems, etc. The development of the information system represents a management task whose neglect jeopardizes successful project orientation (Figure 11.1).

11.1 REQUIREMENTS OF A PROJECT-ORIENTED INFORMATION SYSTEM

> *What demands must be made on the IS?*

Information is *knowledge oriented to a specific purpose* – i.e. data that the recipient can use to perform his tasks. To make such knowledge available, the information system of a project-oriented company must perform the following functions:

- It must support the implementation *of* individual projects by providing suitable information, and at the same time must
- Supply information for a company-wide management *with* projects.

> *Which information recipients are relevant?*

The information system receives information from the projects and the processes running in them and distributes it to the relevant recipients. As Figure 11.2 shows, the management levels in the project as well as at corporate level are the principal information recipients in project-oriented companies.

> *What characterizes a project-oriented IS?*

The information system of project-oriented companies will therefore differ from that of a conventional company in the following ways:

- It must satisfy the requirements of various projects and diverse information recipients in a **flexible** way.[2]
- But it also needs standardized structures and consistent data storage in order to ensure comparability between the projects.

Figure 11.2 Support function of the information system in a project-oriented
company

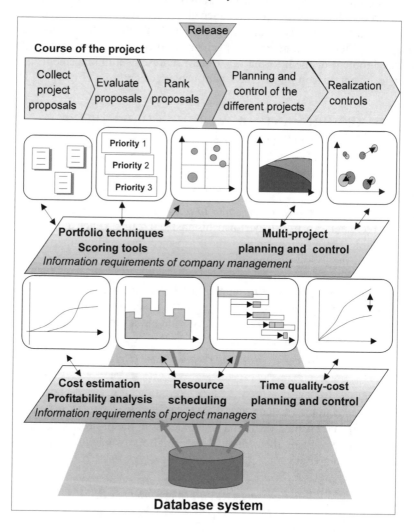

Figure 11.2 shows that a whole series of very diverse types of information is required in the course of the development of a project. Leaders of individual projects require much more detailed information than members of the corporate management. The latter in turn need a total overview of the relationships and statuses of the individual projects as well as of those activities without reference to projects.

11.2 CREATING A PROJECT-ORIENTED INFORMATION SYSTEM

> *Which structure is recommended?*

For the effective support of corporate management policies oriented to projects, an information system with a specific structure is recommended. In particular, it must allow the data recorded within individual projects to be aggregated so that the information requirement of both project leaders and corporate managers is satisfied. Integrated client-server systems with consistent data storage are well suited to this purpose.

Let us consider the example of planning and monitoring costs: in project-oriented companies, estimation of the costs incurred in the various cost centres is important for purposes of planning, controlling, monitoring and documentation. **Cost accounting** represents a basic information tool for this purpose. At the same time, however, it must be possible to determine the costs at project level incurred for the various projects and the work packages contained in them during a particular accounting period.[3] A **project cost calculation** must cover this information requirement.

> *Are suitable software tools already available?*

Whereas many highly sophisticated software tools are now available for supporting project management functions, there are hardly any comprehensive tools designed for the systematic support of management *with* projects. Companies are thus forced to create their own solutions. Let us take a look at an innovative software tool, which is optimally suited to fill this gap.

Table 11.1 summarizes some parts of a project-oriented information system which have already been described.

Table 11.1   Elements of a project-oriented information system

Recipient Function to be supported	Project management (e.g. project leaders, team leaders)	Corporate management (e.g. board members, division heads)
Planning	– PM standard software (e.g. TimeLine, MS Project, Primavera, CA Super Project) – Resource information systems (RAPS) – Project cost calculation	– Systems for collecting product ideas and project suggestions, – Portfolio methods,- Ranking/ scoring tools, – Tools for estimating expenditures (COCOMO, Price, etc.) – Profitability analysis and investment planning methods
Monitoring	– Project reports, – Resource information systems – Time recording systems – Earned value analysis (e.g. Primavera, TimeLine) – Project cost calculation	– Portfolio methods, – Reporting systems extending beyond individual projects – Resource information systems – Time recording systems – Cost calculation – Financial calculation
Organization	– PM standard software – Resource information systems	– Resource information systems
Personnel management	– Resource information systems	– Resource information systems – Portfolio methods for strategic resource management
Controlling	– Use of all tools listed above – Also participation in their design	– Use of all tools listed above – Also participation in their design

---

Case study 11.1   TopInfo

TopInfo is an integrated information system for supporting management tasks in project-oriented companies. Its scope of performance comprises a broad range of functions, some of which are listed below:

- Comprehensive support of the definition cycle (see Use of TopInfo in the definition process, p. 17).
- Standardized reporting procedures relating to all projects and products of a company and its divisions inclusive of their particular history (e.g. MTA).
- Integration of project reporting procedures for business data/key figures (expenditures, costs, quality), e.g. via interfaces to SAP systems.
- Standardized schedule administration of the projects.
- Active notification of those involved in the project or interested in the product in the event of situations such as schedule deviations or product announcements.
- Consistent document management.
- A finely meshed authorization concept – i.e. access authorizations can be defined individually for each view level and information sector. Authorizations are assigned by the teams responsible for the relevant view level.

Thanks to these functions, the managers of a project-oriented company can:

- Obtain a rapid overview of the current product and project portfolio because the programme reveals interrelationships between current and planned projects and products.
- Find out the current status of products as well as both current and planned projects at any time.
- Establish a standardized escalation process (traffic-light reports).
- Have flexible access to various levels of aggregation (country, regional, organizational units, product and project views).

The data used by TopInfo is acquired in a distributed and team-oriented way. Its three-layer architecture provides the basis for supporting the project orientation even of companies with an international presence. This is because access to this system is via www browsers (e.g. in the Intranet), which limits local installation and maintenance expenditures and ensures simple system extendibility.

NOTES

1 Küpper (1997), p. 105, offers a comprehensive discussion on the importance of the information system for corporate management.
2 This is also described by authors such as Turner and Speiser (1992).
3 Guserl (1997), p. 6 f., describes the structure of such a system.

12 Project-oriented controlling

The management functions of a company are too diverse and comprehensive to be tied completely to a single person or department. They are consequently assigned to various agents within the company such as organization and IT departments, the personnel department or marketing and strategy departments. This distribution results in an inevitable separation of these functions. And yet, successful corporate management requires integrated cooperation and coordination of all management functions. An example is the necessity of coordinating business strategies with strategic resource planning and appropriate human resources measures already described:

What is the core of controlling?

- Controlling is a set of tools, which supports the corporate management in coordinating the individual management functions with respect to each other in order to reach a specific goal (see Figure 12.1).[1]

In project-oriented companies, such a coordination requirement occurs at two different levels: in each individual project and across all projects. Project-oriented controlling thus covers the following functions:

What does project-oriented controlling do?

- Controlling supports the *company* executive in its management tasks. This is done with the aid of coordination functions within the

271

Figure 12.1   Controlling in a project-oriented company

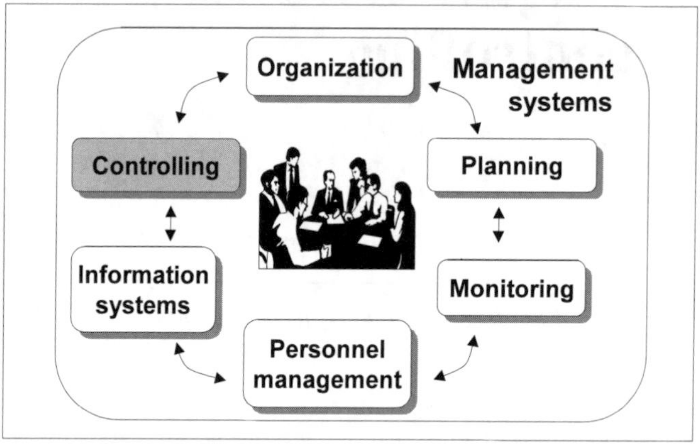

management system of a project-oriented company. The following are among the principal tasks of **multi-project controlling**:

(a) Coordination within the project portfolio – i.e. between projects
(b) Embedding individual projects within the higher-order corporate strategy, as well as
(c) Orientation of the management tools to support the project portfolio.

• **Project controlling** supports the *project* management in the coordinated management of a single project.

> *Who performs controlling?*

The management *function* of controlling must not be equated with the *person* who acts as the controller. After all, there is no single information manager who performs all information management tasks or a single project planner who carries out planning activities. In the same way, there need not be a project or multi-project controller to perform these controlling functions. In practice, however, project-oriented companies have found that it makes sense to establish a *know-how pool* for project managers. It is therefore a good idea to assign some of the controlling tasks described below to specially created project-controlling agencies.

12.1 PROJECT CONTROLLING

> *Who performs project controlling?*

The controlling of individual projects provides important support for project management. The relevant tasks are performed either by an agency specifically designated for the project controlling function or by the project leaders themselves. The coordination tasks in the management system of a project cover a number of principal activities. Some of these will now be examined.

An initial important task of project controlling is to coordinate and support **project planning** with the other management functions:

> *How does project controlling support planning?*

- By participating in the process of product and project structuring, project controlling ensures that the derived work packages can be realized within the existing organization and with the available resources. For example, it is involved in issuing and correctly merging the **structure plans** relating to the product, project and organization as described in Part I.
- Project controlling also contributes to ensuring that all persons required to make a sufficiently accurate estimate of the project expenditures are convened in an expert session.
- By including personnel management aspects in the planning process, it endeavours to ensure that the tasks assigned to the individual units are sufficiently **motivating**. Thus it supports project management in coordinating the tasks assigned to individual employees as well as the responsibilities associated with their skills. Resource information systems represent a useful aid for this purpose: they show not only when employees are available but also their primary expertise and their personal preferences as regards deployment to specific tasks.
- In complex projects, it ensures that the various subplans contribute to attaining the project targets. For example, it supports the derivation of low-level plans from high-level ones as well as their later aggregation.
- In addition, project controlling ensures that project planning satisfies the requirements of **higher-level process guidelines** or process specifications at all times.

- Project controlling continuously monitors whether the **value-added created** in the project corresponds to the initial targets. This is done by analyzing whether the original project aims still appear to be attainable. Examples are earned-value analyses and suitable software tools, which are used to check that the use of resources in the project is on schedule.

How are information, demand and supply coordinated?

Another task of project controlling is to coordinate the project-referred **information system** with the other management functions. This ensures that the project managers receive all the information relevant to plan and monitor a project at the level of aggregation required for the job in hand. This is done by coordinating the acquisition and analysis of deviation information with the planning of suitable countermeasures. This task also means that project controlling is significantly involved in shaping the reporting procedures within the project.

What role does project controlling play in the project organization?

In defining the **project organization**, project controlling ensures among other things that the defined competence levels of the individuals involved in the project correspond to their tasks and responsibilities. This is done by applying suitable systems to determine the capacities available for a project in both quantitative and qualitative terms. This qualitative determination of free capacities is not performed in order to assess individual employees, but to find out in which sectors they would prefer to be deployed. Social aspects must already be included in the early phases of a project in addition to technical ones. For example, the project leader will tend to select the members of his project team principally on the basis of technical criteria. However, if social aspects are ignored in the early phases of planning and organizing a project, conflicts can arise at a later stage. An example is the creation of a team in an international project. Here, it may be necessary to consider aspects of social class (caste) or tribal relationships in order to ensure that the project runs efficiently from the very outset.

> *How is personnel management supported?*

In **human resources** management, the project controlling agencies are involved in drafting target agreements in order to promote particularly critical project activities. In the same way, their presence is helpful in selecting project-referred bonus and incentives schemes.

Finally, the project controlling coordinates the **monitoring** process with the other management functions:

> *Does project controlling support monitoring?*

- By a suitable selection of control criteria and times it checks that all the information produced and delivered is relevant to the monitoring process.
- It ensures that personnel management aspects are not neglected in shaping the type and performance of checks within the framework of project control. This is because checks always have an effect on the motivation of the employees. Depending on the way they are organized, they can either block the course of the project or promote it. Project controlling must obviously aim to implement checks, which promote efficiency.

> *Which tools are used in project controlling?*

In order to perform these tasks, project controlling makes use of a series of **coordination tools**. These have already been explained within the framework of presenting project execution in Part II as well as in identifying the other management functions earlier in Part III. They are thus merely summarized in brief in Figure 12.2.

Project controlling on the one hand can deploy various management tools from the sectors of planning, monitoring and organization, as well as the information system and personnel management for coordinating a project. In addition to that it also has access to integrative controlling tools, which comprise components of several management functions:

What are integrative controlling tools?

- **Change management** was examined in Part II. This term involves monitoring changes as well as selecting and planning all incoming change requests and organizing the best ways of handling them.
- In complex projects, project controlling makes use of internal **target systems** to coordinate the activities of individual subprojects with a view to higher-level project targets. For example, the quality targets of the overall product are broken down into their subcomponents. In this process, it is the task of project controlling to match the weighting of individual targets to the importance of the schedule, quality and cost targets from the standpoint of the overall project. Cost targets may be of comparatively secondary importance in product-innovation projects whereas they may play a significant part in determining the realizable profit in customer-order projects.

Figure 12.2   Instruments for the coordination tasks of project controlling

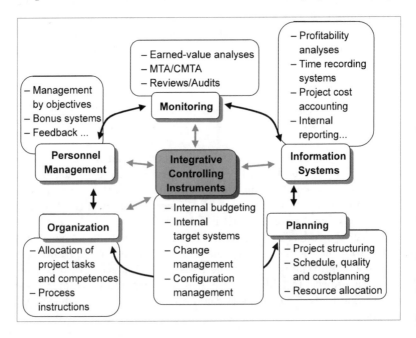

- Target systems also make **key figures** available which facilitate the process of tracking the progress of the project. Error rates in software development are one example of such figures.
- Among the tasks of project controlling is to divide up the **project budget**. Scarce financial resources must be allocated to individual activities according to their importance. Adherence to the subbudgets must be monitored in the course of the project.
- On the whole, therefore, project controlling plays a **significant part in supporting project management**. For complex projects in particular, including an explicit project controller in the project team in order to establish this function solidly in project practice is recommended.

12.2 MULTI-PROJECT CONTROLLING

> *What does multi-project controlling do?*

In contrast to individual project controlling, multi-project controlling is a trans-project management task and is therefore of strategic significance. It comprises the following subtasks:

- The portfolio of projects running in the company must be aligned to the corporate goals and thus to the corporate strategy.
- The corporate management system must be coordinated to ensure that the projects can work within framework conditions, which are optimally designed for target attainment.

> *What tools are used in multi-project controlling?*

Like project controlling, multi-project controlling has access to a series of coordination tools some of which are summarized in Figure 12.3. Of special importance are integrative controlling tools with an explicitly trans-project character:

- Multi-project controlling plays an important part in the distribution of **resources,** which are allocated to individual projects in a company. This task also involves defining the minimum information which must be present for the project release, as the resource allocation is also decided at this point.

Figure 12.3   Coordination instruments for multi-project controlling

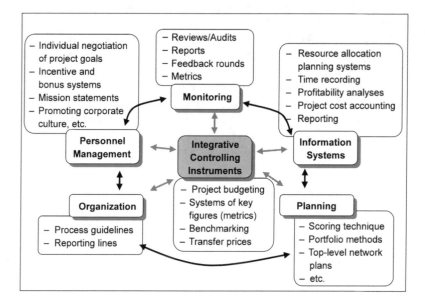

- Together with project budgeting, multi-project controlling affects the distribution of critical corporate resources among individual projects by setting **transfer prices**. These are internal prices that projects must pay for using resources. Examples are hourly cost rates or fees charged for the use of test laboratories or for the internal procurement of preliminary products. The higher the price of an internal good or service, the more sparingly will the projects make use of them.
- **Systems of key figures** make it easier for the corporate management to ascertain the current development of the project portfolio and to make control decisions on this basis. As an example, the following sections will look at **process metrics** designed to support the assessment of corporate structures.
- Key figures may also be specified as target parameters for individual projects. They are then derived from the higher-level corporate targets within a **target system** and specified as project targets. Examples are target rates of return in customer projects or target manufacturing costs in product-innovation projects.
- Finally, **benchmarking** offers an obvious way of comparing the interaction of the individual management functions of the company

with the procedures in use at particularly successful external partners. It allows improvement potentials to be identified and changes to be planned and implemented. However, benchmarking requires significant modifications in project-oriented companies, so a separate subsection has been devoted to this method (see Section 12.2.2).

Is project-oriented controlling worthwhile?

We have seen that controlling is a management function, which faces a series of new tasks in project-oriented companies. Because of its great importance for achieving the corporate goals, it makes good sense to establish the relevant tasks and tools in specific project-controlling agencies.

The benefit of project-oriented controlling cannot be directly quantified. Successes in the company or of individual projects cannot simply be traced back to the existence of a project controlling function. Any negative consequences because of a missing controlling function are usually more apparent than the benefits of applying it, as a lack of coordination between the management functions will show up in problems and inefficiencies. The establishment of multi-project controlling agencies must thus be carefully considered. This is no less than a strategic management decision.

Finally, two controlling tools with a broad scope of application will now be described more closely as they are highly promising for a project-oriented company: they are **metrics** and **benchmarking**.

12.2.1 Metrics as a tool for supporting continuous organizational learning

---

Why are metrics needed?

One of the tasks of controlling in project-oriented companies consists in encouraging continuous improvement of the company by suitably coordinating its management functions. Metrics and metric systems represent a set of tools specifically designed for this purpose:

- Above all, metrics aim to contribute to the **continuous improvement** of a project-oriented company. Improvement measures can be applied effectively only if initial data is available which can be used to assess the success of the implemented measures at a later point. For example, process restructuring makes sense only if its effect can be assessed on the basis of *before and after comparisons.*

- Metrics **prepare empirical values** in order to increase the quality of the estimates in the early phase of new projects, and in order to
- **Metrics support** individual **project leaders** in planning, monitoring and controlling their projects.

> *Are metrics easy to develop?*

In the section on project control in Part II it was mentioned that project measurement is no easy task. The uniqueness of projects also makes them hard to compare. For this reason, the development of suitable metrics represents an important but at the same time also a problematic task of controlling in project-oriented companies.

> *Which mistakes must be avoided?*

The mistake most commonly committed when developing a metrics system is an attempt to compare incommensurate quantities. Metrics must take into account the differences between projects in order not to produce unusable results. Thus a complex new development project can be as little compared with a simple redevelopment project as the construction of a power plant with that of a private detached house.

Another mistake often made when applying metrics is to limit measurements exclusively to processes. However, a faster completion of a product, which later turns out to be unsuccessful will hardly be of much use to the company.

To avoid these mistakes, an integrated and standardized metrics system must be established. It covers the following three sectors:[2]

> *How is an integrated metrics system characterized?*

- Dimensional parameters for the **characteristics** and **input parameters** of the projects
- Variables relating to the **processes** traversed by the projects, as well as
- Parameters for measuring the **outputs** of the projects.

Ways of determining project input and project characteristics

> *How are projects made comparable?*

The more diverse the projects which are performed in a company, the more important it is to make them comparable before making any measurements. Two factors may be used for this purpose, which also have a significant effect on the difficulties associated with a project. They not only influence the duration of the project, but also its costs and quality targets. They are:

- The **complexity** of the project, and
- The **novelty** or **uniqueness** of the project compared with previous projects in the same sector.

> *What is project complexity?*

Project complexity is a measure of:

- How comprehensive the project is altogether
- How many different performance features, components, technical peculiarities, product functions etc. must be implemented
- How many different persons, functional sectors, etc. work together on the project
- And how greatly these differ in each case: for instance, the inter-disciplinary cooperation of engineers, marketing specialists and technicians is more complex than cooperation between different development sectors.

> *How can complexity be measured?*

Although complexity is one of the most important criteria for comparing projects, it cannot be easily measured in an objective way. However, there are ways of obtaining a key figure for the complexity of a project. The procedure described here is based on a benefit value method. It has already been described in Section 3.1.3 in Part I, together with its advantages and drawbacks:

(1) Initially, criteria must be determined which contribute to the complexity of a project – e.g. the number of technical sectors involved, the number of product components to be manufactured, the level of technical difficulty, etc.

(2) A weighting factor is then applied to the selected criteria. For example, the difference of the specialist sectors involved may turn out to be more problematic for the project management than the number of product components to be manufactured. Experience from previous projects is thus helpful in defining the weighting factors.

(3) In addition, a maximum bandwidth is defined for each criterion. It can be used to classify individual projects. Example: number of employees in the project between 1 and 100 $\Rightarrow$ 100 employees in a project = 100 per cent.

(4) Each project can be simply classified in the criteria catalogue established in this way. For example, if some 50 employees were involved in a project (corresponding to 50 per cent with this criterion) and this criterion was weighted as 30 per cent, this means that the *number of employees* has contributed to the complexity to the tune of 15 per cent. A percentage value is obtained for each project by performing a summation over all the criteria. It reflects the complexity of the project as an approximation referred to individual target parameters. It runs along a scale from 0 to 100 per cent.

> *How is the novelty of a project measured?*

The **novelty** of a project is easier to estimate than its complexity. Here, the percentage change in the project compared with preceding projects may be used as a basis. In addition, a distinction may be made between the novelty of the product itself and of the processes to be traversed in order to manufacture it.

In product-innovation projects, the novelty may be a percentage change of the product compared with the preceding version (100 per cent = new development, < 10 per cent = adaptation development). In customer projects, in contrast, a useful approach may be to estimate the proportion of adaptation activities and individual modifications for each customer.

Measuring the processes traversed

What are the preconditions for process measurement?

Process metrics endeavour to measure and evaluate the processes which are traversed by the projects. To do this effectively, at least a rough formal process scheme must exist which may be used as a basis for assessing the various projects. The process guidelines mentioned in Section 4.2 offer an initial approach to develop such schemes, which must be supported by a corresponding configuration of the corporate structures. For example, employees must be assigned to specific sub-processes and it must be possible to allocate costs to processes.

What are examples of process metrics?

Comprehensive metrics can be based on established processes, which are applicable to all projects and are used to measure their scheduling, cost and quality efficiency. One of the most fundamental metrics is certainly the measurement and comparison of the duration of each individual phase. The same or similar comparisons may also be applied to the factors listed below:

What can be measured in this way?

- The distribution of project expenditures among the functional sectors or organizational units involved
- The distribution of the manpower deployment over the various subprocesses (cf. Figure 12.4)
- The defects/errors which were detected/open/eliminated in individual subprocesses (e.g. in software development)
- The proportion of products which passed specific test phases with no defects at the first attempt (known in hardware development as **First Pass Yield, FPY**)
- Percentage overruns of the schedule, cost or quality targets in individual subprocesses (possibly determined from the MTAs and CMTAs of preceding projects, etc.).

Figure 12.4   Evaluation of process metrics

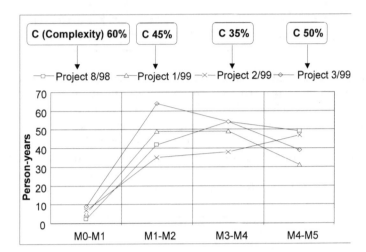

In Figure 12.4 the degree of complexity of the respective projects has been entered into the diagram as supplementary information. Evaluations may also be made on the basis of this criterion – for instance, to reveal the necessity of individual subprocesses for projects of different levels of complexity.

> *What is learned from process metrics?*

In order to support continuous improvement in a company, the results should be expressed in the form of a temporal sequence which goes beyond individual projects. It then becomes apparent whether specific subprocesses have been traversed more quickly or more slowly over a period of years, or how process quality has developed. This can in turn be a source of ideas for corporate improvement.

> *How do metrics support individual projects?*

Process metrics offer the managers of individual projects a basis for their planning and controlling tasks. Thus previous projects supply a wealth of empirical information as to how long individual subprocesses might take relative to each other (cf. Figure 12.5).

Figure 12.5   Evaluating past projects (example)

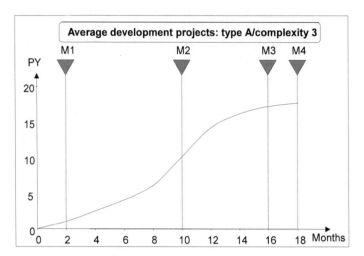

Measuring project output

Why must the output be measured?

A significant part of the metrics to be applied in practical project management relates to information about the processes traversed. To allow the information derived from these to be correctly evaluated, it is important to compare not only the inputs, but in particular the outputs of the project. A metric system must therefore try to determine systematically whether the product manufactured in the project has satisfied the set targets.

Among the most important output targets of a customer-oriented company are:

Which outputs are relevant?

- The satisfaction of the **customer requirements**.
- The **profitability** of the product.

Within the framework of a stakeholder orientation, the estimates made not only by the employees, but also by external suppliers and partners must be included. Concluding reports and manoeuvre critiques are two examples of tools suitable for this purpose. They have already been presented in Part II (Section 6.4).

Although the profitability and customer-satisfaction targets are not independent of each other, they can be measured in different ways.

> *How is customer satisfaction measured?*

For example, the **customer satisfaction with the progress of the project** can be determined in the customer-order sector by including the customer in systematic project conclusion rounds (feedback rounds, manoeuvre critiques). In addition, relevant surveys should also be carried out some time after the end of the project (e.g. last milestone + 1 year). They provide a good way of **assessing the customer's satisfaction with the manufactured product**.

> *How is project profitability measured?*

It is relatively straightforward to evaluate the **profitability** of the project output in customer-order business, as all the necessary data is available as soon as the project has been concluded. The profits obtained as well as any cost deviations can be determined directly within the scope of a subsequent project calculation. It is more difficult to assess profitability in product-innovation projects. It is no easy task to allocate concrete successes to an individual project, particularly in the case of adaptation developments. In most cases, the success of the project can only be quantified after several years – e.g. by re-running the economic product planning (EPP) routines at the end of the set planning horizon, but this time with the actual figures.

> *What is the use of a metrics system?*

- An integrated metrics system, which takes into account the factors described above supplies important basic information for continuously checking developments in a project-oriented company.

Additional details on the current status of one's own company can be obtained by making a comparison with similar companies, which are particularly successful.

12.2.2 Continuous learning via benchmarking in project-oriented companies

> *What is benchmarking?*

Metrics are (in addition to the realization, premise and progress checks dealt with in Chapter 3) a first step to assessing whether the management of the company and its individual projects has in fact been successful. They form a basis for organizational learning, whose encouragement represents an important controlling task. They can be significantly enriched by including other corporate sectors or companies in the comparison. The comparison of products, processes and structures of a company over several sectors has been practiced for many years under the designation of **benchmarking**.[3]

> *Does benchmarking in the project sector present problems?*

Despite the great successes which benchmarking has already shown in corporate learning, this concept has hitherto scarcely been extended to a comparison of project management practices. This is due primarily to the following problems:

- Projects are very diverse even within a single company. It is consequently not easy to compare them systematically.
- It is no simple matter to link the success of a project to unequivocal success criteria. Therefore it is difficult to compare the success of various projects.
- The relationship between the management and the success of a project is not always clear-cut. Good project management will not always lead to successful projects, and projects can run successfully despite careless management. It is thus risky to immediately assume that successful projects necessarily imply good management.

> *Is benchmarking nevertheless useful?*

Despite these problems, it is nevertheless very helpful for project-oriented companies to compare themselves with internal or external benchmarking partners. A somewhat modified and pragmatic benchmarking procedure was developed for this purpose and will now be presented.

Figure 12.6   The benchmarking-process

> *What steps does benchmarking comprise?*

A **benchmarking process** comprises the five subprocesses shown in Figure 12.6.[4] In order to be effective, it should be established permanently in the company. This also means that responsibility for benchmarking must be assigned in the organization and the top management must be involved in the process. An example of how it can be applied to a project-oriented company will now be described:

Defining a benchmarking object

> *What is defined?*

In defining the benchmarking process, the following must be established:

- Who is the customer of the benchmarking process?
- What goals are pursued by the benchmarking?
- What is to be benchmarked (products, processes, subprocesses . . .)?
- What is the necessary effort in terms of time and money?
- Who is to finance the benchmarking process?
- What resources will be required for benchmarking?

> ### What is a realistic object of examination?

In project-oriented companies the process organization – i.e. the project-related business procedures within the company – forms a central object for benchmarking. The chosen object of investigation should initially be delimited as clearly as possible. This involves not only restricting the type of projects to be examined (product innovation projects, customer order projects) but also setting the degree of detail to be considered. The greater the degree of detail with which a project management process is analyzed, the more difficult will it be to compare different projects and companies. As a starting point therefore, a relatively abstract view of project management as was described in Parts I and II should suffice.

In order to limit the extent of the benchmarking, it may also make sense to restrict it to a particularly critical part of the overall process, such as project selection or project completion.

Forming benchmarking teams

> ### Who is to participate?

The decision as to who is to be involved in benchmarking should be made on an individual basis. Here too, a good idea is to aim for an interdisciplinary team, especially as the object of examination tends to have an equally interdisciplinary character. This also ensures openness *vis-à-vis* all types of potentials for improvement.

> ### Which members are helpful to its success?

It can be helpful to include persons external to the company (consultants, university institutes) in the team. This avoids the effect of *corporate blindness* which can otherwise lead to new suggestions being rejected prematurely as inapplicable to one's own company.

In addition, it is recommended to acquire a patron at top management level. Such people can act as powerful promotors who can facilitate both the implementation of benchmarking and the later performance of any changes.

> *How is a fair exchange of information ensured?*

Finally, an important part is played by a **clearing agency**. Especially if external companies are to be acquired as comparison partners, a neutral agency must be set up to ensure a fair exchange of information. All partners involved can then benefit from the results obtained, and no company can one-sidedly exploit the information of the other partners. The existence of a clearing agency is a confidence-building measure which facilitates the recruitment of benchmarking partners. Cooperation with university institutes has proved to be of benefit in this field.

12.3   SELECTING BENCHMARKING PARTNERS

> *Which partners are of interest?*

The quality of the results of benchmarking depends decisively on the selection of the companies selected as benchmarking partners. The better the partners, the greater the likelihood of deriving promising improvements from it. However, if the quality difference is too great, potential benchmarking partners may be scared off because they could derive only limited benefit from such participation.

Depending on the selected partners, a distinction is made between various approaches to benchmarking as listed in Table 12.1.[5]

> *How are benchmarking partners selected in a pragmatic way?*

Generic benchmarking offers a particularly promising approach: in order to identify suitable comparable companies, the benchmarking object should initially be examined for factors, which affect it particularly strongly in one's own company. Sectors are then identified in which these factors are even more strongly marked than in the own one. Companies, which are particularly successful in these sectors are then contacted as potential benchmarking partners. Table 12.2 shows an example of how a company in the telecommunications sector has sought partners for generic benchmarking of product-innovation projects.

Table 12.1   Types of benchmarking

	Benchmarking partner	Advantages	Disadvantages
Internal benchmarking	Internal divisions with similar activities	Data easily available	Often limited viewpoint
Competitive benchmarking	Competitors in same sector	Good comparability, good knowledge of partners	Difficult data acquisition
Generic benchmarking	Companies from other sectors	New angle, innovative results	Time-consuming, some results not transferable

Table 12.2   Criteria for selecting suitable comparison partners

Critical variables for product innovation projects in the own company	**Sectors**, in which those factors are particularly strongly marked	Particularly successful and innovative **companies** in this sectors
Technology push	Semiconductors	(…)
International competition	Automobile	(…)
Technical complexity of products	Aerospace	(…)
(…)	(…)	(…)

12.3.1   Collecting and analyzing information

Why are analyses of the status quo problematic?

In order to compare the techniques and procedures used by different companies, an **analysis of the status quo** must initially be carried out. This raises particular problems in the project sector because many companies tend to be rather careless with their project and process documentation and evaluation. Benchmarking can offer a welcome opportunity to eliminate such defects.

> *Are quantitative comparisons mandatory?*

Because of the difficulty of standardizing and comparing projects, suitable comparative criteria of a quantitative kind usually cannot be found. The common elements and above all the differences between the benchmarking partners must therefore be analyzed at a qualitative level. Meetings to discuss the positive and negative experience gained with relevant subproblems offer the greatest promise of success.

> *Why is a clearing agency important?*

In this subprocess of benchmarking, the participation of a neutral clearing agency is of considerable advantage. It coordinates the collection and analysis of information in the companies involved and, as an outside observer, helps to reveal particularly interesting differences between companies. A trust relationship can consequently develop between the benchmarking partners which may become the first step to a longer-term exchange of information and know-how.

12.3.2 Deriving appropriate measures

> *What output should be aimed for?*

The aim of benchmarking is naturally to implement some of the potentials for improvement recognized in one's own company. These may be minor adjustments capable of immediate realization. More extensive measures constitute separate **project proposals**, for example with respect to internal reorganization projects. They must flow into a definition cycle as was described in Part I.

> *What is the conclusion of Part III?*

It was shown in Part III that the endeavour to apply a project orientation in order to become a customer-oriented company makes major demands on the corporate management. In order to establish project management as a viable concept, adjustments must be made in almost all sectors of corporate management, the mere implementation of a series of projects is not sufficient to transform a conventional company into a project-oriented one. The management *of* and *with* projects must be supported by the management system of the company in an optimal way.

Why is corporate culture a significant factor?

In addition to developing suitable methods of project-oriented corporate management, another factor is important for their success: corporate culture! This is, however, significantly more difficult to influence. Ultimately, all employees apply all the tools described so far so that they may perform their tasks effectively. But if the values and attitudes of the employees are opposed to working with and in projects, even the most sophisticated tools cannot lead to success. An effective project orientation of the company must therefore be based on a **project-oriented corporate culture**. What this means and how efforts can be made to promote such a culture will be the object of Part IV of this book.

NOTES

1   A comprehensive description of controlling as a separate discipline within business management may be found in Küpper, Weber and Zünd (1990) as well as in Küpper (1997).
2   Cf. also Griffin (1993), p. 115.
3   Cf. also Leibfried and McNair (1993), p. 48, for example.
4   For details of this benchmarking process, see Spendolini (1992).
5   Cf. Spendolini (1992), p. 17.

Part IV Project-Oriented Corporate Culture

> *Why is corporate culture so important?*

Parts I and II have shown in detail which processes must run in project-oriented companies in order to support management of and with projects. Part III showed which structures help a company to effectively implement a project orientation. As in other management concepts, the success of management with projects does not, however, depend merely on establishing relevant structures in the company. Project management must become second nature to its employees if it is to be successful in the long term. It must be solidly anchored in the company culture. Corporate culture thus forms the very basis of the project management concept (cf. Figure IV.1).

Case study IV.1 *The concept of corporate culture*[1]

The concept of corporate culture represents an attempt to transfer a phenomenon familiar in social life to the corporate situation. A company is a place in which employees spend a large part of their time. It thus forms something like a *society in miniature* in which a specific culture, known as the **corporate culture**, can emerge. This affects the actions of the people who live and work within it. In a similar way longer projects may also be distinguished by a specific **project culture**.

A culture in general and a corporate culture in particular are a complex phenomenon. It is made up of components from three different levels (Figure IV.1).

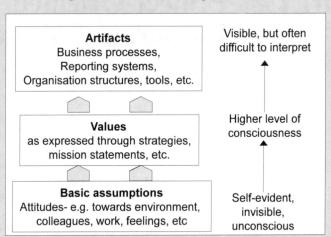

Figure IV.1   Levels of a corporate culture

The externally visible level of a culture is represented by its *artifacts*. These include anything which can be seen, heard or felt, and which distinguishes one cultural group from another. Examples would be a style of architecture, a language, technology, etc. Artifacts are apparent from the outside. However, it is not easy to infer the deeper levels of the culture from them. Although they form part of the corporate culture, the core of the culture is to be sought at two other levels.

Artifacts are based on a deeper-lying level of the *declared values* of the members of a culture. Values determine what is regarded as desirable, as correct or as false. It is not only individuals who possess values; groups can also develop common values. The values of a group may be declared by the formulation of strategies, philosophies and mission statements. This presupposes that the values reach the awareness of the members of the culture.

The declared values and artifacts of a culture are based on the *underlying assumptions* of its members. These include views, attitudes, perceptions, feelings, etc. which remain below the threshold of consciousness. Such basic assumptions can also be found in single individuals as well as in groups. They are taken for granted and are not further questioned. In a western company, for example, it would be inconceivable to introduce corporal punishment for mistakes. This would contradict the fundamental attitudes of our society, which also hold sway in corporate cultures.

This multi-layer consideration of (corporate) culture makes clear the great importance of basic unconscious assumptions for the values of a society, and thus its role in the acceptance of structures, processes, tools, etc. Any attempts to influence a corporate culture by introducing processes, strategies or mission statements which do not resonate with the basic values of its members is bound to fail. The only viable approach is to gradually influence the basic assumptions and unconscious values of the employees (Figure IV.2). However, this is a lengthy process.

NOTE

1   This summary of the discussion on corporate culture in the established literature as well as the further descriptions in this main part have their origin in Schein (1995), pp. 29 ff., as well as Rosenstiel (1992), pp. 353 ff. These publications also contain references to further sources on this topic.

Figure IV.2 Corporate culture as the basis of project management

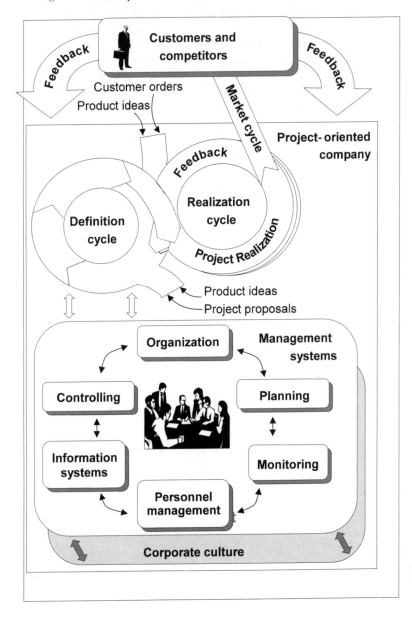

13 Project-oriented corporate culture as a basis for project management

Why are the employees so important?

Project management depends to a particularly high degree on the employees of the company. Their contribution is vital to the success of projects and therefore also to the overall success of a project-oriented company. This includes not only the members of the project teams, but also all the other employees in the company: each of them can affect the success of the projects in a positive way.

How are structure and culture related?

A conventional company can be transformed into a project-oriented one and continue this orientation successfully in the long term only when the project focus is firmly anchored in the corporate culture. Changes in corporate structures must be in tune with the fundamental values and assumptions of the employees:

- In project-oriented companies, a fit must be established between the project-oriented structures and the corporate culture (cf. Figure 13.1).

How is a company given a project orientation?

The endeavour to transform a company into a customer-oriented enterprise by introducing project-oriented management concepts must combine both aspects addressed in Figure 13.1. Project-oriented structures must be established in a stepwise and integrated way. Side-by-side with this, constant efforts must be made to encourage a project-oriented corporate culture, which brings these structures to life.

Figure 13.1   Necessary conditions for successful project management

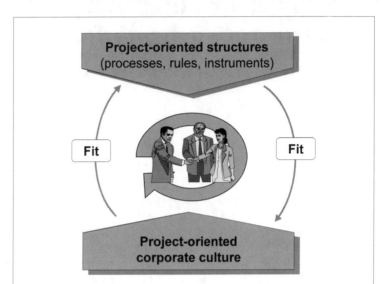

How is PM introduced via new rules?

When reorienting a company, however, most weight often is placed on introducing new **rules and guidelines**, as these are relatively easy to change:

- Processes and guidelines are designed to motivate employees to act efficiently.
- A new process organization redefines and redistributes authorities: for instance, who is to perform supportive work for a particular department.
- Plans and checklists are used to specify what tasks are to be performed by which employees by a specific time.
- A formal reporting procedure specifies who has to report what to whom and at what time.
- Project-internal and trans-project *business regulations* stipulate what meetings should be held at what times and with which participants, etc.

> *Is a change of rules and structures sufficient?*

As Parts I to III have shown, rules of this kind are indispensable to ensure well ordered mutual cooperation in the company. They also allow empirical know-how from the past to be drawn upon to develop corporate efficiency in an ongoing way.

However, a mere modification of corporate structures in line with a project focus will not suffice to attain optimum results. Such *superficial* measures designed to change structures can indeed change the behaviour of the employees. But if the rules, guidelines or specifications which are introduced are not in tune with the fundamental values and attitudes of the employees, they will not be implemented optimally if at all. The underlying roots of employee behaviour, which are not apparent from outside, can hinder the project-orientation of a company in the long term.

The promotion and explicit inclusion of the corporate culture is significantly more important in project-oriented companies than in conventional ones:

> *Why is culture especially important in project orientation?*

- Projects comprise novel tasks, which must be handled in a flexible way. It is consequently impossible to control a project-oriented company down to the last detail via rigid rules. The employees of such a company require considerable **discretionary freedom of action** to perform their functions. The best way of ensuring that such freedom is used to optimally satisfy the corporate goals is to anchor these goals in the corporate culture. For example, customer orientation is best implemented when the individual employees feel that it is worth striving for on their own initiative. In contrast, prescribed modes of action will be of little value.
- In addition, customer orientation frequently implies that a company simply cannot depend on its rules and specifications. Employees must be able and willing to adapt their conduct to the procedural specifications of the project customer and still act in harmony with the corporate goals.
- Project-oriented companies are subject to a faster rate of **continuous change** than that observed in conventional companies. Consequently, flexibility is a significant factor for their success.[1] The employees must be the originators and implementers of this process of change.[2]

> *Should employee values be influenced?*

It would appear desirable to influence the values of the employees to ensure that project orientation becomes second nature to them and is implemented and further developed on their own initiative. The inclusion and modification of company values represents an important task within the development of the **corporate culture** (see The concept of corporate culture, p. 295).

Chapter 14 will show exactly what characterizes a **project-oriented corporate culture**.

NOTES

1 'Flexibility' is a concept which is frequently used without looking more closely into its actual meaning. A further-reaching and scientifically well founded discussion of flexibility in companies may be found in Janssen (1997).
2 Janssen (1997), p. 139 f. sees the ability of employees to handle newly arising situations and uncertainties as an important potential for flexibility with roots at a deep structural level.

14 Characteristics of a project-oriented corporate culture

A project-oriented corporate culture cannot be described in an abstract way. However, it is possible to identify some aspects, which may either facilitate or hinder the successful implementation of project orientation in a company:

> *Why is proprietary thinking obstructive?*

- Proprietary thinking blocks successful project work. Restrictions in the flow of information represent a particularly serious obstacle.

Successful project management thrives on transparency. To ensure integrated planning, control and monitoring of all the functions involved in a project, the relevant information must flow as quickly and freely as possible to the project management agencies. However, as soon as possession of information in individual technical sectors of the company is regarded as a source of power, the open exchange of information is blocked. The great importance of the information and communications culture for the management of projects has already been described in some detail in Part II (5.1.2):

- Work in project-oriented companies requires willingness to change.

> *Is project work more stressful than line activities?*

Employees in conventional companies are used to constant activity in transparent and relatively stable hierarchical structures. In contrast, projects can mean working in various professional roles, involve tasks which are of limited duration and are relatively poorly structured as well as uncertain follow-on activities under the supervision of more than one immediate superior. This can lead to stress for employees and constitute a reason for dissatisfaction. If that is the case, the status of project work will drop among the staff in the mid term. It will then become increasingly difficult for project leaders to motivate their employees for projects:

- The position of the project leader as an *entrepreneur within the enterprise* must be accepted in the company.

> *Project leaders versus technical superiors?*

Managers from technical or line departments have hitherto often felt their authority threatened if project leaders want to access 'their' resources. In the same way, project employees continue to feel responsible to their line superiors rather than to the project leader. Such attitudes hinder efficient working and reduce the attractiveness of project participation for employees:

- Teamwork should become a matter of course for employees.

> *When is teamwork efficient?*

Project work invariably also means teamwork. Effective group work is a critical success factor for projects. Project teams are specially formed for specific project tasks. Empirical studies have shown that project groups require approximately 1.5 years to develop their full efficiency.[1] In view of the short period in which projects generally run, this appears to be a very long time. It is therefore decisive for the project duration as to how quickly such teams take to reach a high degree of efficiency. If work in individually created teams becomes a habitual and popular form of activity for employees, this will clearly have a positive effect:

- Employees in project-oriented companies must be prepared to accept responsibility. In return, managers must be prepared to delegate responsibility to their employees.

> *Who holds and who delegates responsibility?*

The delegation of responsibility (**empowerment**) is regarded as an important means of motivating employees. But it is also a necessary way of increasing the efficiency of project work because empowerment reduces reaction times in the project. For instance, employees can often solve problems on site quickly and in an uncomplicated way before they escalate those problems to higher decision authorities. In contrast, long discussions with superiors and bureaucratic hurdles will retard solutions to a problem.

Project work therefore implies a considerable acceptance of responsibility. This means that managers must delegate part of their apparent authority to the members of their project team:

- Successful project management calls for a *collective* awareness of responsibility. Every employee who can influence the success of the project directly (e.g. in a project team) or indirectly (e.g. as an employee in a service sector) must feel responsibility for the project.

> *Why is individualism less useful?*

Joint acceptance of responsibility contradicts a number of basic assumptions of our society. At school, performance is assessed exclusively on the basis of individual marks and reports. This strong focus on individual goals often continues beyond universities into the corporate world. This must be seen as a reason why the establishment of the team concept is particularly difficult in western industrial societies. In project management, this implies the danger that the project leader is seen as the person with sole responsibility for the project. During project crises in particular, this assumption can be very problematic, as motivation in the teams drops and a solution to the conflict is made more difficult:

- Acceptance of responsibility must be encouraged by the corporate structures.

> *What blocks creativity?*

One-off failures must be accepted and need not lead immediately to negative sanctions. An excessive success orientation, possibly encouraged by strongly performance-oriented forms of remuneration, can restrict creativity in the company and reduce the willingness to accept responsibility:

● Customer orientation must become second nature to all employees.

> *Why is customer orientation rarely practised today?*

In many companies, only a very small part of the workforce has direct customer contact. However, if employees are unfamiliar with the customer and his requirements, it becomes understandably difficult to orient their day-to-day work toward enhancing customer satisfaction. And yet this is precisely the goal of a project. Successful project work implies a customer-focused approach. If this attitude is already established in a company, the transition to project orientation will also become easier. Otherwise, a customer focus must first be gradually introduced to the individual employees:

● The set of tools used for project management must be applied and accepted as a self-evident way of working in the company.

> *Can planning be dispensed with?*

Project management means integrated planning, control and monitoring of all relevant activities. Especially in companies with a strong technical orientation, however, a certain distaste can often be observed for planning as such and commercial planning in particular. This leads to an underweighting of planning aspects and can have a negative effect on the success of the project.

> *Is monitoring an expression of distrust?*

In both Part II and Part III it was shown why it is important in project-oriented companies to be aware of deviations in individual projects at an early stage in order to initiate suitable adjustments. Monitoring measures, such as reviews, support the project management and the team members in this process. Monitoring must therefore be seen as a support service, and under no circumstances as an expression of distrust.

NOTE

1 Cf. Rosenstiel (1992), p. 272 f.

15 Ways of promoting a project-oriented corporate culture

Changing the corporate culture is a difficult and lengthy process. However, this should not dissuade anyone from trying to develop a project focus in a company. On the contrary, it should act as an incentive to influence the corporate culture in a positive sense at an early stage and continuously thereafter.

15.1 CHANGES IN CORPORATE CULTURE INITIATED BY THE CORPORATE MANAGEMENT

> *What do change-processes look like?*

The endeavour to modify the corporate culture constitutes an integrated management task. It must be continuously applied and involves the following substeps:

(1) The elaboration of a **target idea** about the kind of corporate culture appropriate to the company.
(2) A **diagnosis** of the current corporate culture. This may be performed with methods of organizational diagnostics of the kind familiar from organizational psychology.[1]
(3) An **analysis** of the discrepancies between actual and ideal corporate cultures and the reasons for them.
(4) Careful selection of possible **changes** which can affect the corporate culture. This will in particular include suitable initiatives for encouraging a **willingness to change** within the company. Crises, particularly positive news or other events that shake up a company, can create a good breeding ground for activities designed to change the corporate culture. If such 'thawing' of the company is neglected, all efforts aimed at changing its culture will peter out.

An example is that of spontaneous poster and mission-statement initiatives which are often used in vain to affect the attitudes of employees.

(5) **Planning** the implementation of efforts designed to change the corporate culture as well as necessary flanking measures. These can result in transient informal activities as well as more complex projects, which must in turn traverse the project management cycle whose start was described in Part I. An example of more easily applicable measures is a modified way of **hiring staff**. This can be used to preferentially attract employees whose values and attitudes are suited to a project-oriented company. These may include keenness for teamwork, flexibility, openness, responsibility awareness and the willingness to take calculated risks. A series of sophisticated appointment tests can be used to identify such personal qualities which can otherwise be recognized only with difficulty.

(6) Assuring and continuous checking of the **implementation** of these measures.

(7) One of the most important steps, which is indispensable for any change in the corporate culture, is **the consistent day-to-day example of introducing the planned changes in one's own way of working!**

(8) **Checking** the effects of efforts made to introduce changes.

15.2 PROMOTING THE CORPORATE CULTURE AS A TASK OF ALL COMPANY MANAGERS

> *Is cultural change the exclusive province of top managers?*

Influencing the corporate culture is not the sole preserve of corporate management. Ultimately, it must have the active support of all employees who exercise leadership functions. Although corporate management can initiate impulses for promoting a project-oriented corporate culture, it must be represented and diffused by managers along all echelons of the company hierarchy. Of particular importance are those people who act as nodes of relationship networks. Such employees can influence many of their colleagues simply by virtue of their role. The best example of these are project leaders, group leaders and other line superiors.

How do managers influence the corporate culture?

Values are a fundamental component of a corporate culture and are significantly affected by positive and negative **experiences**. If positive experience is linked to an activity, its future attractiveness will increase for an individual. Managers at all hierarchical and technical levels should be aware that they affect the values of their employees whenever they expressly provide them with positive or negative experiences. Successful participation in projects thus offers the individual the best opportunity of gaining positive experiences with project-work and nurtures a project-oriented corporate culture:

Which concrete measures affect the corporate culture?

- As far as possible, all employees should be actively involved in projects several times in the course of their careers. This also applies to employees in the service sectors, who then obtain a better insight into the problems of the project world through their own experience. Career paths should therefore run via participation in projects. Job rotation can encourage employees to work in various positions within projects.
- Special successes of individual projects must be adequately communicated in the company.
- The conclusion of a project should always be appropriately celebrated. This celebration should also include those persons outside the project who have contributed to its success (e.g. in the service sectors). They will then become more willing to commit themselves to future projects.
- Project leaders should be aware of how they can contribute to creating a positive corporate culture with a project focus. Motivating employees to work in a project not only helps to attain the project targets, it also makes project work a positive experience for the employees, which in turn affects their attitude to projects and project work.
- Individual employees should always be made aware of the importance of their activity for the customer and the company. They should be given direct feedback about the consequences of their activities, as far as possible by putting them into direct contact with

the customer. Within the scope of job rotation, therefore, product developers may be sent to visit the customer for a certain time together with service or sales employees in order to experience his problems at first hand.

- The project leader as well as the other managers in a project-oriented company should actively encourage teamwork. Employees must be given the opportunity to gain positive experience in connection with such work:

    - Delegation of responsibility to the teams, group feedback etc. are good ways of enhancing intrinsic motivation in groups.
    - The attractiveness of a group will be increased if its members feel they are at a similar level and have something in common. The project leader should endeavour to utilize this feeling. The selection of a meaningful project name is often the first step in this direction. Outwardly visible signs such as common project T-shirts, ballpoint pens, etc. are other ways of achieving this end.

- Particular importance is attached to the spatial proximity of project groups. After all, 'togetherness' has been shown to engender sympathy![2]
- The establishment of common rituals is seen as a way of influencing the corporate culture. One example is that of regular 'complaints meetings' in which an open exchange of information is encouraged between everyone involved.

15.3 THE WILL TO ONGOING DEVELOPMENT AS A PRECONDITION FOR LONG-TERM SUCCESS IN PROJECT ORIENTATION

Why is organizational learning vital?

The project management concept has the advantage of offering a wealth of opportunities for continuous organizational learning (Table 15.1). At the same time, the ongoing development and improvement of corporate structures, tools and culture represents a critical factor which allows project management to be successful in the long term. A project-oriented company cannot rest on its laurels either but must always strive to improve its performance.

Table 15.1 References to ways of supporting learning in a project-oriented company

Topic domain	Section	Keywords
Selection of projects	Part I	Continuous checks of filter criteria
	Part III	Realization checks
Process improvements	Part II	Project audits Deviation analyses Project temperature charts Method of the 'five whys' Manoeuvre critiques Concluding rounds Feedback from customer
	Part III	CIP teams Realization checks Project controlling Metrics systems Benchmarking
Personnel development	Part III	Project leader pools Mentor programmes Career paths
Promotion of corporate culture	Part IV	Action by corporate management Active example by managers at all levels

> *How does organizational learning take place?*

Repeated reference has been made at diverse points in this book to tools, structures and routines that can be introduced in management with projects and management of projects in order to establish this learning process. Table 15.1 reviews these in brief. It makes no claim to completion.

> *Are tools sufficient for this purpose?*

It became clear in Part IV that it is not sufficient merely to provide relevant structures for facilitating corporate change. The vital point is to motivate the employees to continually push these changes through. That is why effective customer orientation via project management can be successful only over the long term if the employees have the will to improve the company's performance as well as their own way of working in an ongoing way.

NOTES

1   A number of basic features of his programme, which not only provides a well founded corporate analysis but also forecasts the effects of possible measures, can be found in Rosenstiel (1992), pp. 358 ff. References to more detailed sources are also given there.
2   Cf. Rosenstiel (1992), p. 264.

Appendix: Checklist for project completion

A checklist represents a good way of giving the project completion phase the status of an established procedure in the company. It gives project leaders a rapid overview of the activities, which must be performed in order to complete the project in a systematic way. The checklist for assuring that the project has been correctly concluded should include the following points:

DECISION OF COMPLETION

- Have the project targets been reached?
- If the targets were not reached, have measures been prepared and applied to avoid/minimize overrunning schedules and costs?
- Has the customer been informed and approval for the project completion been granted?
- Has a record been made of all outstanding activities?
- Have all those involved in the project been informed?
- Has closure of the project accounts been initiated by the due date?
- Are the current team members motivated for the project completion?
- Has the termination of all in-house project tasks been planned?
- Have arrangements been made by the management to relieve the project leaders of their responsibilities?

HAND-OVER OF RESULTS

- Has the project hand-over been planned and scheduled?
- Have the follow-on activities been defined?
- Have outstanding points and possible deviations been listed and action taken for their solution?
- Has the hand-over protocol been published?
- Have the requisite preconditions for transferring the project and performing the hand-over been created?
- Have the project results been secured and has the know-how transfer been initiated?

DEMOBILIZATION OF RESOURCES

- Have the efforts of the project team members been evaluated and remunerated?
- Has transfer of the project team members to new functions been initiated?
- Have resource utilization plans been issued?

PROJECT EVALUATION

- Has a project evaluation report been issued giving details of schedule and budget fidelity, realized performance features, achieved quality, achieved operating result, competitiveness of the product and achieved targets?
- Has a project experience report been issued giving a description of the factors having positive/negative effects on the project together with the recommendations derived from these for subsequent projects?
- Has a project completion report been issued giving data on the time of the project completion and results hand-over, the designation of responsibilities for follow-up activities, the department responsible for assuring the know-how, a list of the resources still tied up together with a personnel transfer plan?

Bibliography

Note:

As this book originally was published in the German language, most of the following sources are written in German. If you are looking for relevant English texts, please feel free to contact the authors.

Ahsen, Anette von (1996) *Komponenten und organisatorische Umsetzung einer unternehmensweiten Qualitätskonzeption*, Frankfurt.

Altrogge, Günter (1994) *Netzplantechnik*, 2nd edn, Oldenburg 1994.

Anderson, Stuart D. (1992) 'Project Quality and Project Managers', *International Journal of Project Management*, 3, pp. 138–44.

Ansoff, Igor H. (1976) 'Managing Surprise and Discontinuity – Strategic Response to Weak Signals', *Zeitschrift für betriebswirtschaftliche Forschung*, 28, pp. 129–52.

Backhaus, Klaus, Erichson, Bernd, Plinke, Wullf and Weiber, Rolf (1996) *Multivariate Analysemethoden*, 8th edn, Berlin/Heidelberg/NewYork.

Blazek, Alfred (1990) *Projekt-Controlling – Denken und Handeln in Projekten zur Verwirklichung der Selbstkontrolle*, 3rd edn, Munich.

Blohm, Hans and Lüder, Klaus (1991) *Investition – Schwachstellen im Investitionsbereich des Industriebetriebes und Wege zu ihrer Beseitigung*, Munich.

Boehm, Barry W. (1986) *Wirtschaftliche Software-Produktion*, (ed.) Wolfgang Heilmann, Wiesbaden.

Boehm, Barry W. (1988) *Software-Engineering Economics*, Englewood Cliffs.

Böhnisch, Wolf and Nöbauer, Brigitta (1995) 'Soziale Kompetenz', *Handwörterbuch der Führung*, 2nd edn, Stuttgart 1945–58.

Bühner, Rolf and Tuschke, Anja (1997) 'Zur Kritik am Shareholder Value – eine ökonomische Analyse', *BFuP Betriebswirtschaftliche Forschung und Praxis*, 49, pp. 499–516.

Burghardt, Manfred (1995) 'Leitfaden für Planung', *Überwachung und Steuerung von Entwicklungsprojekten*, 3rd edn, Munich.

Coenenberg, Adolf Gerhard and Raffel, Andreas (1988) Integrierte Kosten- und Leistungsanalyse für das Controlling von Forschungs- und Entwicklungsprojekten', *krp Kostenrechnungspraxis*, 32, pp. 199–207.

de Wit, Anton (1988) 'Measurement of Project Success', *International Journal of Project Management*, 6, pp. 164–70.

Deutsches Institut für Normung e.V. (1987) *DIN 69901 – Projektwirtschaft: Projektmanagement – Begriffe*, Berlin.

Diekmann, James (1992) 'Risk Analysis: Lessons From Artificial Intelligence', *International Journal of Project Management*, 10, pp. 75–80.

Dunst, Klaus H. (1983) *Portfolio-Management – Konzeption für strategische Unternehmensplanung*, 2nd edn, Berlin/New York.

Edgett, Scott , Shipley, David and Forbes, Giles (1992) 'Japanese and British Companies Compared: Contributing Factors to Success and Failure in NPD', *Journal of Product Innovation Management*, 9, pp. 3–10.

Franke, Armin (1987) 'Risk Analysis in Project Management', *International Journal of Project Management*, 5, pp. 29–34.

Franke, Armin (1993) *Risikobewusstes Projekt-Controlling*, Cologne.

Frese, Erich (1968) *Kontrolle und Unternehmensführung*, Wiesbaden.

Frese, Erich (1995) *Grundlagen der Organisation – Konzepte – Prinzipien – Strukturen*, 6th edn, Wiesbaden.

Frey, Bruno S. and Osterloh, Margit (1997) 'Sanktionen oder Seelenmassage? Motivationale Grundlagen der Unternehmensführung', *DBW Die Betriebswirtschaft*, 57, pp. 307–21.

Gälweiler, Aloys (1990) *Strategische Unternehmensführung*, 2nd edn, Frankfurt/New York.

Gareis, Roland (1991) 'Management by Projects – The Management Strategy of the "New" Project-Oriented Company', *International Journal of Project Management*, 9, pp. 225–48.

Gareis, Roland (1992) 'Management by Projects – Spezifische Strategien, Strukturen und Kulturen projektorientierter Unternehmen', *Projektmanagement-Forum '92 Dokumentation*, (ed.) Gesellschaft für Projektmanagement Deutschland (GPM), Munich, pp. 145–55.

Globerson, Shlomo (1994) 'Impact of Various Work-Breakdown Structures on Project Conceptualization', *International Journal of Project Management*, 12, pp. 165–71.

Gong, Daji and Hugsted, Reiar (1993) 'Time-Uncertainty Analysis in Project Networks with a New Merge-Event Time-Estimation Technique', *International Journal of Project Management*, 11, pp. 165–74.

Griffin, Abbie (1993) Metrics for Measuring Product Developing Cycle Time', *Journal of Product Innovation Management*, 10, pp. 112–25.

Grosse-Oetringhaus, Wigand F. (1993) 'Sozialkompetenz – ein neues Anspruchsniveau für die Personalpolitik', *ZfbF Zeitschrift für betriebswirtschaftliche Forschung*, 45, pp. 270–95.

Guserl, Richard (1997) 'Praxisrelevantes Führungskonzept für projektorientierte Unternehmungen: Die Führung von 'Unternehmungen' in der Unternehmung', *Zeitschrift für Betriebswirtschaft – Ergänzungsheft*, 3/97, pp. 1–29.

Halman, Joop and Keizer, Jimme A. (1993) 'Diagnosing Risk in Product-Innovation Projects', *International Journal of Project Management*, 12.

Hammer, Michael and Champy, James (1993) *Reengineering the Corporation – A Manifesto for Business Revolution*, New York.

Hartmann, Yvette (1998) *Controlling interdisziplinärer Forschungsprojekte – Theoretische Grundlagen und Gestaltungsempfehlungen auf der Basis einer empirischen Erhebung*, Stuttgart.

Hofstede, Geert (1993) *Interkulturelle Zusammenarbeit: Kulturen – Organisationen – Management*, Wiesbaden.

Horváth, Péter, Niemand, Stefan, and Wolbold, Markus (1993) 'Target Costing – State of the Art', in Péter Horváth (ed.), *Target Costing – Marktorientierte Zielkosten in der deutschen Praxis*, Stuttgart, pp. 1–27.

318 *Bibliography*

Janssen, Holger (1997) *Flexibilitätsmanagement – Theoretische Fundierung und Gestaltungsmöglichkeiten in strategischer Perspektive*, Stuttgart.

König, Eckard (1992) 'Soziale Kompetenz', *Handwörterbuch des Personalwesens*, Stuttgart, pp. 2046–56.

Kolks, Uwe (1986) 'Probleme und Möglichkeiten des Konfigurations-Managements in der versionsorientierten Entwicklung – eine empirische Untersuchung', in Wilfried Krüger (ed.), *Projekt-Management in der Krise – Probleme und Lösungsansätze*, pp. 289–351.

Kreikebaum, Hartmut (1993) *Strategische Unternehmensplanung*, 5th edn, Stuttgart/Berlin/Cologne.

Krystek, Ulrich and Müller-Stewens, Günter (1993) *Frühaufklärung für Unternehmen – Identifikation und Handhabung zukünftiger Chancen und Bedrohungen*, Stuttgart.

Krystek, Ulrich and Zur, Eberhard (1991) 'Projektcontrolling – Frühaufklärung von projektbezogenen Chancen und Bedrohungen', *Controlling*, 3, pp. 304–11.

Küpper, Hans-Ulrich (1997) *Controlling – Konzeption, Aufgaben und Instrumente*, 2nd edn, Stuttgart.

Küpper, Hans-Ulrich and Weber, Jürgen (1995) *Grundbegriffe des Controlling*, Stuttgart.

Küpper, Hans-Ulrich, Weber, Jürgen and Zünd, André (1990) 'Zum Verständnis und Selbstverständnis des Controlling – Thesen zur Konsensbildung', *Zeitschrift für Betriebswirtschaftslehre*, 60, pp. 281–93.

Küpper, Willi, Lüder, Klaus and Streidtferdt, Lothar (1975) *Netzplantechnik*, Würzburg/Vienna.

Larson, Erik W. and Gobeli, David H. (1988) 'Organizing for Product Development Projects', *Journal of Product Innovation Management*, 5, pp. 180–90.

Leibfried, Kathleen H.J. and Mc Nair, Carol Jean (1993) *Benchmarking – Von der Konkurrenz lernen, die Konkurrenz überholen*, Freiburg i.Br.

Litke, Hans-Dieter (1995) *Projektmanagement – Methoden, Techniken, Verhaltensweisen*, 3rd edn, Munich/Vienna.

Madauss, Bernd J. (1994) *Handbuch Projektmanagement: mit Handlungsanleitungen für Industriebetriebe, Unternehmensberater und Behörden*, 5th edn, Stuttgart.

Meredith, Jack R. and Mantel, Samuel J. Jr. (1989) *Project Management – A Managerial Approach*, 2nd edn, New York.

Michel, Kay (1987) *Technologie im strategischen Management – Ein Portfolio-Ansatz zur integrierten Technologie- und Marktplanung*, Berlin.

NN (1995) *Selbstbewertung – Richtlinien für Unternehmen*, European Foundation for Quality Management, Geschäftsstelle Brüssel, Avenue des Pléiades 19, 1200 Brüssel.

Oakland, John S. (1994) *Total Quality Management – The Route to Improving Performance*, 2nd edn, Oxford.

Pavia, Teresa M. (1991) 'The Early Stages of New Product Development in Entrepreneurial High-Tech Firms', *Journal of Product Innovation Management*, 8, pp. 18–31.

Perridon, Louis and Steiner, Manfred (1993) *Finanzwirtschaft der Unternehmung*, 7th edn, Munich.

Picot, Arnold, Reichwald, Ralf and Wigand, Rolf T. (1998) *Grenzenlose Unternehmung – Information, Organisation und Management*, 3rd edn, Wiesbaden.

Reichert, Rainer, Kirsch, Werner and Esser, Werner-Michael (1991) 'Suchfeldanalyse – Die Erarbeitung neuer Betätigungsfelder für die Unternehmung', *Beiträge zum Management strategischer Programme*, (ed.) Werner Kirsch, Munich, pp. 575–604.

Rickert, Dierk (1995) *Multi-Projektmanagement in der industriellen Forschung und Entwicklung*, Wiesbaden.

Riegler, Christian (1996) *Verhaltenssteuerung durch Target Costing – Analyse anhand einer ausgewählten Organisationsform*, Stuttgart.

Rosenstiel, Lutz von (1992) *Grundlagen der Organisationspsychologie – Basiswissen und Anwendungshinweise*, 3rd edn, Stuttgart.

Schein, Edgar (1995) *Unternehmenskultur – Ein Handbuch für Führungskräfte*, Frankfurt.

Schelle, Heinz (1996) *Projekte zum Erfolg führen*, Munich.

Schmelzer, Hermann J. (1992) *Organisation und Controlling von Produkentwicklungen – Praxis des wettbewerbsorientierten Entwicklungsmanagements*, Stuttgart.

Schultz, Volker (1995) *Projektkostenschätzung – Ermittlung in frühen Phasen von technischen Auftragsprojekten*, Wiesbaden.

Schweitzer, Marcell and Küpper, Hans-Ulrich (1998) *Systeme der Kosten- und Erlösrechnung*, 7th edn, Munich.

Seicht, Gerhard (1994) 'Industrielle Anlagenwirtschaft', in *Industriebetriebslehre – Das Wirtschaften in Industrieunternehmen*, (ed.) Marcell Schweitzer, 2nd edn, Munich, pp. 327–445.

Seidenschwarz, Werner (1993) *Target Costing – Marktorientiertes Zielkostenmanagement*, Munich.

Seiler, James (1985) 'Cost and Schedule Data Analysis and Forecasting', *International Journal of Project Management*, 3, pp. 45–9.

Spendolini, Michael J. (1992) *The Benchmarking Book*, New York.

Stedry, Andrew C. and Kay, Emanuel (1966) 'The Effect of Goal Difficulty on Performance – A Field Experiment', *Behavioral Science*, 11, pp. 459–70.

Stock, Ulrich (1990) *Das Management von Forschung und Entwicklung*, Munich.

Stockbauer, Herta (1991) 'F&E-Budgetierung aus der Sicht des Controlling', *Controlling*, 3, pp. 136–43.

Studt, Jürgen (1983) *Projektkostenrechnung*, Frankfurt.

Turner, Rodney J. (1993) *The Handbook of Project Based Management – Improving the Processes for Achieving Strategic Objectives*, London.

Turner, Rodney J. and Speiser, Arnon (1992) 'Programme Management and its Informations Systems Requirements', *International Journal of Project Management*, 10, pp. 196–206.

Wideman, Max R. (1990) 'Managing the Project Environment', *Dimensions of Project Management – Fundamentals, Techniques, Organizations, Applications*, (ed.) Hasso Reschke and Heinz Schelle, Berlin, pp. 51–69.

Wiendahl, Hans-Peter (1987) *Belastungsorientierte Fertigungssteuerung – Grundlagen, Verfahrensaufbau, Realisierung*, Munich/Vienna.

Womack, James P., Jones, Daniel T. and Roos, Daniel (1994) *Die zweite Revolution in der Autoindustrie – Konsequenzen aus der weltweiten Studie aus dem Massachusetts Institute of Technology*, Frankfurt a.M./New York.

Yeo, Khim-Teck (1991) 'Project Cost Sensitivity and Variability Analysis', *International Journal of Project Management*, 9, pp. 111–26.

Index